FINGERPRINT
TECHNIQUES

Inbau Law Enforcement Series

FINGERPRINT TECHNIQUES

ANDRE A. MOENSSENS

CHILTON BOOK COMPANY

RADNOR, PENNSYLVANIA

To T. DICKERSON COOKE, whose contributions to fingerprint training and to the identification profession, most notably by continued publication of *Finger Print and Identification Magazine,* are without equal.

CONTENTS

Preface

The public takes it for granted today that identity can be positively established through fingerprints, but the accurate and widespread use of fingerprinting is relatively recent. Less than a century has elapsed since it was discovered that fingerprints could determine the identity of criminals, although various uses for finger designs, some dating back thousands of years, have been recorded throughout the history of man.

Probably as a result of the influence of movies and crime novels, fingerprints are popularly associated with the detection of crime and the apprehension of criminals. It is true that in modern law enforcement fingerprints play a fascinating and essential role. But fingerprints have many other equally valuable uses. As well as protecting society in general, they protect or comfort the individual, law-abiding citizen.

In the delivery rooms of many hospitals, the footprints of newborn infants are recorded along with the fingerprints of the mother to guarantee that identity can be proved beyond question should the mother suspect that the wrong baby is sent home with her. Even when no hospital error is suspected, infant footprints can prove valuable. In 1953, the officer in charge of an Indiana police identification bureau received a letter from a mother who told him of her frustration at being uncertain of the identity of the beautiful twin girls she had. She did not know for sure which was Carolin and which was Norene. Since they resembled each other in the most minute details, the mother believed that at some time or other she had become confused about their individual identities. Fortunately, a set of the girls' footprints had been taken at birth in the hospital and the mother wondered if it would be possible to use them to tell which daughter was which. Captain Birk C. Harl, of the Evansville, Indiana, Police Department, recorded the footprints of the twin sisters at the mother's request (see Figure 1). After comparing the new sets of footprints with those recorded shortly after birth, the mother found out, to her delight and comfort, that she had been calling the girls by their correct names.

Unfortunately, many baby footprints recorded in maternity hospitals are worthless for identification purposes because nurses often lack training in the delicate printing process and are content to press an infant's ink-smeared foot onto paper without concern for legibility. When properly taken, however, baby footprints provide a means of accurate personal identification throughout life.

The results of airplane and train wrecks, explosions, earthquakes, fires and drownings all demonstrate the frailty of the human body. Many interested persons must depend upon the identification of unrecognizable human remains by means of fingerprint comparisons. Disaster victims, mutilated beyond recognition, can be positively identified even if only a small area of finger skin is preserved in a relatively intact condition. Insurance companies do not readily pay off life insurance or accident policies unless adequate proof is forthcoming that the victim is indeed the insured party, and the probate of an estate depends upon proof of the identity of the deceased.

In fatal accidents involving the destruction of visually identifiable features of the body, thousands of victims whose identity was unknown have been identified by fingerprints. In one instance, a victim of a maritime disaster off the Florida coast was positively identified after a shark was caught in the coastal waters and the remains of a human hand were found in its bowels. The skin on the hand was sufficiently preserved to permit identification.

The armed forces maintain fingerprint collections of all military personnel so that mutilated battle casualties can be identified and the next of kin notified. As unpleasant as notification of death is, relatives generally prefer establishing positive identity of war casualties to the torture and uncertainty that accompany a report of "missing in action."

By using fingerprints, banks can identify depositors who cannot sign their checks. Educational institutions, civil service commissions and employers can prevent impersonations during examinations for

Figure 1. In 1953, Captain Birk C. Harl, in charge of the identification bureau of the Evansville, Indiana, Police Department, recorded the footprints of two twin sisters at the request of their mother and compared the prints with those recorded on the birth certificates to establish the separate identities of the identical twins.

admission and employment by requiring each candidate to impress his fingers on his test papers so that the impressions can be compared with official records of identity.

The examples cited here are but a few of the many ways in which fingerprinting can be used in noncriminal cases. Imagination can provide many more. With the advances of science and the development of ever more encompassing computer technology, we may eventually witness many of the projections described by science fiction writers—for instance, a society in which fraud or imposition might no longer be possible, and burglary or intrusion of a home nonexistent, because of technological developments in human identification. Not too far away may be a computerized system of individualized charge-account crediting and debiting by means of a credit card with fingerprints on it. Money could be deposited automatically to the credit of each individual's account; purchases could be made by depositing the credit card in a computer-controlled device resembling a slot machine; the computer would automatically add the amount of the charge to the account and match the fingerprint on the credit card with the fingerprint in a central memory bank and with that of the individual using the card, thus making forgeries or unauthorized use of the card impossible. A man's home might truly become his castle once again if keys were to go out of style and burglarproof locks responded only to the fingerprints of the person or persons having legitimate access to the premises.

Are such futuristic views of fingerprinting mere fantasy? No, they are not, because computer technology and research in the optical scanning and coding of fingerprints may make all of these "dreams" realities within a decade or so, although more time will probably be required for widespread practical application. The challenges of the future include many other uses for fingerprints, all of them in noncriminal services.

I wish to express my gratitude and deep appreciation to the many identification experts around the world who have generously contributed research material and photographs; to Major Georges F. Defawe, whose inspiration and guidance initiated my fingerprint studies some twenty years ago; and to the Institute of Applied Science for making freely available to me its incomparable library on fingerprinting.

Chapter 1

The History of Fingerprinting

To discover the earliest uses of fingerprints is almost as impossible as establishing, in precise terms, the date of the emergence of man. For thousands of years no writings or carvings existed. Then primitive man began to use tools and started making inscriptions and crude drawings, but it remains impossible to determine the meanings of a great number of those primitive works. Fingerprints, too, have been discovered on artifacts and prehistoric pottery, and more than likely they were placed there unintentionally when the artists impressed their fingers into the wet clay.

Most historians agree that the intentional use of finger impressions dates back many centuries. Probably the oldest demonstration of primitive interest in the strange patterns on the friction skin of the fingers is an aboriginal carving in stone that was discovered in Nova Scotia. The carving depicts the outline of a hand and fingers (see Figure 2). In crude markings, the artist illustrated simple whirling ridges on three of the fingers. The pictograph does not establish use of fingerprints for personal identification; more than likely, the curiosity of the artist had been aroused by what he considered to be unusual markings and ridges on the skin.

In the Neolithic caves and burial grounds on the island of Gavrinis, off Brittany, carvings have been found that resemble friction skin ridges (see Figure 3). These granite slab illustrations are in fact attributed to ancient observations of finger and palm impressions by their discoverer, the Belgian scientist Stockis. Other researchers, however, claim that such carvings more nearly depict primitive observations of the line patterns found on wind-swept sandy beaches

1

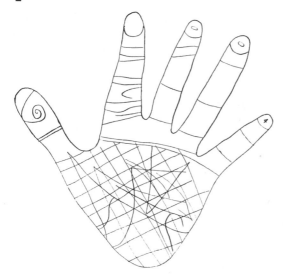

Figure 2. An aboriginal Indian pictograph discovered on a slaty rock near Kejimkoojik Laks, Nova Scotia. (Courtesy: Institute of Applied Science.)

undisturbed by human or animal imprints, on the hides of zebras, in the grain of wood, or in the circular patterns formed by a stone tossed into a pond.

The fingerprint author and historian B. C. Bridges writes about

Figure 3. Photograph of carvings resembling friction skin patterns discovered on granite wall slabs on the island of Gavrinis.

the use of palmprint impressions in a criminal trial during the Roman Empire, nearly two thousand years ago. He draws his information from a work of the Roman legal scholar and author Marcus Fabius Quintilianus, *Paries Palmatus* (The Handprints on the Wall). The Roman advocate, born in the year A.D. 35, successfully defended a blind boy accused by his stepmother of murdering his own father by showing that a set of bloody handprints along the walls from the scene of the crime to the boy's sleeping quarters could not have been made by the defendant, but had been planted by the true criminal, the stepmother. No claim is made by Bridges that the Romans knew anything about fingerprint identification, but he does note that some early use of similar impressions in criminal trials is recorded.

Archeological expeditions in the Middle East and Egypt have unearthed numerous artifacts bearing fingerprints, some clearly the accidental deposits of handcrafters, some attributed to intentional markings in the nature of seals of property (see Figure 4). Intentional uses of fingerprints are recorded in Chinese writings dating from the seventh century to the present. Kia Kung-yen, a Chinese historian of the T'ang Dynasty (A.D. 619 to 906), makes mention of fingerprints in his writings of A.D. 650 while commenting on an older method of preparing legal documents. In translation, his nota-

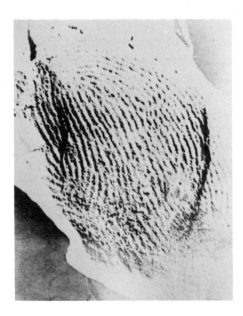

Figure 4. Impression on a Palestinian lamp of the Byzantine period (fourth or fifth century A.D.), believed by some to have been intentionally placed.

tion reads: "Wooden tablets were inscribed with the terms of the contract, and notches were cut in the sides at identical places so that the tables could later be matched, thus proving them genuine. The significance of the notches was the same as that of the fingerprint [Chinese word *hua chi*] of the present time."

The Chinese law book of Yung-Hwui of about the same period, in describing the code of domestic relations in China, states that to divorce a wife the husband must give a document in his own handwriting setting forth the charges, and adds, "but in case he is unable to write, he must sign with his fingerprints." It is generally accepted that the Chinese use of fingerprints on contracts, deeds and other legal documents was ceremonial only, and was in effect the counterpart of our medieval wax seals. Hindus and Chinese also shared the mystical belief that anything touched by the human hand in the course of a transaction became a sacred and binding symbol of the transaction. A few fingerprint pioneers believed that the Chinese use of finger seals, reported to date back some two to three thousand years, had its origin in the belief that fingerprints were individual and could establish identity. According to those authors, in subsequent centuries the knowledge of or belief in personal identification by fingerprints was gradually lost until the practice became merely symbolic. But no credible evidence for or against that theory has been discovered.

The earliest European writing on fingerprints yet discovered appeared in 1684 and was authored by Dr. Nehemiah Grew, an English botanist noted for his works on vegetable anatomy and physiology. Grew was born in 1641 at Manchester and graduated from Cambridge in 1661. He received a doctor of medicine degree from the University of Leiden, Holland, in 1664. He practiced medicine for a while at Coventry and then went to London, where the publication in 1671 of his book *Anatomy of Vegetables Begun* secured his admission to the Royal Society as a Fellow of the College of Physicians and Surgeons. In 1677, he became secretary of the Royal Society.

In 1684, Dr. Grew presented a report before the Royal Society on his observations of patterns on the fingers and palm. He described the sweat pores, the epidermal ridges and their arrangements, and presented a drawing of the configurations of one hand (see Figure 5). That same year the report was published in the volume *Philosophical Transactions* of the Society. In the paper, Grew said:

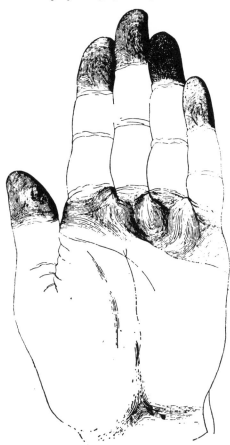

Figure 5. The hand drawing that accompanied the report on friction ridge detail published in 1684 by Dr. Nehemiah Grew.

"If any one will but take the pains, with an indifferent glass, to survey the palms of his hands, very well washed with a ball, he may perceive innumerable little ridges, of equal size and distance, and everywhere running parallel to each other. And especially on the ends and first joints of the fingers and thumbs, on the top of the ball, and near the root of the thumb a little above the wrist. In all which places, they are very regularly disposed into spherical triangles and ellipses. On these ridges stand the pores, all in even rows, and of such a magnitude as to be visible to a good eye without a glass. But, being viewed with one, every pore looks like a little fountain, and the sweat may be seen to stand therein as clear as rock-water, and as often as it is wiped off, they spring up within them again. . . ."

Grew apparently did not notice or examine the permanence of these ridges, nor did he envision the possibilities of using the skin ridges for identification purposes. Purely anatomical in nature, his lengthy thesis describes the purpose of his research: "What nature intends in the position of these ridges is that they may the better suit with the use and motion of the hand." Almost two hundred years later, another English fingerprint pioneer, Sir Francis Galton, would make similar observations before the Royal Society, ignorant, apparently, of Grew's thesis, since Galton's earliest reference dates to an 1823 publication in Prussia.

One year after Grew's presentation before the Royal Society, Govard Bidloo, an anatomist from Holland, had published a book on human anatomy (*Anatomia Humani Corporis*, Amsterdam, 1685) wherein he illustrated the friction ridges and the pores of a thumb. His work makes no mention either of the permanence of the ridges or of possible identifying characteristics. Bidloo's work was followed in 1686 by the publication in London of an anatomical treatise, *De Externo Tactus Organo*, by Professor Marcello Malpighi of the University of Bologna, Italy. Malpighi's research in anatomy is recognized as so outstanding that one of the layers of the skin is named after him (*stratum Malpighi*).

In his anatomical studies, Malpighi utilized the recently invented microscope. With respect to the friction skin, he wrote: "Finally, we have to examine the hand. On its palm certain well-marked wrinkles describe various patterns; at the finger tips, however, these wrinkles curve spirally and, if examined through a microscope, show open pores for sweat along the middle of a protracted ridge."

In the 1700s, several other works on anatomy mentioned or described the existence of friction ridge patterns on the palmar surfaces of the hand. Among them are the books of Christian J. Hintze (1747), Bernard S. Albinus (1764), and J. C. A. Mayer (1788). Mayer's work went virtually unnoticed until its rediscovery in the 1900s by the world-renowned authority on dermatoglyphics, Professor Harold Cummins, who wrote that Mayer was the first author to clearly expound the principle that patterns of friction skin have a close similarity in appearance yet are different in minute detail. No explanation is given in Mayer's work for how he reached his conclusion.

The beginning of the nineteenth century saw the publication of a few other studies, notably those of Prochaska of Vienna in 1812 and

Johan Friedrich Schroter of the University of Leipzig in 1814. The most significant event in scholarly anatomical research, from the viewpoint of fingerprint technicians, was the publication of the Purkinje thesis in 1823.

Johannes Evangelist Purkinje was born in Libochovice, Bohemia, in 1787. Following his primary studies, he decided to become a scientist and believed that he could best achieve his goal by studying medicine. Upon graduation from the medical school at Prague, he sought to engage in further research. His wish seemed close to fulfillment when he was offered a professorship at the University of Breslau, Prussia (now Wroclaw, Poland). In a dissertation written in Latin while at that institution, Purkinje described fingerprints, distinguished among and named various types, and formulated rules for classification. *Commentatio de Examine Physiologico Organi Visus et Systematis Cutanei* (A commentary on the physiological examination of the organs of vision and the cutaneous system) was dated December 22, 1823. It must be regarded as revolutionary in its concepts relating to fingerprints.

In describing the variety of friction skin patterns he had observed, Purkinje divided them into nine groups (see Figure 6) and

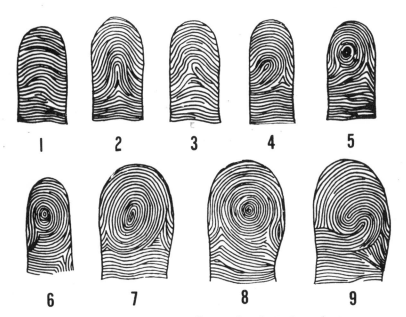

Figure 6. The nine patterns illustrated in the Purkinje thesis.

assigned to the patterns these names: (1) Flexura transversas, (2) Stria centralis, (3) Stria obliquus, (4) Sinus obliquus, (5) Amygdalus, (6) Spirula, (7) Ellipsis, (8) Circulus, and (9) Vortex duplicatus. Comparing those divisions with modern terminology, the Latin names have these equivalents or near equivalents: (1) arch, (2) tented arch, (3) and (4) loops, (5) and (6) central pocket loops, (7) and (8) whorls, and (9) double loop.

Although Purkinje's work received little notice immediately after publication, it nevertheless constituted a significant step in the development of modern fingerprinting. It was the first time patterns had been subdivided into a logical scheme, and the work obviously influenced later researchers developing classification schemes of their own, although they seldom bothered to refer to their source. Purkinje's studies, which when first published appeared to be extensive, did not include mention of the possible use of the finger patterns for personal identification, but Purkinje did urge that further research be done and pointed the way for the many others who followed him.

Another anatomical study of friction skin formation on the hands and feet of man and monkeys was published in 1867 by the French scientist Alix. Ten years later, the French physician Aubert, in connection with studies of skin diseases and their manifestations in glandular excretions, recommended the use of a silver nitrate solution to develop fingerprints on paper.

Modern fingerprinting developed in the last two decades of the nineteenth century. The impetus was provided by a letter published in the British science journal *Nature* on October 28, 1880, by Dr. Henry Faulds. Made a licentiate of the Royal Faculty of Physicians and Surgeons in Glasgow in 1871, Faulds was sent to Japan two years later as a medical missionary for the United Presbyterian Church of Scotland. He arrived at Yokohama in early March, 1874. Shortly thereafter, he became the editor of a medical journal and was offered, but declined, the post of physician to the Prince of Japan.

During his stay in Japan, Faulds' interest in fingerprints was awakened after observing the intricate designs of human finger imprints on prehistoric pottery found among the low cliffs surrounding the beautiful beaches of the Bay of Yedo. He began to study them in the mid 1870s, comparing ancient imprints with those of his contemporaries, and soon was struck by the thought that some degree of persistence in the patterns could be observed. At that early time, he supposed that skin patterns change, but set out to investigate his premise. He described his experiments in a pamphlet called *The Hidden Hand,* which was published during his years of retirement in Scotland:

> "I had under training in biology some very acute and enthusiastic Japanese pupils, many of whom afterwards attained good positions as doctors. Under my guidance those students set out to test such points carefully. We began by shaving off the ridges which contained the patterns near the fingertips till no pattern should be traced. Yet whenever the skin grew up the old pattern came again into view with unimpeachable fidelity. Then we used pumice-stone, sand paper, emery dust, various acids, caustics, and even spanish fly. . . . Special attention was given to the earlier months of infancy when changes are rapid. An epidemic of scarlet fever, then new to Japan and very virulent, gave me a remarkable opportunity for observing the patterns—after the severe peeling of the old skin—in a great number of cases. None of them were ever observed to have changed in the least. For more than two years this had gone on before I wrote, and observations have been kept up till the present time. During the period before October, 1880, many thousands of digital impressions were taken and compared mutually, while the same fingers were many times reprinted and re-examined with the greatest minuteness.
>
> "They were scrutinised even with some little bias in favour of variation, but no single change was discovered in any one of the patterns. . . ."

Having made an extensive study of the phenomenon that presented what he considered to be a potentially valuable means of personal identification, Faulds decided to share his findings with the world. The letter published in *Nature* represents the first writing describing fingerprints and advocating their use for the detection of criminals. The letter said, in part: "When bloody finger-marks or impressions on clay, glass, etc., exist, they may lead to the scientific identification of criminals. Already I have had experience in two such cases, and found useful evidence from these marks. In one case greasy finger-marks revealed who had been drinking some rectified spirit. . . . In another case sooty finger-marks of a person climbing a white wall were of great use as negative evidence." Faulds also suggested that fingerprints might be useful in establishing the identities of unknown bodies and predicted that one day experts might be able to use general hereditary traits in patterns to prove kinship, a field of studies that is now under investigation by medical researchers.

Faulds' letter spurred another European living in the Far East to action with a claim to prior discovery of fingerprinting. Sir William J. Herschel had been engaged in the Civil Service in India from 1853 to 1878. While acting as administrator of the Hooghly District of Bengal, India, Herschel was troubled with numerous native impersonations. In 1858, he started the practice of recording the handprints of natives on contracts to prevent refutation of signatures. The first such instance that Herschel recalled was that of Rajyadhar Konai. Herschel's idea at that time, as he admitted later, was totally unrelated to modern concepts of fingerprint identification. He stated, "I was only wishing to frighten Konai out of all thought of repudiating his signature hereafter." The Konai contract (see Figure 7) testifies to that purpose: although the hand friction ridges are clearly visible, little useful detail can be noted in the fingers. Later, Herschel purportedly requested permission to initiate the fingerprint system in the jails, but that request was said to have been denied in 1877. He did not publish anything about his activities until after Faulds' letter to the editor of *Nature* was published, but from that time on he claimed prior discovery based on his earlier experiments.

Herschel recorded some fingerprints along with hand impressions, although by direct admission of his later defender, Sir Francis Galton, the fingerprint collection that Herschel later turned over to Galton for further study consisted only of the prints of some fifteen different persons. A careful study of the objective evidence leads the unbiased observer to the conclusion that Herschel's contribution to modern fingerprinting was minimal. He himself admitted that at no time had he envisioned the use of fingerprints as a means of discovering criminals. It might therefore be believed that when he started making hand prints Herschel was merely utilizing the mystical idea, held by Hindus and Chinese, that a trace of bodily contact was more binding than a signature.

In a lively correspondence in *Nature*, continuing for several years after 1880, Faulds and Herschel each claimed to be the originator of modern fingerprinting. Sorting out the available data, it is now incontrovertible that Faulds had prior right of publication

TO:

Mr. Dabnue Moharasen Sahel

I am writing you this agreement that at the house of Raghunath Ganga I will bring 2000 millions of "Mand", (80 lbs per mand) of marbles, and will receive 4 Rupees out of 100 Rupees from you. Now I have written this agreement after receiving the value of 15 pounds of Rupees from you. Dated the 28, July.

(Facsimile of)

The agreement between W. J. Herschel and Rajyadhar Konai made in Bengal in 1858 from which originated the modern system of personal identification by means of "finger-prints"

Figure 7. A copy of the contract between Herschel and Konai that was discovered by Herschel's son among his father's papers. The typewritten portion is the translation of the Hindu script. The English notation at the bottom is in Herschel's handwriting. (Courtesy: Institute of Applied Science.)

because his concept of the use of fingerprints as a means of personal identification in criminal cases was original and preceded Herschel's. Nearly all historians of fingerprinting in this country, and in other countries except England, are in agreement on this point. Undoubtedly because of the English-Scottish rivalry of the time and the substantial patronage that the nobility serving in or directing the affairs of Britain's India Colony afforded Herschel, all English texts published in Great Britain claim Herschel as the orginator of fingerprinting; a few English texts do not even mention Faulds. While both were pioneers in their own right and contributed to modern fingerprinting in different ways, Faulds' efforts were certainly the more valuable to the development of fingerprint techniques for personal identification.

In 1886, Faulds offered to set up a fingerprint bureau at Scotland Yard at his own expense to test the practicality of his method, but a report unfavorable to Faulds and recommending the adoption of a system of anthropometric measurements developed by Alphonse Bertillon caused a rejection of Faulds' system, which nevertheless was adopted at "The Yard" less than two decades later. After that, in July, 1921, Faulds began publication of a bimonthly journal on fingerprints titled *Dactylography,* but only seven issues of the journal were published, the last one dated October 1922. During the last years of his life, he wrote numerous books and monographs on fingerprints, but only after an Englishman had preceded him with the first textbook on fingerprints in 1892. In 1958, while investigating historical documents relative to the centennial anniversary of Keio University in Japan, Dr. Yasoshima discovered the site of Faulds' residence, where a permanent monument to his accomplishments as a fingerprint pioneer was unveiled in 1961.

The studies of Sir Francis Galton, born in 1822 at the Larches near Sparkbrook, Birmingham, England, had a far greater impact on the development of modern fingerprinting than the efforts of Herschel. Astronomer, geographer-explorer, inventor, author, and blood relative of Darwin, Galton became interested in anthropometrical measurements in 1882. Six years later, when he gave a lecture at the Royal Institution on Bertillon's system of identifying humans by measuring their bodily dimensions, Galton became interested in fingerprints, especially their reported use by the Chinese. Writing a letter to *Nature* asking for information, he started corresponding with Herschel. Using Herschel's findings, and assisted by F. Howard Collins in his research, Galton published the 1892 textbook on fingerprints, the first of its kind. He had given careful consideration to the discoveries of his predecessors and contemporaries, supplementing their work with a great deal of personal investigation. His textbook discussed the anatomy of finger patterns, offered practical methods for recording them, and described techniques for classifying fingerprints, which he divided into three groups: arches, loops and whorls.

At the insistence of Galton, the Right Honourable Henry H. Asquith, K. C., appointed a special committee on October 21, 1893, to investigate the subject and merits of fingerprinting. Members of the committee chaired by Charles Edward Troup of the Home Office were Major Arthur Griffith, inspector of prisons, and Melville Leslie Macnaghten, chief constable of the London Metropolitan Police. The committee was greatly impressed by its studies in Galton's laboratories and indicated as much in its report dated February 12, 1894. On that date, fingerprints were officially adopted by the British government as supplementary to the Bertillon method of bodily measurements.

Following in Galton's footsteps and basing much of his original data on the great scientist's discoveries, Sir Edward Richard Henry ultimately devised the modern classification system that bears his name and is still in widespread use today. Born in London in 1850, Henry was appointed assistant magistrate collector in the Indian Civil Service in 1873; he became inspector general of police in Bengal in 1891. Two years later, he visited Galton, then returned to India to introduce fingerprints as a national aid to identification. First he used only thumb prints, but later he added a separate record of all ten digits.

Henry set out to devise a more workable system of classification than that suggested by Galton, so that he might be able to handle his unwieldy collection of fingerprints. This work occupied most of his free time during 1894–97. At the end of that time, he felt sufficiently secure about the validity of his results to invite the government of India to appoint an independent committee to investigate his system. The report of that committee was adopted, by resolution of June 12, 1897, by the Council of the Governor General of India, and that same year India discarded anthropometry in favor of an identification system based on fingerprints alone. The Indian legislature passed Act V in 1899, amending the law of evidence to declare relevant the testimony given by those who had become proficient in personal identification by fingerprint decipherment. The same year, Henry read a paper at Dover, England, before an assembly of the British Association for the Advancement of Science, detailing his system and the use it had been put to in India. In 1900, Henry's paper was published in enlarged and revised form, titled *Classification and Uses of Finger-Prints,* under the sponsorship of the government of India. In later years, the book went through numerous editions, all of which were published by H. M.'s Stationery Office in England. Called to London in 1901 to become assistant commissioner of police in charge of criminal identification at New Scotland Yard, Henry was responsible for bringing fingerprinting into effective use in England. The Henry system, with modifications and extensions, is still used today in most English-speaking countries, including the United States, and it forms the basis for several other systems as well.

In recent years, Indian fingerprint researchers have claimed that most of the work on primary classification, the basis for the system, was not the work of Henry but of two police officials in Bengal working with Henry, Khan Bahadur Azizul Haque and Khan Bahadur Hem Chandra Bose. A 1957 *Patna Journal of Medicine* article describes the work of Henry's assistants:

> "Haque, who was very strong in mathematics, took up very seriously the problems of fingerprint classification, to which work he was assigned. Henry had employed a number of selected men to work on the problem under his general supervision. The problem . . . was to find out a way to classify finger-prints 'not merely of the different types (a simple matter), but of their combinations and permutations in any given set of ten digits.' The officer who actually 'did the trick' was young Haque.
>
> "Azizul Haque devised the present system of ten-digit classification and handed over the papers to Henry. The Inspector General of Police studied it for a week with Haque but failed to understand it. He then took the papers to his residence 'to study alone.' Henry was now quick to realise that 'the formula presented to him was the key to the whole problem and fully met the practical purposes of a system of identification.'"

Indian researchers contend that Henry unflinchingly monopolized all the credit for the new system because he never mentioned Haque in his book. But since Henry was known as a mild-mannered, fair-minded man, it seems unjust to attribute such sinister motives to him. More likely, he followed the prevailing pattern of behavior existing in colonial England that held that native labor performed for the English belonged to the latter. Other sources corroborate that, in 1911–12, Henry, who at the time was commissioner of police in London, visited India as a member of the Royal Visit entourage of King George V and attended a meeting of the officers of the Bengal police at Calcutta, where he presented Haque to the audience as the man "mainly responsible for the now worldwide fingerprint system of identification." In official Indian reports honoring Haque, it is also stated that, in March 1897 at the request of Henry and with the sanction of the government of India, a committee of experts met in Calcutta to apply scientific tests to the anthropometrical and fingerprint systems. Haque demonstrated the system he designed and was put to all possible tests by the committee. In a letter dated May 10, 1926, to P. H. Dumbell, then secretary of the Services and General Department, India Office, Henry made it clear that in his opinion Azizul Haque contributed in a conspicuous degree to the perfection of his classification system. Henry paid similar homage to the labors of Chandra Bose, particularly for his system of subclassifications and for his efforts in developing a single-digit classification system.

As a result of the writings of Grew, Purkinje, Faulds, Herschel, Galton and Henry, fingerprinting for personal identification came of age as the nineteenth century drew to a close. Full acceptance was not yet forthcoming, though, because a different system of personal identification had meanwhile gained a firm foothold in criminal investigation.

While Galton was busy studying fingerprints, European and American police departments were using a system of personal identification based on bodily measurements devised and introduced by the French police expert Alphonse Bertillon. His father a physician who had taken up the study of skulls and anthropology, Bertillon learned the methods used by anthropologists in measuring skeletal remains. As an undergraduate, Bertillon flunked out of three schools. He lost half a dozen jobs in France and Great Britain, then served in the military. His father got him a job as clerk at the Parisian Préfecture de Police. Discovering that there was no way to determine if arrested persons had previous criminal records, Bertillon set out to adapt the anthropological measuring techniques with which he had become familiar through his father's hobby. He soon had "invented," as he termed it, the system of criminal identification he called anthropometry. In 1882, Bertillon was named head of the new identification bureau at the Préfecture, and in 1883 he demonstrated his system in Amsterdam, Holland. Two years later, he again gave a short description of anthropometry before an international Prison Congress meeting in Rome, and in 1893 he published *Instructions signalétiques*. An English version of that book was published in the United States in 1896.

Bertillon's system of anthropometrical measurements was based on three fundamental ideas: the fixed condition of the bone system from the age of twenty until death; the extreme diversity of dimensions present in the skeleton of one individual compared to those in another; the ease and relative precision with which certain dimensions of the bone structure of a living person can be measured using simply constructed caliphers. In all, Bertillon recommended eleven measurements of the following parts of the human anatomy:

    Body: Height—standing
           Reach—arms outstretched, middle fingertip to middle
               fingertip
           Trunk—height of person sitting erect

    Head: Length of head
           Width of head
           Length of right ear
           Width of right ear (Later discontinued and replaced by
               the bizygomatic distance; that is, the width of the
               face across the cheek bones.)

    Limbs: Length of the left foot—full weight resting on it
            Length of the left middle finger
            Length of the left little finger
            Length of the left forearm

In practice, the system was often reduced to nine measurements (see Figure 8). Even then, the process was lengthy and time-consuming, since accuracy of measurement was of the greatest importance. But experience soon revealed that the Bertillon system of measurements did not live up to its originator's claims. Successive measurements of one individual by several police officers would vary appreciably, largely because of the difficulty experienced by

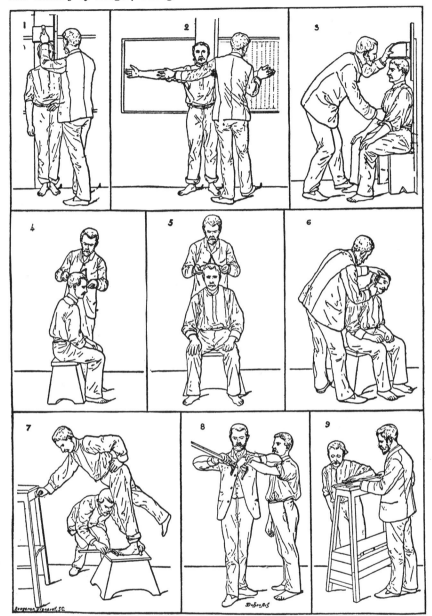

Figure 8. Bertillon's system of bodily measurements, called anthropometry, as used in the United States in the early 1900s.

technicians in reading minute graduations on the calipers. Another problem was that the measurements were usable only for adults because growth made data meaningless until physical maturity was reached.

In spite of all the difficulties and disadvantages, anthropometry spread rapidly throughout France, England and much of the world. Identification men in police departments became known as Bertillon officers. So profound was the influence of that early professional label that to this day some lawyers and laymen erroneously refer to identification men as Bertillon experts and believe that Bertillon was the inventor of fingerprint identification.

As head of the Paris identification service, Bertillon always considered his own measurement system superior to fingerprints, and he refused to accept fingerprinting long after all other police agencies abandoned anthropometry. In France, criminal identification records were filed by anthropometrical classification formulas until Bertillon's death in 1914, although, in various stages, he had added fingerprints to his anthropometric cards as a supplemental means of establishing identity.

Bertillon records were not filed according to a fingerprint formula. In order to identify fingerprints found at a crime scene, the name of the suspect would have to be known so that his Bertillon card could be pulled and the prints compared. The only alternative was for all the Bertillon cards to be searched—an obviously impossible task. When the *Mona Lisa* was stolen from the Louvre in Paris, a clear set of fingerprints was discovered at the scene. The prints could not be identified even though it was later discovered that the criminal had been arrested shortly after the theft on a different charge and that his anthropometric card and fingerprints were on file with the Paris police.

While Bertillon never conceded the superiority of fingerprint identification over anthropometry, he was too much of a scientist not to realize the value of finger impressions. Accordingly, he was the first man to identify a criminal solely by the fingerprints in his record when the culprit was not yet a suspect and his identity was still unknown. The case occurred in Paris in 1902. A man was found murdered in his apartment. In the drawing room, the glass door of the cabinet had been broken and fingerprints were discovered on a portion of the glass remaining in the door. Bertillon was assigned the task of investigating the traces. Going through his files, then still fairly modest, he matched the latent impressions with those of one Henri-Léon Scheffer, who had been previously arrested for various crimes (see Figure 9). As a result of Bertillon's report, Scheffer's photograph was circulated among French investigation services and he was ultimately arrested and convicted.

The death knell for anthropometry came in 1903 when a prisoner by the name of William West was taken to the identification bureau of an American penitentiary. Comparing Bertillon measurements and photographs of the prisoner with filed data, the identification man discovered that there was already a prisoner by the name of Will West incarcerated in the institution. Upon comparing the cards, he discovered that both prisoners' photographs looked alike and that their anthropometrical measurements were so similar that the insignificant differences might well be attributed to inaccuracy. When both prisoners were fingerprinted, it was clearly established that fingerprinting was a far superior method of establishing identity (see Figure 10). After that, anthropometry speedily declined in

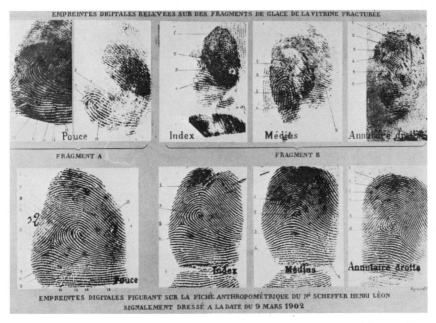

Figure 9. The five latent fingerprints shown in the top row were found by Bertillon on pieces of broken glass at the scene of a 1902 murder. The four prints in the lower row are the record impressions of Scheffer. Bertillon identified the latent prints when he searched for them through his anthropometrical file. (Courtesy: Préfecture de Police, Identité Judiciaire, Paris.)

Figure 10B. Right index of William West.

Figure 10A. Right index of Will West.

favor and fingerprinting soon gained acceptance throughout the world.

While unverified claims have circulated that fingerprints appeared as seals on American government documents as early as 1800, the first use of fingerprints in the United States of which we have evidence seems to have occurred in 1809 when Thomas Bewick (1753–1828), a famous wood and copperplate engraver, started using his thumb or finger print as a colophon, first in the book *British Birds* and later in other volumes (see Figure 11). It is surmised that Bewick got the idea after seeing Chinese finger seals on museum documents, but he may have read of the practice in one of the early anatomical writings of seventeenth or eighteenth century European scientists.

The first legal use of fingerprints in the United States occurred when Gilbert Thompson of the United States Geological Survey used fingerprints during an expedition to New Mexico in 1880–1882. Galton suggested that Thompson used the prints as a

Figure 11. A wood engraving by the famous Thomas Bewick, used as a frontispiece in his books around 1810.

guard against forgery, mostly on his commissary orders. He was probably inspired by Faulds' letter in *Nature*. Beyond Galton's statement, little evidence has been found of Thompson's practice.

The first criminal use of fingerprints was made by a fictional detective. In 1893, Mark Twain's novel *Pudd'nhead Wilson* was published in serial form in *Century Magazine*. In the story, Pudd'nhead identifies the two "twins" of Dawson's Landing by their fingerprints, and he assures the conviction of a murderer by showing the jury enlarged drawings and fingerprints. In *Life on the Mississippi*, Twain referred to the gruesome identification of a corpse in a morgue by means of fingerprints. His character, Carl Ritter, talks about an old French prison guard who told him "that there is one thing about a person which never changes from the cradle to the grave—the lines of the ball of the thumb—and he said that these lines were never exactly alike in the thumbs of any two human beings." The first half of *Life on the Mississippi* was written before Faulds' 1880 letter appeared in *Nature* and did not mention fingerprints. When the complete book was published in 1883, the passage on fingerprints was included. It is therefore likely that Mark Twain was inspired by Faulds' letter, which furnishes all of the technical data Twain used.

The first systematic and official use of fingerprints for personal identification in this country must be credited to Dr. Henry P. de Forest, medical examiner for the New York City Civil Service Commission, who in 1902 introduced a system for fingerprinting all civil service applicants. While in London as a member of the United States Civil Service Commission, de Forest had visited New Scotland Yard and there studied Henry's fingerprint system. Back in the United States, he applied it in his own way:

> "A complete set of finger prints was taken at the time the applicant for a position filed his formal application. On a duplicate sheet, when the candidate took his physical examination, the rolled impressions of the right hand were taken. When the papers of the mental examination were turned in, the rolled impressions of the left hand were taken on the same sheet. When the candidate began his work as a probationary officer, the plain impressions of the left hand were taken simultaneously and when he finally received his official appointment, three months later, the plain impressions of the four fingers of the right hand were taken. This sheet was then compared with the

original finger prints taken when the application to take the examination was filed."

The following year, 1903, Captain James Parke initiated the fingerprint system in the New York State Department of Prisons at Albany. He also tried to interest immigration officials in fingerprinting, but they informed him that "the Bertillon system is the most advantageous for the needs of this Service." Parke's efforts represent the first official state use of fingerprints.

The major breakthrough for fingerprinting in the United States occurred at the 1904 World's Fair held in St. Louis, where Sergeant (later Inspector) John Kenneth Ferrier of the fingerprint service of New Scotland Yard instructed several American police officials in fingerprint identification. Ferrier had been sent by his superintendent, Arthur Hare, to the fair as part of a detachment of Scotland Yard detectives to guard the British crown jewels. The nine students instructed by Ferrier came from police departments in Missouri and Illinois and from the Royal Canadian Mounted Police. Later on, Ferrier instructed policemen from other states, and his pupils then went on to instruct people in their own departments. Ferrier is therefore the man primarily responsible for the rapid growth in the use of fingerprinting in the United States after 1904.

After the St. Louis Fair, fingerprinting began to be used in earnest in all of the major cities of the country. In 1905, the United States War Department adopted fingerprinting for the Army, followed in 1906 by the Navy and in 1908 by the Marines. The first state supreme court to uphold the admissibility of fingerprint evidence was the Illinois Supreme Court in the celebrated 1911 case of *People v. Jennings.*

Fingerprint experts met in California in 1915 to found the first professional organization of identification experts, the International Association for Identification, a group still in existence with regional divisions throughout the world. In 1916, the Institute of Applied Science became the first school especially organized for teaching fingerprinting to the law enforcement profession. In 1919, that school started publication of *Finger Print and Identification Magazine,* the only professional fingerprint journal that has followed the growth of fingerprinting throughout the world from its infancy to date.

As far back as 1896, the International Association of Chiefs of Police had started a national Bertillon file for the purpose of creating a central repository for identification records, which some time later were moved to Washington, D.C. After fingerprint files had been added, the central bureau's files were ultimately combined, in 1924, with the fingerprint records of the federal penitentiary at Leavenworth, Kansas, to form the nucleus of the identification division of the newly created Federal Bureau of Investigation, headed by J. Edgar Hoover. Henry's classification system, which proved inadequate for the collections housed in the U.S. files, was modified and enlarged in 1917 by A. J. Renoe to accommodate files encompassing millions of fingerprint cards and was extended again in later years. The FBI now houses the largest fingerprint collection in the world.

While early western researchers in fingerprints during the seventeenth and eighteenth centuries were mostly anatomists and physicians, when law enforcement became involved in fingerprinting for personal identification in the late nineteenth century the medical profession's interest in the subject somewhat waned. In the past fifty years or so, however, medical science has taken a renewed interest in fingerprints. The impetus was provided by the famous Dr. Harold Cummins, now professor emeritus of the medical school of Tulane University. In 1926, at a meeting of the American Association of Anatomists, Dr. Cummins introduced the term dermatoglyphics to describe fingerprints in the context of his anatomical and biological studies of friction ridge designs. Since then the term has been widely adopted by anatomists, physical anthropologists, geneticists and other researchers in embryology as a description of the prints of fingers, palms and soles.

Dr. Cummins' interest in the subject was aroused in 1921 when the anatomy lab of Tulane University received the body of an adult male Negro. In examining the body, Cummins discovered that the man had an extra big toe on each foot, and Cummins decided to dissect the feet to study their internal structures. During his preliminary investigation, he devoted some study to the external surfaces of the toes as part of the routine dissection. Not knowing much about friction skin patterns on the human body, Dr. Cummins decided to research the subject, but he could find little of value aside from the use of fingerprints for identification. From that time until his retirement in 1964, he spent a great deal of time studying dermatoglyphics. His 1926 paper was the result of his first research efforts, in which he was assisted by Dr. Charles Midlo. Together, they authored many articles and two books on the subject. Many others have since joined them in their medical research.

By the time fingerprinting had spread throughout the United States, many other countries were already using the new method of personal identification. As far back as 1888, the German veterinary surgeon Wilhelm Eber urged the Prussian government to adopt fingerprinting for criminal identification. Eber must have been inspired by Faulds' letter to *Nature,* for he proposed to use the new technique to identify criminals by matching the latent impressions they left at the scene of a crime. He also advocated the use of iodine fumes for the development of latent prints, a technique still used today. Even though the Prussian government turned down his proposal, Eber should be considered one of the pioneers of fingerprinting because he had devoted considerable study to it before Galton announced his first experiments.

The other foreign fingerprint pioneer who deserves special mention is Dr. Juan Vucetich of La Plata, Argentina. Born on the Dalmatian Island of Lessina in 1858, Vucetich emigrated to Argentina in 1884 and joined the police force in La Plata. He happened to read an article on Galton's experiments in the May, 1891 issue of the *Revue Scientifique,* written by Henri de Varigny. Fascinated by the subject, he immediately started working with fingerprint identification, and less than three months later he had worked out a system of classification. He called it "icnofalangometrica," derived from the Greek words for finger track. At the suggestion of another pioneer, Dr. Francisco Latzina, Vucetich later discarded the term in favor of "dactyloscopy."

Vucetich's system was put into practical use in the La Plata Police Department in 1891; he was, therefore, the creator of the first system of identification by fingerprints to come officially into use. He announced his method at the second Latin American Congress of Science held in Montevideo, Uruguay, in March 1901 and in 1904 he published the fingerprint textbook *Dactyloscopia comparada.* On July 1, 1907, the Académie de Sciences of Paris voted Vucetich's method the best classification system, a judgment shared by several English authors. Vucetich's system of fingerprint classification is widely used today, with local modifications, in all Spanish-speaking countries. It serves as the basis for many other local systems.

Fingerprints have always held a great fascination for Latin

Figure 12. The Cuban government some years ago honored one of its civil servants, Juan Steegers, as a fingerprint pioneer by issuing these stamps in his memory.

American researchers and policemen. A number of Latin American countries pioneered, and then abandoned, the idea of fingerprinting all citizens. In 1921, Cuba honored its fingerprint pioneer, Juan Steegers, by issuing special commemorative postage stamps (see Figure 12). The Spanish-language literature on fingerprinting is almost as voluminous and varied as that in English. Latin American friction skin identification experts were as estimable forerunners as those in England who were primarily responsible for the development of fingerprint classification systems and as those in Germany and France who helped to develop techniques for making crime-scene finger impressions visible.

Chapter 2

The Nature of Friction Skin

Fingerprints are graphic representations of the patterns of the ridged skin on the distal phalanges of the fingers and thumbs. A graphic representation may be an inked impression or some unintentional impression. The palmar surfaces of the hands and the plantar surfaces of the feet are covered by a layer of friction skin, so designated because nature has provided those surfaces with corrugated skin to insure a firmer grasp and to resist slippage. Friction skin may be likened to a miniature series of roads along mountaintops separated by valleys. The mountain roads represent the friction ridges, while the valleys in friction skin are referred to as furrows or grooves. Friction skin has also been compared to automobile tires, with their road-gripping treads and the grooves in between. In a fingerprint illustration, the ridges are normally depicted by black lines and the white spaces in between the ridges represent grooves (see Figure 13).

Anatomically speaking, friction skin consists of two main layers: the epidermis or outer skin and the dermis or inner skin. The epidermis is also called the stratum Malpighi. The dermis is also known as the cutis or corium (see Figure 14).

The friction ridges are dotted with irregularly spaced and shaped pore openings; perspiration is discharged through the ducts from the sweat glands located in the corium. Perspiration, which serves as a lubricating agent for the friction skin, also provides a means by which criminals can be connected with objects or scenes of crimes. When a finger touches a smooth surface, the perspiration coursing over the ridges causes an imprint of the ridge pattern to be left on

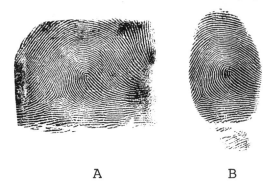

A   B

Figure 13. A represents a rolled impression of a
thumb. B is the plain impression of the same digit.

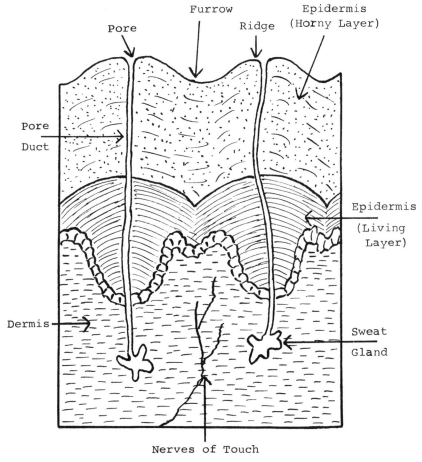

Figure 14. A diagrammatic sketch of friction skin.

that surface. Such an imprint is usually, though not necessarily, invisible to the naked eye and is referred to as a latent print, or a chance impression. Latent prints can be made distinct through the proper use of powders or the application of certain vapors or chemical solutions (see Figure 15).

Perspiration that exudes through the pores in friction skin consists largely of water (about 98.5 percent). The remainder is made up chiefly of organic acids, salts (mainly sodium chloride), neutral fats and cholesterin, and extracts (including urea) with epithelium. Perspiration exuded by the friction skin's sweat glands does not contain a significant quantity of oil. Oils are secreted mainly by the sebaceous glands adjacent to hair follicles. Approximately 62.5 cu mm of perspiration is excreted at a finger tip in one hour.

Skin thickness varies in different regions of the body. On the average, the skin on the ball of the fingers of an adult male is 1–2 mm thick, measured from the top of the ridge inward to the junction of the epidermis and the dermis. Ridge width also varies but is generally about .45 mm on adult males. The friction ridges of women are usually finer and narrower. Cummins suggests that the anatomical dimensions of friction skin should not be taken by directly measuring single ridges, since differences of ridge breadth may occur on the same individual, but by counting the average number of ridges that transversely cross a one-centimeter line. According to his data, the average number of ridges per centimeter on the ten digits of 200 white adult males is 22.3.

The size and age of the body are in direct correlation with the

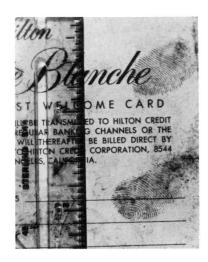

Figure 15. Latent print on a credit card, developed by the ninhydrin process.

width and coarseness of ridges, as are the types of employment men engage in. It might be stated parenthetically that the same type of friction skin present on humans can also be found on the plantar and palmar surfaces of anthropoid apes such as the orangutan, chimpanzee and gorilla. In fact, striking similarities exist between the fingerprints of certain monkeys and those of humans. Our lesser brothers' fingers show friction ridge designs that can be properly classified as loops and whorls, but little time has been devoted so far to a thorough study of this natural phenomenon. Going beyond such studies, it has occasionally been suggested that the nose prints of dogs are as individual as the fingerprints of human beings (see Figure 16).

Fingerprints form definite patterns that appear to have a general resemblance in shape and design. Their resemblance allowed fingerprint pioneers to devise systems of classification for fingerprint patterns; now they allow practical use to be made of large collections

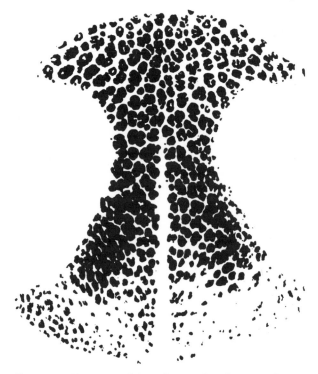

Figure 16. Noseprint of the Belgian police dog "Alex." Noseprints have been said to be as reliable an index of identity for dogs as are fingerprints for humans.

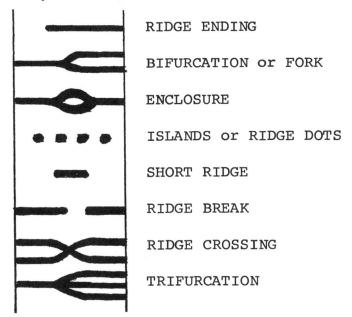

RIDGE ENDING

BIFURCATION or FORK

ENCLOSURE

ISLANDS or RIDGE DOTS

SHORT RIDGE

RIDGE BREAK

RIDGE CROSSING

TRIFURCATION

Figure 17. The minutiae or ridge characteristics by means of which identity is established. Some technicians, probably in an attempt to increase the number of ridge characteristics found to be identical in two compared prints, mark an enclosure as two bifurcations, just as they indicate a short ridge or a ridge break as being two end ridges. This practice, while not recommended, does not affect the validity of a finding of identity between a known and a suspect print unless an insufficient total number of matching ridge characteristics exists.

of prints that can be filed according to a definite scheme. Identification—the process by which two fingerprint impressions are determined to have been made by the same finger of the same person—is established not by comparing general shapes or designs but by quantitatively and qualitatively comparing the ridge characteristics, or minutiae, that compose a fingerprint pattern. Minutiae are also sometimes referred to as Galton details; primarily, they comprise ridge endings, bifurcations or forks, enclosures, islands or ridge dots, and short ridges. Other characteristics sometimes mentioned include ridge breaks, ridge crossings, and trifurcations (see Figure 17). In the process of identifying fingerprints, then, general patterns serve as class characteristics, while ridge minutiae constitute individual characteristics. Identification must be established by individual characteristics; class characteristics alone can never be the basis for finding identity.

By studying fingerprint patterns, one can observe that in some prints there appear, between the fully developed friction ridges, a number of finer and less developed fragmentary ridges. Such incompletely developed ridges are called incipient, or nascent, ridges. They typically lack pore openings and are not considered for the purposes of identification and classification because they lack the permanence of fully developed ridges (see Figure 18).

Figure 18. Between the heavy black lines, which represent the friction ridges of the pattern, there appear narrow ridge fragments. These fragments are called incipient or nascent ridges. They are not used for classification or identification purposes.

FRICTION SKIN FORMATION

The friction skin patterns on the palms of the hands and on the soles of the feet are fully developed at birth. While it is impossible to determine exactly when during fetal development the patterns start forming, it has been found that the ridges first appear in the third or fourth month of prenatal development. The embryo is covered with an epidermis about one cell thick at three weeks. As growth progresses, several layers in the form of strips develop underneath the epidermis. Called primary ridges, these strips multiply by outgrowth and by splitting away, and eventually sweat glands sprout from them.

Through the process of differential growth, the strips ultimately develop into ridge minutiae. Within the skin, and especially at the junction of the epidermis and the dermis, series of irregularly distributed pegs, referred to as dermal papillae, determine the ways in which friction ridge patterns are formed. Since the epidermis is in fact molded by the dermal papillae, it follows that the underlying layer, the dermis, has the same ridge patterns as the epidermis. As a result, when the epidermis is injured the ridges grow back after healing in the exact patterns they took before. If the injury reaches deep enough into the dermis and destroys the dermal papillae, then growth of new epidermal cells is impaired and a permanent scar is created. In Figure 19 observe that, where the epidermis is missing, similar friction ridge patterns occur in the underlying dermis.

In essence, the outermost layer of the epidermis is composed of an accumulation of dead, cornified cells that constantly slough as scale from the exposed surface. The underlayers of the epidermis, however, consist of living cells that constantly multiply to replace the dead scales lost from the surface of the epidermis. In the intermediate layers of the epidermis, the cells undergo progressive cornification as they approach the outer surface. Every epidermal cell begins its existence as an active, live cell in the lower part of the epidermis and is gradually shifted to the surface.

One of the principal premises upon which fingerprint identification rests is that ridge patterns never change during the life of an individual. In terms of embryology and histology, that premise is incompletely stated because, as we have already seen, where the dermis is injured permanent scars may develop, altering the patterns of the friction skin.

CONGENITAL ABNORMALITIES

Physical or biological malfunctions during prenatal growth can, in rare cases, produce aberrant formations of the epidermal ridges and can cause congenital malformations of the digits, resulting in odd-

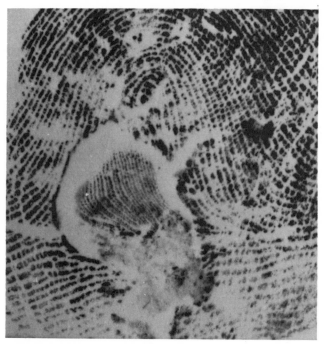

Figure 19. A piece of the epidermal skin has been torn away in this fingerprint and unveils part of the underlying dermal layer of the skin, which also shows dermal ridges. (Courtesy: Kriminalpolitisentralen, Oslo, Norway.)

shaped friction skin patternings. Among the latter, Cummins notes brachydactyly (abnormal shortness of the fingers or toes), ectrodactyly (congenital absence of one or more digits—also referred to as oligodactyly), macrodactyly (abnormal largeness of fingers or toes), polydactyly or hyperdactyly (more than five digits on a hand or foot), symphalangy (end-to-end fusion of the phalanges of the fingers or toes), orthodactyly (fingers or toes cannot be flexed, ordinarily as the result of symphalangy), and syndactyly (congenital side-to-side fusion of the digits, from simple webbing to intimate bodily union).

Even though the intimate study of the abnormal ridge formations belongs to medicine and anatomy, fingerprint technicians should be familiar with common abnormalities. The most frequently seen include the following:

Dissociated Ridges

Dissociation occurs, it is believed, as a result of disturbances during the third and fourth months of pregnancy when the finger ridges form on the fetus. According to Cummins, dissociation happens when individual ridge elements are formed but for the most part fail to consolidate into continuous ridges. The condition can be localized in a small area of the fingerprint or it can cover significant friction skin areas (see Figure 20). Medical studies have revealed that a marked tendency for disturbed or dissociated ridge patterns can be found in the fingerprints of schizophrenics, epileptics and others affected by such disorders and deviations as albinism and mongolism. Dissociated ridge patterns also occur in people not suffering from such afflictions.

Dysplasia

A term used in fingerprinting to refer to the incomplete or faulty development of friction skin, resulting in patternless surfaces. This

Figure 20. An example of the dissociation of friction ridges.

condition is sometimes referred to as ridgeless skin, but that is really incorrect, because ridge elements are present; as a result of faulty embryological development, the pebblings fail to align in continuous ridges (see Figure 21).

Figure 21. The extreme dysplasia shown in this illustration is caused by faulty development of the friction skin in the prenatal stage. (Courtesy: Institute of Applied Science.)

Split Ridges

An abnormality caused when, in the embryological process of differential growth, the spacing among the ridges diverges from the norm to produce the appearance of split or paired ridges (see Figure 22).

Figure 22. The irregular pairing of the ridges here is the result of abnormal embryological development.

Cuspal Patterns

The German anatomist Dr. Otto Schlaginhauffen, in his studies of configurational friction pattern types in nonhuman primates, discovered certain oddities in pattern shapes that are rarely seen in man. He defined them in a study published in 1905. One, cuspal patterns, has been found several times on human beings (see Figure 23). It is a condition in which the ridges flow upward rather than form loops or whorls, and they do not group in any recognizable pattern.

Figure 23. These two odd pattern formations on the thumbs of an individual are called cuspal patterns.

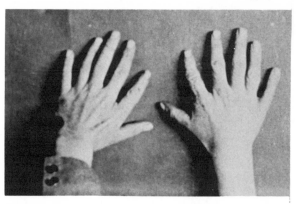

Figure 24. In this example of polydactyly, an African native has six fully formed digits on each hand. (Courtesy: R. Heiby, Tananarive, Malagasy Republic.)

Of the digital anomalies noted by Cummins that result in freak friction ridge patterns, these are perhaps the most common:

Polydactyly

The appearance of supernumerary digits is not uncommon. It is not always easy to determine the identity of the digits when more than five are found on a hand or foot. Sometimes it is found that a

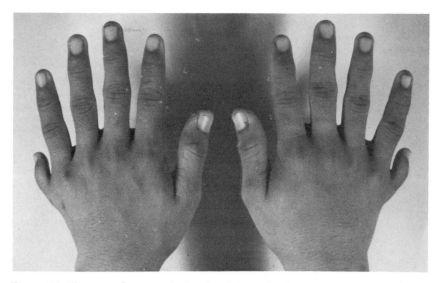

Figure 25. The extra digits on the hands of this individual are incompletely formed and resemble appendages. (Courtesy: R. Heiby, Tananarive, Malagasy Republic.)

person has five perfectly formed fingers in addition to a thumb (see Figure 24); on other occasions the additional digit appears to be incompletely formed and resembles an appendage (see Figure 25). Supernumeraries also occur on the feet (see Figure 26). When extra digits are formed normally, they have ridge patterns that in most instances are as normal as those on the other digits (see Figure 27). Patterns on the extra digits can be identified, classified and interpreted.

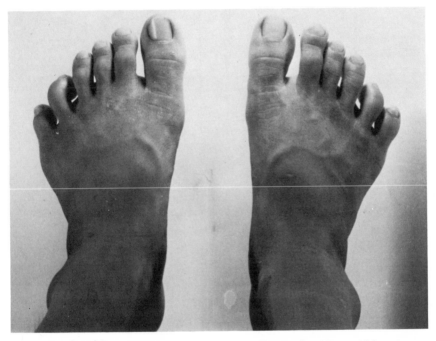

Figure 26. The same individual whose hands are illustrated in Figure 25 has six normally formed toes on each foot. (Courtesy: R. Heiby, Tananarive, Malagasy Republic.)

Syndactyly

The side-to-side fusion of two or more digits, this condition is commonly known as webbed fingers or toes (see Figure 28). In fingerprinting webbed digits it is frequently observed that two complete patterns exist side by side (see Figure 29). Sometimes the patterns are separated by a slit or furrow (see Figure 30), either at the top of the pattern or down to the base of the ridge image, especially on a split thumb.

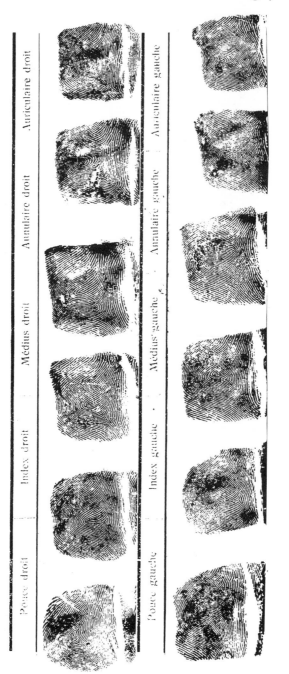

Figure 27. Normally formed supernumeraries show normal ridge patterns.

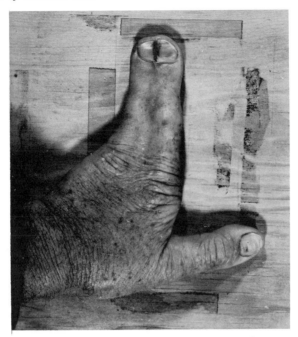

Figure 28. An example of syndactyly or webbed fingers. (Courtesy: Sheriff's Identification Bureau, Washoe County, Nevada.)

Figure 29. Webbed fingers frequently show two complete patterns. (Courtesy: Sheriff's Identification Bureau, Washoe County, Nevada.)

Figure 30. An example of a split thumb. (Courtesy: R. Heiby, Tananarive, Malagasy Republic.)

Ectrodactyly

Some people congenitally lack one or more digits on a hand or foot; they may be born with only four or three or, rarely, two digits on a hand (see Figures 31 and 32). In one known instance, a Mexican male's right hand had only one digit; the peculiar feature was that friction skin wholly covered the lone finger.

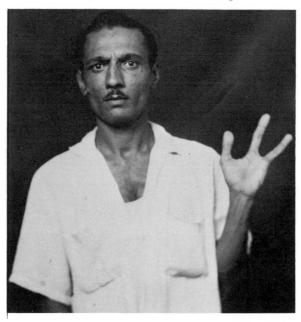

Figure 31. The congenital absence of one or more digits on the hand is called ectrodactyly. (Courtesy: Fingerprint Bureau, CID, Bombay, India.)

Left thumb.	Left index.	Left middle.	Left ring.	Left little.

Figure 32. The rolled prints of the three digits shown in Figure 31. (Courtesy: Fingerprint Bureau, CID, Bombay, India.)

COMMON POSTNATAL MARKS

Unnatural skin formations or marks that occur after birth generally do not impair classification or interpetation. Creases show up in fingerprints as straight white lines without puckering at the ridge ends (see Figure 33). Creases are caused mainly by flexion and by buckling of the skin because of the kind of work done or because of cracking of the epidermis as a result of dryness. They can be numerous on one finger and nearly absent on the next, but they

Figure 33. The creases in this fingerprint pattern show up as white straight spaces but do not affect pattern interpretation.

Figure 34. Warts show up in recorded fingerprints as white spots surrounded by black circles.

usually occur on nearly all of the digits on a hand. Warts also show
up conspicuously in fingerprints. They register as white spots each
surrounded by a black circle (see Figure 34). A wart is a mound
that rises above the normal surface and in so doing causes conges-
tion of the surrounding ridges. After a wart disappears, friction skin
normally returns to the exact pattern that existed before the wart
appeared; in rare cases, a permanent ridge defect resembling a scar
is left. Knife, paper and razor cuts also show up in prints. In appearance resembling creases, cuts are generally narrower and more
uniform in width (see Figure 35). When the skin heals, ridge patterns assume their previous characteristics, provided the cut is superficial. If the cutting instrument reaches the dermis, permanent

Figure 35. The fine white line across the pattern is caused by a skin cut.

Figure 36. The odd ridge formation here is caused by the puckering of the ridges as the result of a permanent scar, which disfigures the whole pattern area.

damage can be done to the dermal papillae, resulting in a scar. Scarred patterns show extensive ridge puckering; in some cases, puckering is mistaken for a congenital defect such as patternless skin or dissociated ridge images (see Figure 36).

Figure 37. The right print is that of a Japanese taken before World War II. The subject was severely burned in the explosion of the atomic bomb dropped on Hiroshima. The left print was taken after the burn wounds had healed and shows that no change in ridge pattern occurred as a result of exposure to intensive atomic radiation. (Courtesy: Institute of Applied Science and National Police Identification Section, Tokyo, Japan.)

Certain skin diseases can also permanently deform or mark the friction ridge patterns, especially in the cases of leprosy, eczema and keratosis. But when only scarification results, identity is not affected and the individual can still be positively identified by his fingerprints. Atomic radiation does not appear to have any effect on ridge patterns, as is illustrated in the two impressions in Figure 37. The left print was taken years after the 1945 explosion of the atomic bomb on Hiroshima, Japan; the right print is one of the same subject taken before he was subjected to the burns in the explosion. When digits are amputated, friction skin on the remaining stub often shows the puckering characteristics of scarring (see Figure 38), although the skin in some cases seems smoothly cut.

Figure 38. The top part of the print shows what remains of the partially amputated digit. The bottom part shows friction ridge patterns on the proximal phalanx.

OCCUPATIONAL MARKS

Just as certain diseases sometimes alter the appearance of friction skin patterns, a person's occupation or hobby can leave marks on his fingers that are characteristic of his occupation or hobby. Stone cutters' hands usually bear distinctive marks. Guitarists' hands show evidence of frequent contact with their instruments' strings, and the right thumbs of saxophone players are usually peculiarly marked. Some marks point to particular jobs, as the little white specks that show up in a shoemaker's fingerprints indicate his use of the awl, but it is generally difficult to discern the cause of marks by seeing the abnormal fingerprint alone.

In dividing all occupations into groups according to the degree of exposure to which hands are subjected while at work, we might recognize three categories: work using mainly the intellect, light manual work, and heavy labor. In the first category are lawyers, teachers, doctors, clergymen, executives, salesmen, students and people in a host of other occupations. People doing light manual work include cooks, housewives, opticians, painters, photographers, watchmakers, bartenders, taxi drivers, waiters, nurses and gardeners. Heavy manual work would be expected of mechanics, bricklayers, plasterers, carpenters, sanders and electrical construction workers doing wire pulling.

While it might be expected that people doing other than manual work would show no characteristic ridge defects—which is the general rule—it has nevertheless been found that constantly handling papers over a period of years can cause the ridge elevations of the fingers to wear down to such an extent that it becomes difficult to record legible inked fingerprints. Such persons would probably leave latent impressions that are difficult to identify because of the relative flatness of the ridges. This situation has been observed in secretaries, teachers and executives, but it could happen in any occupation involving prolonged paper handling. The same general flattening or eroding of ridge elevations is usually noted in people whose hands are immersed in water for long periods of time, as is the case with many housewives and laundry women. Cases have also been observed in which the right index finger of elevator operators exhibited extensive flattening of the ridges due to the constant pushing of buttons, while the other fingers of the hands showed normal ridge elevations. Here, then, we may speak of a truly occupational marking that is characteristic of a certain job.

Skilled and unskilled laborers who do heavy manual work most often show some signs of their occupation in the ridge structure or patterns of the finger. Some representative cases are illustrated in Figures 39–42. Welders and solderers often get burned and thereby damage extensive ridge areas of the fingers and hands. Since most of their burns are superficial and destroy only the epidermis the skin regains its original patterns, upon healing, without leaving scars. A permanent scar results only if the dermis has been dam-

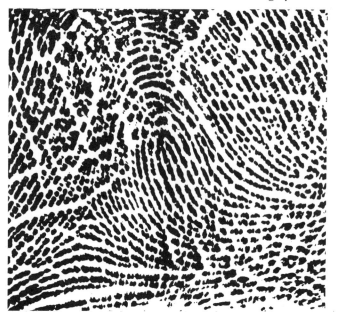

Figure 39. The fingerprint of a plasterer, showing definite ridge breaks that are the result of his occupation.

Figure 40. A print of the right thumb of a bricklayer.

Figure 41. A right thumbprint of a steel worker whose job it is to tie construction steel with wire.

aged. Comparing the impressions of the hands of laborers with those of persons not involved in heavy manual labor illustrates the difficulty of using the characteristic marks in the investigative process as a means of determining the occupation of a person from his fingerprints. A study of the fingerprints of a professional photographer illustrated in Figure 43 compared with those in Figures 39–42 reveals no clear characteristics that serve to distinguish the occupationally affected finger designs of the manual laborers from those of other individuals. The prints in Figure 43 are those of a person whose hands are constantly immersed in or in contact with photo-

Figure 42. The left index fingerprint of a welder.

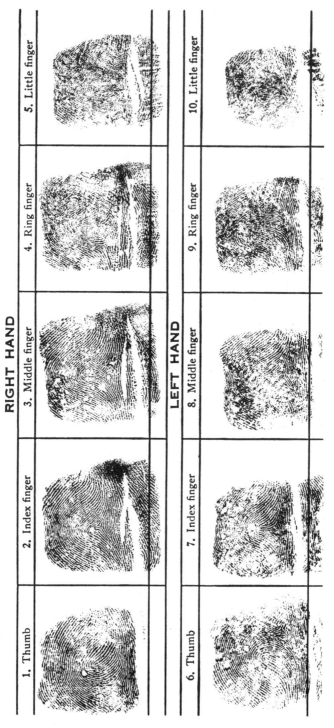

Figure 43. The fingerprints of a photographer whose hands are frequently immersed in photographic chemicals.

6. Thumb | 7. Index finger

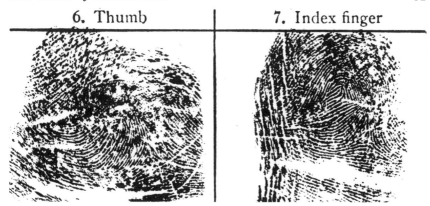

Figure 44. An example of the appearance of infectious dermatitis in a fingerprint.

graphic chemicals. As a result, the skin on his fingers and palms is rough and it is difficult to obtain a legible set of fingerprints.

People occasionally contract a disease that results in a partial or complete destruction of the friction ridges, as in the case of patients suffering from leprosy. Ridge destruction caused by disease may be of a temporary or permanent nature, depending on the disease. Skin marking is observed on hands affected by infectious dermatitis (Figure 44) and by jungle rot (Figure 45). Such marks are often mistaken for occupational damage. And a general flattening of the ridge relief is not necessarily caused by manual work, either; it can be the result of disease. Truly characteristic occupational marks show themselves in ridge patterns as creases, cuts, punctures, flat-

Figure 45. A right thumb print affected by jungle rot.

tened ridges, partial ridge abrasion and callosities. Unless the damage is total, it does not affect the identification processes, although it frequently interferes with proper classification procedures.

MUTILATION

Whenever the epidermal skin is injured to the extent that its texture is damaged, the friction ridges heal as scar tissue. Accidental injury is responsible for the appearance of many oddly mutilated fingerprint images. Intentional injury usually causes less damage to the skin because it is most frequently directed toward only certain portions of the finger.

Superficial damage to the epidermal skin results in a temporary scar that gradually disappears. In all cases in which minor injury affects only the friction ridges, the skin patterns assume the same detail they had, to the most minute characteristics, before the injury. Controlled experiments of limited mutilation of the friction skin by cutting and burning have repeatedly confirmed that statement. When damage reaches the dermis, affecting the ridge-building dermal papillae, a lasting disarrangement of the skin patterns in the form of a permanent scar results. Such permanent disturbances may be minor, resulting in a small area of puckered ridges in the patterns, or they may be serious, resulting in a ridge image that defies classification. In some cases, the scar causes the fingerprint to appear to be of a different pattern from that of before the injury. Generally, however, it is easy to recognize the presence of scar tissue in a fingerprint. And scarred patterns usually do not present any difficulty insofar as identification is concerned because identity can be established by considering only the portion of an impression that contains clearly defined, unscarred friction skin. Stated summarily, mutilation of the skin, provided the dermal papillae are affected by the injury, causes some pattern difference after healing, but only in that a scarred design will then exist. Superficial injuries do not change ridge patterns. If any injury is sufficiently deep, the resulting scar itself acquires permanent features and remains on the skin in unchanged form throughout an individual's life.

Throughout the years, criminals have often attempted to "disguise" their identity by intentionally scarring their fingers. Among the means employed have been cutting, stabbing, carving, sanding, scraping, burning, acids, and surgery. In the gangster era of the

1930s, Jack Klutas ineffectually mutilated his ten fingers by carving them. August Winkler supposedly attempted to destroy his fingerprints through an operation, although the Chicago Police Department's identification men maintained at the time that his fingers were damaged in an automobile accident.

The notorious gangster John Dillinger attempted, between September 1933 and July 1934, to destroy his fingerprints, apparently by applying corrosive acid to them. Prints taken at the morgue after he was shot to death, compared with fingerprints recorded at the time of a previous arrest, proved that his attempts at defacement were futile (see Figure 46). Knowing a little about cores and deltas and having been instructed that without cores and deltas an individual's prints could not be classified, Dillinger had a doctor apply acid to the key areas of all ten patterns. (Some sources suggest that the doctor changed the prints by carving.) But, unknown to Dillinger, identification is based on principles totally different from those of classification.

Another convicted criminal attempted to preclude identification by skin grafts. Using an ordinary razor blade, he cut out portions of the pattern areas on some of his fingers and had them grafted upside down on other digits. When he was arrested in Denver in 1953

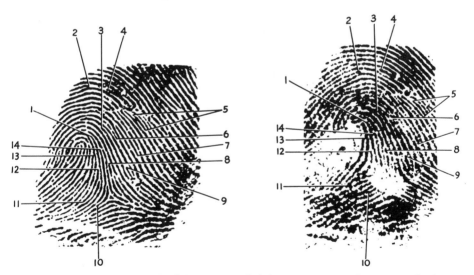

Figure 46. The print on the left was recorded from the right index finger of John Dillinger prior to scarification; the one on the right is the right index taken from the morgue prints recorded after Dillinger was shot. (Courtesy: Institute of Applied Science.)

by the United States Secret Service, it was shown rather dramatically that his attempt to prevent identification had failed, as is illustrated in Figure 47. He claimed to have sewed the patches onto his fingers with a needle and thread, but it is believed that he merely impressed them in place and kept them on the open wounds by means of bandages until the grafts took hold.

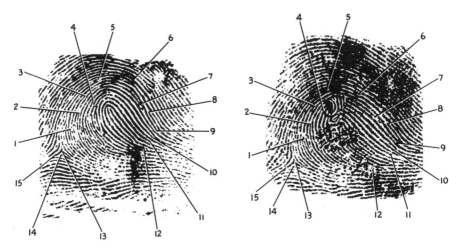

Figure 47. On the left is Donald Darling Roguerre's right thumb print as it appears on an early arrest record card. The print on the right is of the same finger recorded after scarification. (Courtesy: Institute of Applied Science.)

A more spectacular attempt was that of Roscoe Pitts. When Pitts was arrested and fingerprinted by Texas law enforcement officers in 1943, the bulbs of his fingers showed no identifiable ridge detail; his fingertips seemed devoid of friction skin (see Figure 48). Upon questioning, he admitted to having submitted to a very painful and lengthy operation. Pitts had had a doctor cut five two-inch strips of skin from the right side of his chest. The strips were left attached to the chest at one end. The doctor then removed as much of the skin on each finger of the left hand as he could and bound the left-hand digits to the skin strips on the right side of the chest for three weeks, after which the edges of the chest skin strips were severed, so that Pitts had chest skin growing on all of his left-hand fingers. A similar operation was conducted on the fingers of the right hand, transferring strips of skin from the left side of his chest (see Figure 49). His altered finger tips lacked friction skin patterns. After Pitts

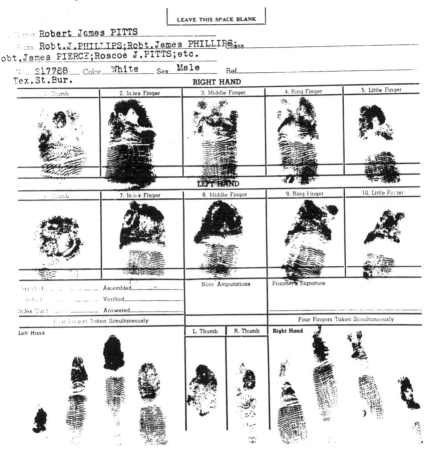

Figure 48. The set of fingerprints of Robert James Pitts, alias Roscoe Pitts, recorded after the transplant of chest skin tissue onto the fingers. Note the clarity of the ridge detail on the second phalanges of the fingers. (Courtesy: Texas State Bureau of Identification.)

had been arrested and told his story, earlier fingerprints were discovered and Pitts was identified by the friction skin on the second joints of his fingers, which shows clearly in the fingerprint card taken after arrest (see Figure 48). Twenty-nine identical points were charted in the alleged and in the known prints of the second joint impression of the left index finger, as shown in Figure 50. Pitts seemed to have gained nothing from his painful operation. If anything, because of the publicity given his case, Pitts was recognized far more readily by the strange, patternless skin on his fingertips than he might have been had he left his fingers intact.

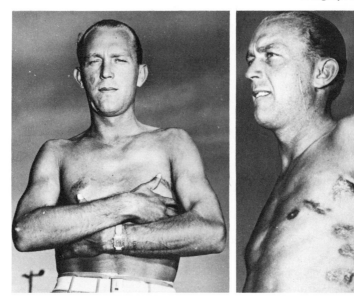

Figure 49. A graphic illustration of the transplant process that was used to obliterate Roscoe Pitts' fingerprints.

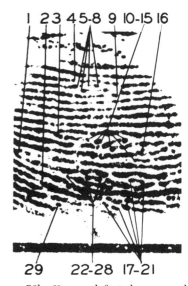

Figure 50a. Alleged left index, second joint impression of Robert James Pitts.

Figure 50b. Known left index, second joint impression of Robert James Pitts.

Figure 50. This identification illustrates the futility of Pitts' attempt to avoid identification by covering his friction ridges. (Courtesy: Texas State Bureau of Identification.)

In the few illustrative cases discussed here, scarification or pattern change was permanent. A 1958 case proved that extreme injury, willfully inflicted, can be merely temporary in nature. A prisoner was found to have burned his finger bulbs by placing them on a hot wire sieve, resulting in an injury of a grill design covering the pattern area of the fingers (see Figure 51). It may be observed, however, that sufficient ridge detail remained unscarred on the sides of the sieve burns to permit positive identification by fingerprints. Then too, after receiving first aid and medical care the burns started healing, and when the prisoner was fingerprinted again some time later the scars had completely disappeared and friction skin was again visible. A comparison with the fingerprints taken

Figure 51. Intentional scarification by burning the finger on a hot wire sieve. The scarification was temporary and after the injuries had healed the pattern returned to its former condition. (Courtesy: Major Abel K Darwish and Criminal Identification Department, Ministry of the Interior, Cairo, U.A.R.)

after the convict's first arrest eighteen years earlier, proved that the ridge details were still identical. In the 1930s, a plastic surgeon grafted skin from the palms onto the right index finger of a man who had accidentally been extensively burned on that finger. Palmar skin had been selected for the graft because of its resemblance to the finger pattern. The graft took hold. The pattern did have an unnatural appearance, however, and an examination of the finger itself clearly revealed traces of the graft. In every case of skin grafting, both for unlawful and legitimate purposes, it has been easy to detect any tampering with the original friction skin patterns. Yet, a skillful surgeon, selecting the proper palm pattern for grafting onto a finger, could conceivably perform a pattern graft that could not be distinguished as artificial in a fingerprint—but not on the finger itself.

Attempts to evade identification by mutilation of finger patterns, then, have proved unsuccessful. The most authoritative voices, obviously, are those of people who have made such attempts. Roscoe Pitts, interviewed in 1958 while incarcerated in a state penitentiary in South Carolina, gave this reaction to a question put to him about the effectiveness of his attempt to evade identification: "Any crook who has his fingerprints rubbed off is nuts. If I had fingerprints, I probably wouldn't be behind bars today. Any policeman in American could spot my marks half way across the room. It's given me nothing but grief."

DERMABRASION

In the latter half of the 1950s, Dr. James W. Burks, an associate professor of clinical dermatology at Tulane University's Medical School in New Orleans, developed a means of treating certain skin afflictions by wire brush surgery. The technique involved anesthetizing the problem area with a local refrigerant and then planing it with a rapidly revolving circular wire brush. Burks suggested that when this method was used for the treatment of friction ridge surfaces, the ridges might be obliterated by dermal planing. When a subject appeared who suffered from a small keratotic lesion on one finger, Burks decided to remove the lesion by the wire brush method. Mindful of the possible implications, he alerted law enforcement specialists in fingerprinting, who recorded the impressions of the fingers before surgery. After the process was completed by planing the skin to a depth in excess of 1 mm—or until minute herniations of fat became visible—postoperative procedures of providing antibiotics and gauze dressings were initiated. After the crust was removed from the finger on the twenty-third postoperative day, pink skin totally devoid of ridge patterns and free from scars was visible. Recording the finger's print at different intervals, the last one twenty-four weeks after the operation, disclosed that the new epidermis that grew over the abraded area remained devoid of friction ridges (see Figure 52). When the operation was later repeated on the finger of another patient who was treated for removal of arsenical keratoderma, the results were identical to those obtained for the first patient. If this technique were applied to all ten fingers encompassing their total friction skin area, it would obviously be possible to remove fingerprints permanently. It would, of course, require the cooperation of a surgeon, and identity could still be established by the friction skin ridges on the second and third phalanges of the fingers, as well as by the ridges on the palms and soles. Moreover, a person being taken into custody with evidence of such intervention would have quite some explaining to do if no legitimate medical reason for the operation could be proved. Obviously, a person would draw greater attention to himself under such circumstances than if he had unaltered finger patterns, and he might find himself reiterating the cogent remarks of Roscoe Pitts.

Figure 52. The print on the left is that of the planed fifth digit of a male patient. The print on the right was recorded prior to dermal planing. (Courtesy: Dr. J. W. Burks, New Orleans, La.)

Fingerprint Individuality

The three basic premises upon which identification by means of fingerprints rests are as follows: the ridge patterns that make up fingerprints differ from individual to individual and also from finger to finger even on the same hand; fingerprint ridges and their patterns never change, except in size during growth, throughout the life of an individual; and although each fingerprint is unique in its ridge characteristics, fingerprint patterns vary only within certain limits, which makes possible a systematic classification according to types of patterns. The first two premises are easily stated but difficult to support.

In the past, fingerprint experts have been prone to offer as proof of those two premises the fact that no two fingerprints have ever been found to be identical. The trouble with that statement is that it would constitute proof of uniqueness only if every one of the millions of fingerprints on file in the identification bureaus of the world had been compared with one another, which obviously has never been done. All of the fingerprints collected in just one bureau have not even been compared. Fingerprints are filed according to a mathematical classification formula based on pattern types occurring in a ten-finger set of fingerprints. Classification, then, deals with class characteristics (pattern types and their subdivisions), and does not specifically take into account individual ridge characteristics.

Positive proof of those first two basic premises may be furnished as recent research in automation and in computer scanning of fingerprints becomes reality. Doing away with traditional classification systems based on pattern interpretation, current research involves the design of computer-controlled scanning of fingerprints essentially for ridge characteristics rather than by pattern types. When a sufficient number of prints has been stored in the computer memory, it will be possible to compare each print with every other print.

The impossibility of fingerprint pattern duplication, then, is difficult to establish, even though it is one of the cornerstones of fingerprinting. Despite the difficulty, sufficient objective data has been accumulated to afford a substantial basis for accepting the premise that prints from two different fingers can never be identical. Starting with the premise that nature never duplicates itself in its smallest details, a premise universally accepted by anthropology and botany, the closest nature comes to duplication is in identical twins. Many twins cannot be told apart even by their parents. Throughout the history of modern fingerprinting, nearly all identical twins have been fingerprinted by scholars eager to test the premise of the uniqueness of fingerprints. While pattern similarities have often been found, not one case has occurred in which twins' fingerprints were ever remotely similar in individual characteristics.

That is not to say that the premise has not been challenged. On an average of three or four times a year, some newspaper or periodical headline reports that identical twins with identical fingerprints have been discovered. Upon investigation, each claim has been proved false. In most cases, the similarity has been in classification formula (based on similar pattern types); in some cases, not even that coincidence has been present.

The fingerprints of all known births of triplets, quadruplets and quintuplets have been recorded and compared, with unvarying results establishing the difference of the patterns in terms of individual ridge characteristics. No two fingerprints from different fingers have ever been found to be identical among the extensive sampling of similar fingerprints in the world's identification collections. Experts have painstakingly compared many thousands of loop patterns with the same ridge count and general appearance and have found them to be different in ridge details. Experts have also attempted to find within a small blocked-out area a number of identical ridge characteristics located in the same positions in any two fingerprints. One expert reported finding, at the most, four such characteristics, but as soon as the area was widened slightly the many differences became obvious.

In attempting to illustrate mathematically the impossibility of duplication of ridge details in any two different fingerprints, researchers have suggested various approaches, all arriving at extremely low figures of probability. The French scientist Victor Balthazard used the following procedure. A transparent grid covering squares of one millimeter each was superimposed upon a fingerprint of normal size. Each square was sized to fit over one ridge characteristic of the fingerprint. Within each square, any of the different types of ridge characteristics might be found. Multiplying the number of different types of ridge characteristics that can occur in one square by the total number of squares in the grid obtained figures that defy conception.

The endurance of ridge patterns during the life of an individual has also been clearly established by the tens of thousands of experiments conducted in the past fifty years all over the world. Many of the fingerprint records that arrive in identification bureaus for filing and classification are those of criminal recidivists. In many instances, up to ten different sets of fingerprints from the same individual, recorded at different intervals by different technicians in different bureaus, come together in central fingerprint repositories such as state identification bureaus and the FBI Identification Division. Some of the prints have been recorded twenty years or more apart. The old sets of prints are compared with each new set received; no natural changes in the pattern details have ever been noted. Before sets of fingerprints are withdrawn from the "active" files because of the deaths of their subjects, the old prints are compared with postmortem prints, a procedure which also has substantiated the unchanging nature of ridge patterns.

The persistence of palmprint patterns is the same as that of fingerprints. This fact was graphically illustrated in April 1939 when *Finger Print Magazine* published two palmprints of William N. Jennings, one taken in 1887 and the other in 1937, fifty years apart. Jennings, a member of the Franklin Institute in Philadelphia, attended a lecture at the Institute in 1887 and heard the speaker say that the skin markings on a human hand do not change during a man's lifetime. Jennings, then aged 27, was so impressed by the idea that he inked and recorded the palm and fingers of his right hand, dated the record sheet, and filed it away with the intention of comparing the palmprint with a new one half a century later. He did exactly that when, in 1937 at age seventy-seven, he again recorded an impression of his right hand and fingers that showed the ridge patterns to be exactly alike in their most minute details.

Through his incomparable collection of fetuses and his study in the field spanning an adult lifetime, the formidable authority on dermatoglyphics, Dr. Harold Cummins, has clearly demonstrated that the complete friction skin pattern is present on the unborn child's palms and soles. Untold numbers of identifications made after death, in many instances from corpses not otherwise recognizable, establish that the friction skin remains unchanged until decomposition or destruction of the skin. If the skin is preserved after death, the patterns will remain indefinitely without change. In 1952, the remains of a man's body were discovered in a Danish peat bog. Archeologists estimated that the man, dubbed the Grauballe man, had been dead since about A.D. 310. The corpse possessed well-preserved ridges on the flat of the right hand and foot. The papillary ridge patterns on the left hand could not be read because the fingers were too mummified. On the right hand, the same was true of the index, ring and little fingers, but the right thumb and the middle finger showed clear ridge details.

The persistence of friction ridges throughout life, then, can be demonstrated by objective evidence. But even though it is more difficult to reduce to a simple formula the evidence for the individuality of finger designs, all fingerprint researchers, even those not connected with law enforcement agencies, are firmly convinced that of all the systems for proving identity only fingerprinting affords infallible identification.

Chapter 3

Pattern Interpretation

All fingerprints can be divided into three classes of patterns: loops, whorls and arches. Some 60–65 percent of all patterns are loops, 30–35 per cent are whorls, and about five percent are arches. These divisions hold true for all systems of classification, although minor variations can occur if specific patterns are variably defined and accordingly classified.

Before we can study specific pattern types, a general familiarization with the terminology used in pattern interpretation is required. In looking at friction ridge patterns, note that while most ridges run parallel to other ridges (as in Figure 53A) special formations of ridges are occasionally observed. Sometimes, ridges running in one direction curve smoothly in the form of a hairpin without touching any angular formations; these are called *recurving ridges* (see Figure 53B), sometimes referred to as looping ridges. When two ridges running parallel suddenly separate to run in opposite directions, we refer to them as diverging ridges (Figure 53C) and we call that general area a divergence. The point at which two or more ridges run into each other to form a point is called a convergence, and the ridges are called converging ridges (see Figure 53D). If, instead of two ridges forming a divergence, only one ridge splits or forks into two lines, each running in a separate direction, we have a bifurcation (Figures 53E and F), or a trifurcation when one line forks into three branches (as in Figure 53G). A short ridge abutting an otherwise smoothly recurving ridge is called an appendage (as in Figure 53H). Whenever such an appendage rests on a recurving ridge, the recurve is said to be spoiled and cannot be characterized as a true

64

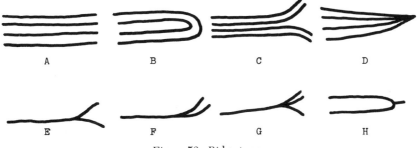

Figure 53. Ridge types.

recurving ridge. True recurving ridges must not touch any angular formations and must not abut any other ridges at an angle.

The process of assigning names to various patterns is called pattern interpretation. It proceeds according to the outlines devised by Henry. Only a portion of a fingerprint is needed for it, and the portion used for determining whether a pattern is a loop, whorl or arch is called the pattern area. It consists of those ridges encircled by typelines which are the two innermost ridges that form a divergence tending to encircle or encompass the central portion of a fingerprint.

Typelines are present in loops and whorls and in a few types of archlike patterns, notably some tented arches, although they are of little or no significance there. At the point of typeline divergence there often appears another characteristic ridge formation somewhat in the form of a triangle, resembling to a certain extent the widened area at the mouth of a river. That location in a fingerprint pattern is appropriately referred to as the delta. Figure 54A illustrates a river emptying into a lake, and the similarity between it and the pattern area of a loop is apparent in Figure 54B, where the detail of the pattern area is purposely omitted. In Figure 54C, the detail has been included and the typelines, formed by the diverging ridges circling the delta, have been drawn in with heavier lines for the sake of emphasis. The area surrounded by typelines is all that is needed to interpret and classify fingerprint patterns.

Since, as we will soon learn more extensively, whorl patterns have at least two deltas, it follows that whorls have at least two sets of typelines, one set for each delta. This is illustrated in Figure 54D. In real fingerprints, of course, ridges do not always continue to run parallel without interruption or joined ridges. Sometimes, two par-

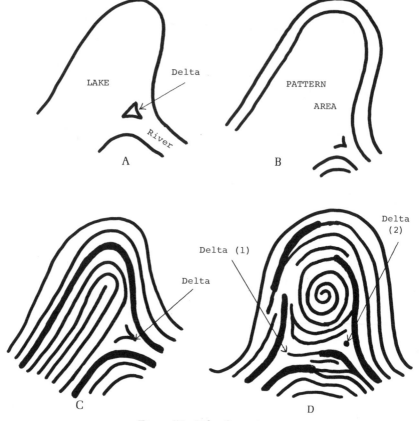

Figure 54. Ridge formations.

allel ridges join smoothly to form a bifurcation, or they stop alto-gether, or they are simply interrupted. When the line being used as a typeline suddenly ends, or when there is a definite break in it, the next outer ridge is considered the typeline. When the ridge traced as the typeline bifurcates, the outer leg of the bifurcation is chosen as the typeline. Both of these possibilities are illustrated in the upper typeline of delta one in Figure 54D.

DELTAS

Two fixed locations within various kinds of patterns are the delta and the core. The delta, sometimes called the outer terminus, is de-fined by the FBI as "that point of a ridge at or in front of and nearest the center of the divergence of the typelines." The delta can be a ridge dot, a short ridge, the forking point of a bifurcation, an ending ridge, or, when no specific ridge characteristic exists in that location, the point on the ridge running in front of the divergence nearest the center between the innermost diverging ridges. The various delta locations are illustrated in Figure 55, which consists of simple loop drawings showing typelines and a recurving ridge as well as the point where the delta is located.

Figure 55. Delta locations.

It must be obvious by now that it can be extremely important to determine not only which ridges constitute the typelines but also exactly where the precise point of divergence is. In Figure 56 the approximate point of divergence of typelines is illustrated. Figure 57 shows a short curved line, marked A-A, which is actually the upper typeline since it runs parallel to the lower typeline B-B before diverging. The line Y-Y, not being one of the two innermost diverging ridges, is outside the pattern area. The delta in Figure 57 is the ridge dot marked D because it is the closest ridge characteristic near the center of the divergence. Figure 58 is essentially the same as Figure 57 with the exception that the short curved ridge Y-Y is located in a slightly different position. That line does not, at any

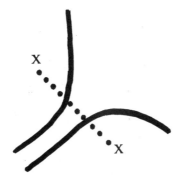

Figure 56. Point of typeline divergence.

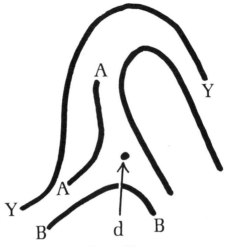

Figure 57.

point, run parallel to the lower typeline B-B before separating from it. For that reason, line Y-Y cannot be a typeline. The upper typeline is the line marked A-A. The delta in Figure 58, however, is located on the lower end of the short curved ridge Y-Y because it is the ridge characteristic closest to the center of the diverging typelines. The ridge dot in Figure 58 is another ridge characteristic, but it cannot be considered to be the delta of the pattern because it is not located near the center of the typeline divergence.

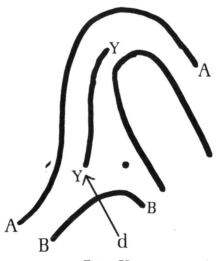

Figure 58.

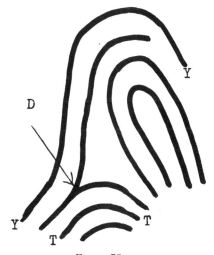

Figure 59.

Bifurcations are never considered to be typelines because two ridges are necessary to form a divergence and a bifurcation is essentially one ridge splitting into two branches. If a bifurcating point occurs near the center of the typeline divergence, however, the point of bifurcation may qualify as a delta, as in Figure 59. If several bifurcations occur in succession, as in Figure 60, the bifurcation

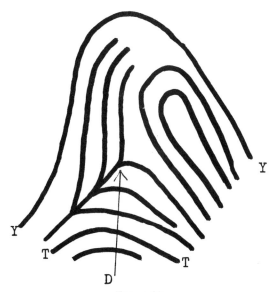

Figure 60.

nearest the center of the pattern, and farthest away from the divergence, is selected as the delta. Such a selection process is valid only
when all bifurcations open toward the center of the pattern. Although we previously asserted that bifurcations cannot be considered to be typelines, in one circumstance this rule does not apply. If
the two legs of a bifurcation continue to run parallel for a while
before diverging, then the two legs constitute typelines, as in Figure 61. The location of the delta in loops and whorls is determined
by the same rules.

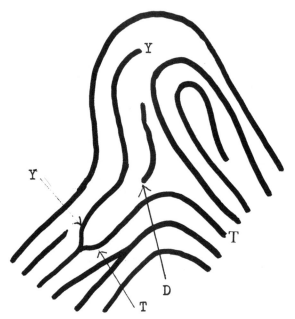

Figure 61.

CORES

The second fixed location within certain patterns is the core,
sometimes called the inner terminus. The core is important for the
correct interpretation of loops, as well as for whorls in a few instances. Whenever we talk about a core, we refer to the specific location within a pattern that has been given that name. Arch patterns do not have cores, although it is customary to talk about the
core area, in the broader sense, as encompassing the core location

as well as the immediate, surrounding ridge detail. The basic rule in determining the exact location of the core in loops is that it is a point located on or within the innermost recurving ridge; that point is determined more precisely by reference to a series of arbitrary rules fixed by Henry, the originator of the system. The principal rules are summarized here.

1. When there is no ridge detail within the innermost recurving ridge, the core is located at the shoulders of the innermost recurving ridge at the side away from the delta (see Figure 62).

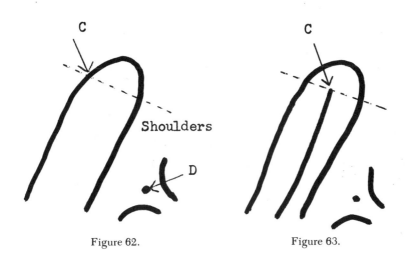

Figure 62.   Figure 63.

2. When a single ridge rises within the innermost recurving ridge up to the shoulders of the recurve, the core is located at the top of that ridge (see Figure 63). Only those rods within the innermost recurving ridge that rise as high as the shoulders of the looping ridge are considered; if a rod remains below the shoulders of the loop, or if any other ridge formation occurs below the shoulders, such ridge details are ignored for the purpose of ascertaining the location of the core (as illustrated in Figures 64 and 65).

3. When an odd number of ridges rise within the innermost recurving ridge up to the shoulders of the recurve, the curve is located at the top of the center rod (see Figures 66 and 67).

4. When two ridges end within the innermost recurving ridge at the height of the shoulders of the recurve, the top of the one farther from the delta is the core (as in Figure 68).

5. When either four or six rods appear within the innermost re-

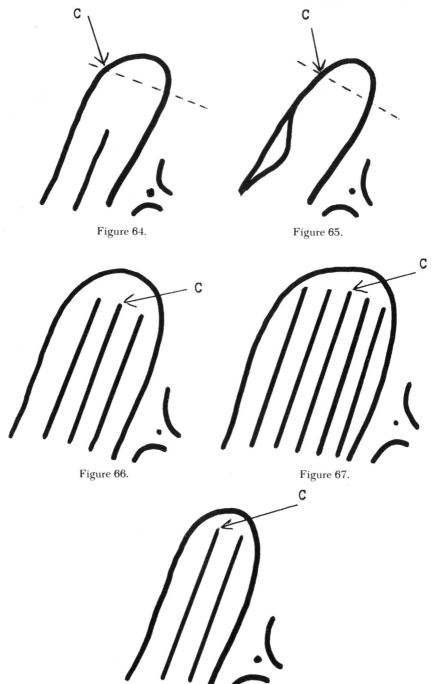

Figure 64.

Figure 65.

Figure 66.

Figure 67.

Figure 68.

curve, only the two innermost are considered and the previous rule applies (see Figure 69). It is important to reiterate that only those rods that rise as high as the shoulders of the loop are considered (as illustrated in Figures 70, 71, and 72).

Since Henry decreed that a recurving ridge is spoiled if an appendage touches it or if another rod flows into it at right angles, it follows that such a recurve can no longer be considered the innermost recurve. The next one accordingly becomes that ridge, which

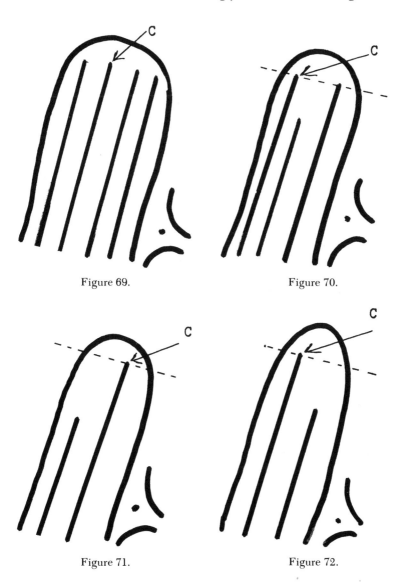

Figure 69.

Figure 70.

Figure 71.

Figure 72.

decides where the point of the core is located (as is illustrated in the various core designs shown in Figure 73). On the other hand, ridges that flow smoothly from recurving ridges in the form of bifurcations do not spoil recurves (see Figure 74).

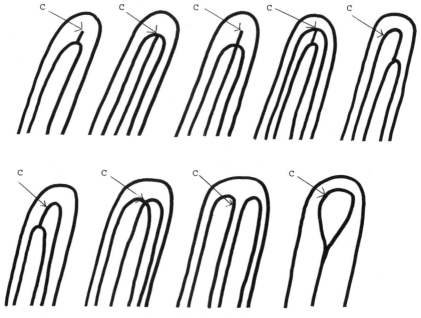

Figure 73. Core designs.

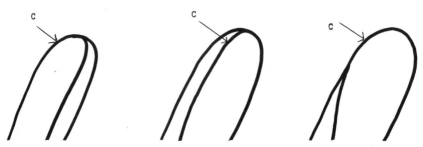

Figure 74. Smoothly flowing ridges.

LOOPS

A loop, of course, contains a looping or recurving ridge, but several requirements must be met before a pattern can be interpreted as a loop. Essentially, a loop must have three features: an unspoiled recurve, a delta, and a ridge count of at least one. Its core is located on or within the innermost recurve.

Figure 75 illustrates two typical loop patterns. In both, many recurving ridges appear between the points marked as cores and deltas. If we know that the ridge count of a loop pattern is ascertained by counting the number of ridges that cross an imaginary line drawn between the core and the delta, we can readily observe that each of these two loop patterns has more than one ridge. In the pattern to the right, the core is formed in the same manner as was illustrated in Figure 63, while in the pattern to the left the core is the same as that in the second drawing of Figure 73. In both loops, the delta is a ridge dot located near the center of the divergence of the typelines (as was also illustrated in Figure 62). Not all loops fall so clearly within the requirements for that type of pattern. Whenever the ridge count is low, a careful study of the pattern is necessary to determine whether or not the essentials of the loop are met. Each of the two loop patterns in Figure 76, for example, has only one recurving ridge.

Loops are further subdivided into ulnar and radial loops. In order to determine whether a loop is ulnar or radial, only the slant of the recurving loop ridges and the hand from which the pattern comes are considered. Ulnar loops slant toward the ulna bone (little finger) of the hand; radial loops slant toward the radius bone (thumb) of the hand. In right-hand patterns, ulnar loops slope to the right and radial loops to the left. In left-hand patterns, ulnar loops slope to the left and radial loops to the right (see Figure 77).

Figure 75. Two typical loops.

Figure 76. Loops with one recurving ridge.

RIGHT HAND FINGERS   LEFT HAND FINGERS

Ulnar   Radial   Ulnar   Radial

Figure 77.

WHORLS

The second most numerous class of fingerprint patterns are whorls. This class is further divided into four distinct patterns: plain whorl, central pocket loop, double loop, and accidental. One characteristic of whorl patterns is that they must have two or more deltas. Plain whorls, central pocket loops and double loops have two deltas; accidental patterns have at least two deltas (see Figure 78d).

Plain Whorl

The FBI defines a plain whorl as one that "has two deltas and at least one ridge making a complete circuit, which may be spiral, oval, circular, or any variant of a circle. An imaginary line drawn between the two deltas must touch or cross at least one of the recurving ridges within the inner pattern area. A recurving ridge, however, which has an appendage connected with it in the line of flow cannot be construed as a circuit. An appendage connected at that point is considered to spoil the recurve on that side." Some of the FBI's plain whorl qualifications become clearer when studying

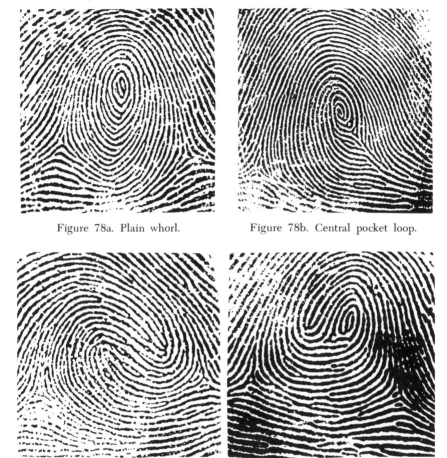

Figure 78a. Plain whorl.   Figure 78b. Central pocket loop.

Figure 78c. Double loop.   Figure 78d. Accidental.

the other types of whorls. Several different plain whorls are illustrated in Figure 79.

Central Pocket Loop

This whorl pattern combines features of both the loop and the whorl. It often resembles a whorl inside a loop, although it may take other forms. There are essentially three variants among central pocket loops: those resembling plain whorls, those resembling loops, and obstruction-ridge central pocket loops. The first type of variant superficially resembles a plain whorl, but when an imaginary line is drawn between the two deltas that line does not cross

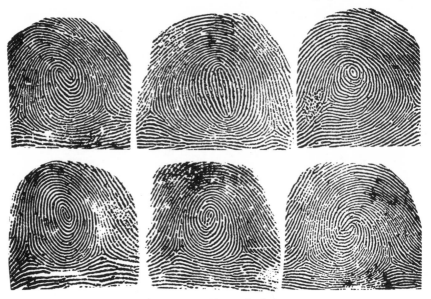

Figure 79. Plain whorls.

or touch any of the circular ridges in the center of the pattern. In discussing plain whorls, we noted that an imaginary line drawn between the two deltas must touch or cross one of the inner circular ridges. If no such line is touched or crossed, the pattern is a central pocket loop rather than a plain whorl. (See Figure 80.) The second variant resembles a loop with a small whorl hidden within its ridges to form what appears to be a pocket. The recurve of the loop turns around a second time below the core to form the pocket, but the second recurve need not be a continuation of—or even connected with—the looping recurve. It can be an independent ridge. Various

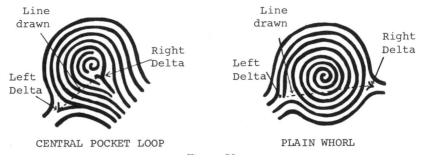

Figure 80.

Figure 81. Second recurving central pocket loops.

types of second recurving central pocket loops are illustrated in Figure 81. At least one of the recurves must be free from right-angle appendage ridges. As with looping ridges and plain whorl circular ridges, an appendage is considered to spoil the recurve. The distinction between loops and central pocket loops is made clear in Figure 82 with reference to "spoiled recurves." Figure 82A shows a pattern resembling a loop that has an apparent second recurve below the core. The second recurving ridges are spoiled by right-angle connecting ridges. For that reason, the pattern is a plain loop, not a central pocket loop. The same is true of Figure 82B, where none of the ridges below the core form a smooth, unspoiled second recurve; that pattern, too, is a plain loop. In Figure 82C, though, the second recurve below the core is smooth and unspoiled by appendages; an imaginary line drawn between the two deltas does not cross any of the circular pocket ridges, so it is a central pocket loop.

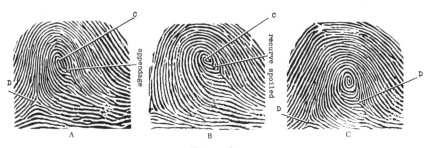

Figure 82.

Central pocket loops can also be formed by an obstruction ridge at right angles to a loop's inner line of flow rather than by a second recurve below the core. Figure 83 illustrates various obstruction ridges, which may be either curved or straight. A ridge dot, of course, cannot be considered to be an obstruction; nor can a convergence of two ridges (as in Figure 84) or obstructions that are not

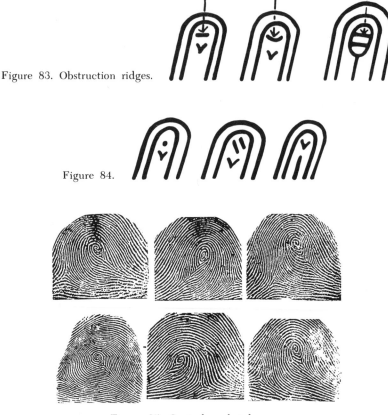

Figure 83. Obstruction ridges.

Figure 84.

Figure 85. Central pocket loops.

at right angles to a loop's line of flow, which always follows the slant of the recurving ridges that compose it. Several different central pocket loops are illustrated in Figure 85.

Double Loop

Double loop patterns consist of two separate and distinct loops that overlap or surround each other. The two loops must have separate sets of shoulders and at least one recurving ridge in each loop must be independent of the other loop formation. Double loops also have two deltas (as in Figure 86A), but the loops need not comply with all of the requirements of a loop pattern. For instance, it is not necessary that both loops should have a ridge count. If an appendage abuts the recurve of one of the loops at a right angle, that re-

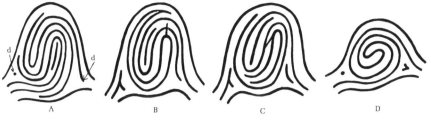

Figure 86.

curve is spoiled and cannot be considered a true recurve (see Figure 86B); that pattern is therefore not a double loop but an accidental pattern. On the other hand, if an appendage does not abut at a right angle and if a ridge flows off sideways in the shape of a bifurcation, the recurve would not be considered spoiled and the pattern is a double loop (as in Figure 86C). If the two sets of shoulders in a double loop are not independent—if one shoulder is shared by both loops in what is called an S core, as illustrated in Figure 86D—the pattern cannot be called a double loop. Because it meets the minimum requirements for a plain whorl, that is how the pattern is interpreted. Several different double loops are illustrated in Figure 87.

The double loop is an American innovation. When Henry designed his classification system and prescribed rules for pattern interpretation, he did not use the term double loop. Henry divided

Figure 87. Double loops.

Figure 88. Accidental whorls.

patterns of that class into two categories: twin loops and lateral pocket loops. Lateral pocket loops consist of two loops, either overlapping or surrounding each other, in which the ridges surrounding the cores of the loops terminate on the opposite side of the delta. In other words, in lateral pocket loops both loop formations flow in the same direction. They differ from twin loops in that the latter consist of loops that terminate on opposite sides of the patterns. The three upper patterns in Figure 87 would be called twin loops in the original Henry system, while the three lower patterns of the same illustration would be called lateral pocket loops. The distinction between the two groups has been abandoned in the United States, where both types of patterns are interpreted as double loops.

Accidental Whorl

This variation in the whorl class is composed of two or more different types of patterns, with the exception of the plain arch. To be more specific, an accidental whorl can be a combination of a loop and a plain whorl, or of a loop and a central pocket loop, or of a loop and a tented arch. In fact, it can be any combination of two different patterns, except a combination in which one of the patterns is an arch. As in all whorls, accidental patterns must have at least two deltas, but they may have as many as four. The term accidental, as used in the United States, does not correspond with the accidental whorl of the original Henry system; it is closer to what Henry called a composite. Figure 88 illustrates two accidental whorls: A is a combination of a plain loop and a plain whorl; B is a loop over a tented arch. A loop over a plain arch is interpreted not as an accidental whorl but as what is variously referred to as a nutant loop, a nascent loop and a nodding loop (see Figure 89). Three accidental whorls are illustrated in Figure 90; each has three deltas.

ARCHES

Even though only about five percent of all fingerprints are arches, it was found convenient to subdivide them into two different groups: plain arches and tented arches.

Plain Arch

This is the simplest of all fingerprint patterns; in fact, it has been said that a fingerprint is a plain arch if its ridges do not form any

Figure 89. Nutant loop.

Figure 90. Accidental whorls with three deltas each.

design. Essentially, in a plain arch the ridges entering the pattern on the left flow smoothly toward the right of the pattern with a small rise in the center resembling a hill. Because of the simplicity of ridge design, plain arches are not easily mistaken for other patterns. In most plain arches, the rise in the center is slight, but now and then a plain arch is found with quite a pronounced rise. The height of the rise does not affect pattern designation as long as no recurving ridges, upthrusts or angular formations are found within the pattern. Several plain arches are shown in Figure 91.

Figure 91. Plain arches.

Tented Arch

This pattern can be formed in three ways: center ridges form an arch in which an angular formation is present, one or several ridges in the center of the pattern form upthrusts or the pattern resembles and had some of the requisites of a loop but lacks at least one of its required characteristics. In Figure 92, A and B are plain arches, C is a tented arch because of the angular formation in the center, and D is also a tented arch because of the end ridge in the center that stands almost straight up (an upthrust). The seven designs in Figure

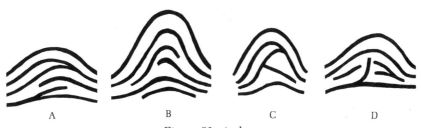

A   B   C   D

Figure 92. Arches.

93 are all tented arches resembling loops. A careful study of the patterns reveals that some of the requisites for a loop are missing in each of them. Drawings A and B have recurves but no deltas. Drawings C and E have insufficient recurves because an imaginary line drawn between the apparent delta and the apparent core will not yield a ridge count across the recurve. Drawing D lacks a re-curve altogether, as does F, where the only recurve is spoiled by a ridge that abuts it at right angles. Drawing G also has a spoiled re-curve and is enveloped by a sufficient recurve, but it has no delta. Several tented arches are illustrated in Figure 94.

In the 1920s, American fingerprint experts decided to put the looped tented arch into a class all by itself and called it an excep-

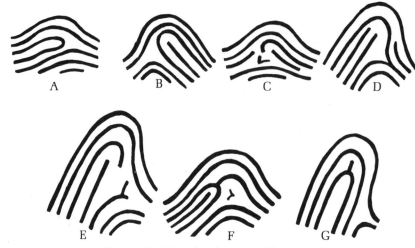

Figure 93. Tented arches resembling loops.

Figure 94. Tented arches.

tional arch. In the mid 1930s, however, the FBI discontinued use of that pattern designation. Other bureaus soon followed suit, reverting to the name of tented arch.

RIDGE CHARACTERISTICS

Identity is established by comparing some of the individual ridge characteristics within each fingerprint. As many as one hundred and fifty individual ridge characteristics can be discerned in the average full fingerprint. In Figure 95A, eleven ridge characteristics represent the most common types charted. In Figure 95B, fifty ridge characteristics are indicated. A close study of Figure 95B reveals that many more ridge minutiae are present in the pattern than have been charted. Of course, some characteristics occur more

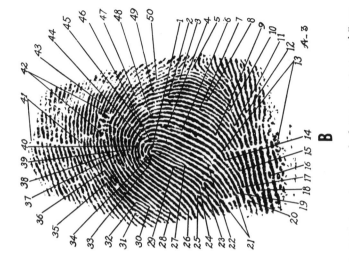

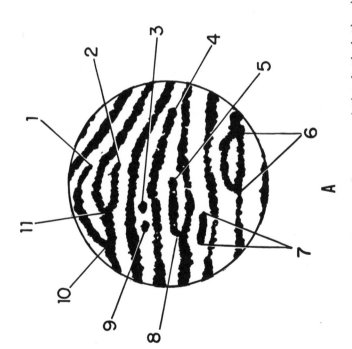

Figure 95. A shows a fingerprint fragment in which individual ridge characteristics have been marked. Points 1, 2, 4, and 5 are ridge endings. Points 8, 10, and 11 are bifurcations. Point 7 is a short ridge. Points 3 and 9 are ridge dots or islands. Point 6 is an enclosure.

In B fifty ridge characteristics have been marked. In the average rolled fingerprint there are well in excess of one hundred ridge minutiae. (Courtesy: Institute of Applied Science.)

frequently than others. The fingerprint pioneer Galton indicated that bifurcations are the most common minutiae, but his conclusion alone cannot be taken as authoritative because he based it on inadequate data.

Surprisingly little serious research has been done on the relative frequency with which the various ridge minutiae appear. Fingerprint experts generally agree that ridge endings and bifurcations are the most common. Beyond them, ranking characteristics according to their frequency of appearance in a fingerprint cannot be done with any degree of accuracy. A survey of eighty-two fingerprint experts, conducted in 1963 by Professor James W. Osterburg, produced the following ranking of characteristics in order of decreasing occurrence: ridge endings, bifurcations, deltas, ridge dots, spurs or hooks, enclosures, double bifurcations, trifurcations and bridges. As Osterburg pointed out in urging additional research, however, the experts based their opinions on their own conclusions, experience and preconceived notions, not on adequate research.

If, as Osterburg suggests, the relative infrequency of each ridge characteristic adds to its weight in establishing identity, then we should have research data based on scientifically controlled examinations. If it were established that several unusual or infrequent ridge minutiae appeared in a certain print, then fewer ridge characteristics would be needed to establish positive identity. The lack of such data has not hampered fingerprint technicians to any significant extent, though, because many ridge characteristics are required to provide positive identification. Additional data would be valuable only when identity had to be established by using fewer than the customary ten to twelve points of identification, provided that no unexplained dissimilarities existed.

RIDGE COUNTING

Ridge counting determines how many friction ridges touch or cross an imaginary line drawn between the core and delta of a loop pattern. It is a means of further subdividing loops. In order to obtain an accurate ridge count, it is important to know the exact core and delta locations. Failure to locate either the core or the delta within a pattern usually results in an erroneous ridge count. The process of ridge counting is illustrated in Figure 96, in which pat-

Figure 96. Ridge counting.

A   B   C

tern A has a ridge count of seven, B a count of ten, and C a count of eight.

A number of rules exist in ridge counting:

1. The count is made of the ridges between the core and the delta, but the core and delta themselves are never included in the count.

2. If the imaginary line crosses exactly at the point of a bifurcation of ridges, two ridges are counted.

3. If the imaginary line passes through a ridge enclosure, either in the center or through the bifurcating end, a count of two ridges is made at that point.

4. If the imaginary line touches a ridge island or dot, a count of one ridge is made.

5. A white space must intervene between the delta and the first ridge count. If no such interval exists, the first ridge must be disregarded. (See Figure 97.)

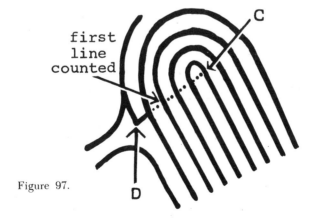

first
line
counted

C

D

Figure 97.

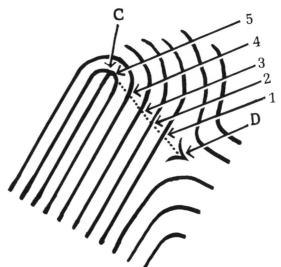

Figure 98.

6. The white space rule in counting loop ridges does not apply in most instances in the core area of the pattern.

In Figure 98, for instance, the imaginary line passes through the shoulder of the innermost loop (core) without showing any white space, but a count of one ridge is nevertheless made because the core is located at the point where the rod joins the innermost recurve. The rule here is that, when the core is located on a rod that touches the inside of the innermost recurving ridge, the recurve is counted as one ridge if the delta is located below a line drawn at a right angle to the rod; if the delta is located above a line drawn at a right angle to the rod, the ridge is not counted. The application of

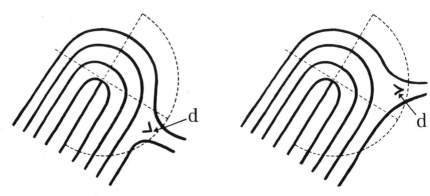

Figure 99.   Figure 100.

this rule is illustrated in Figures 99 and 100. The core of each pattern is located at the point where the rod within the innermost recurve touches that recurve. In Figure 99, the delta of the pattern falls below the dotted line drawn at a right angle to the rod; therefore, the core area recurve is counted as one ridge and the total ridge count for the pattern is three. In Figure 100, the delta of the pattern falls above the dotted line drawn at a right angle to the rod; for that reason, the innermost recurve is not counted and the total ridge count for the pattern is two.

RIDGE TRACING

The process of ridge tracing, is a further subdivision of whorls into I (inner), M (meeting) and O (outer) patterns. No distinction is made in the process of ridge tracing between plain whorls, central pocket loops, double loops and accidental whorls. The technique is based chiefly on the two focal points, the deltas, which are located according to the same rules that apply in locating deltas in loops. In ridge tracing, the ridge emanating from the lower side of the left delta is traced until it comes nearest to or opposite the right delta. By observing the number of ridges between the traced ridge and the right delta, we can determine whether a whorl pattern is Inner, Meeting or Outer according to three rules.

1. A pattern is Inner (I) if the ridge traced from the left delta passes inside or above the right delta and if three or more ridges intervene between the traced ridge and the right delta.

2. A pattern is Meeting (M) if the ridge traced from the left delta exactly meets the right delta, or if it passes over or below the right delta with not more than two intervening ridges.

3. A pattern is Outer (O) if the ridge traced from the left delta passes outside or below the right delta and if three or more ridges intervene between the traced ridge and the right delta.

Figures 101–106 illustrate various whorl drawings; ridge tracing is indicated by a dotted line. Figure 101 illustrates an Inner whorl, Figure 102 shows what is interpreted as a Meeting whorl because there is only one intervening ridge between the traced ridge and the right delta, and Figure 103 illustrates an Outer whorl.

As in ridge counting, a number of rules govern the process of ridge tracing.

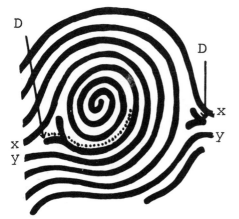

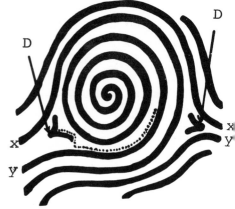

Figure 101. Ridge tracing.   Figure 102.

1. Tracing always starts on the left delta and moves toward the right delta.

2. If the traced ridge ends, the next lower ridge is selected to continue the tracing process toward the right delta. (See Figures 102 and 104).

3. The rule for dropping down to the next lower ridge also applies when the left delta is a ridge dot. (See Figure 103.)

4. The rule for dropping down applies only when there is a definite ridge ending. Short ridge breaks that may be the results of improper inking, the presence of foreign matter on fingers, enlarged

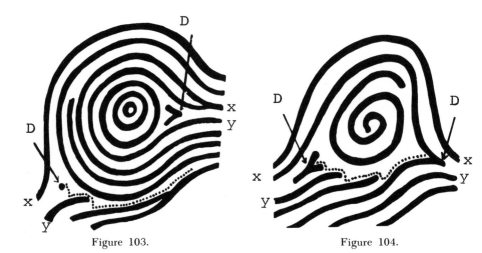

Figure 103.   Figure 104.

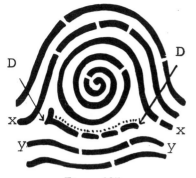

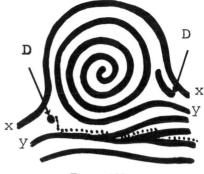

Figure 105.   Figure 106.

pores or worn ridges should not be considered to be definite ridge endings. (See Figure 105.)

5. Should the traced ridge bifurcate, tracing continues onto the lower branch of the bifurcation. (See Figure 106.)

When tracing an accidental whorl that has more than two deltas, tracing extends from the extreme left delta to the far right delta; intervening deltas are ignored. Whorl tracing is always indicated by the capital letters I, M, or O, never by the numerical count of the intervening ridges. Although it was stated earlier that whorls always have at least two deltas, sometimes a whorl is encountered that has only one delta or no deltas at all, usually because the pattern area is so large that there was not enough space between the edges of the friction skin for deltas. In a number of whorls that lack one delta, it is easy to determine ridge tracing. For example, in Figure 107 the right delta is missing. Yet, in tracing from the left delta, it is apparent that the traced ridge runs toward the inner portion of the pattern, making this an Inner whorl. When the left delta is missing or when both deltas are missing, ridge tracing might be extremely difficult, if not impossible. In that case, the pattern is arbitrarily interpreted as an M trace, with reference interpretations to I and O. (See Figure 108.)

Scarred Patterns and Amputations

Certain rules have been devised for the interpretation of scarred patterns and for how amputated digits are to be reflected in a classification formula. Minor scarification in a pattern that does not affect interpretation according to pattern type or subdivision by ridge

Figure 107.

Figure 108.

count in loops or by ridge trace in whorls requires no special rule. The scarred area is simply ignored. The same is true of all scars appearing outside the pattern area. (See Figure 109 for two impressions in which the scarification is minor and without any effect on

Figure 109. Minor scarification.

pattern interpretation.) For some patterns, recognizable by type, an accurate ridge count or ridge trace is impossible. If the corresponding finger on the other hand is of the same pattern type as the scarred impression, the latter is given the same ridge count or ridge trace as its corresponding digit. But should such a corresponding finger be of a different pattern type, suitable reference subclassifications for all possibilities must be assigned to the scarred pattern. Although Figure 110 is clearly a whorl, it is impossible to determine its ridge trace accurately because of the scarred formation in the pattern area. If we know that Figure 110 is from a right middle finger, we can look at the left middle finger. If the left middle finger is also a whorl that has, say, an inner trace, then the right middle finger can also be called an Inner whorl. Should the left middle finger be a loop or an arch, we would interpret the right middle

Figure 110.

Figure 111.

finger as I?M?O (Inner, referenced Meeting, referenced Outer) whorl.

The same rule applies to loops scarred in such a way as to make an accurate ridge count impossible, as in Figure 111. In the event a pattern is scarred to the extent that even the pattern type cannot be determined with any degree of accuracy, then that pattern is given the same interpretation as that on the corresponding finger on the opposite hand. In the event the same fingers on both hands are scarred beyond recognition, the patterns are arbitrarily interpreted as Meeting whorls. The rules for interpreting scarred patterns also apply to amputated digits and to patterns that have dissociated ridges in the pattern area. That is, if the right thumb is amputated, it is given the same interpretation as the pattern that appears on the left thumb. Should both thumbs be amputated, both are interpreted as Meeting whorls.

QUESTIONABLE PATTERNS

Sometimes patterns are encountered which defy interpretation; equally experienced technicians differ on how they should be interpreted. A technician interprets a pattern according to his best judgment, based on his knowledge of the rules of pattern interpretation, and then assigns a reference interpretation after considering the various opinions of other technicians. For example, if a technician feels that a pattern is an ulnar loop with a right count of twelve, but believes that other technicians might call it an outer central pocket loop, he will interpret the pattern as U?W—U meaning ulnar loop and W being the symbol used for all whorls. The fact that two technicians might differ about how a pattern should be interpreted does not in any way endanger the reliability of fingerprint identification. The interpretation of patterns is a preliminary process in fingerprint classification, which itself refers only to locations within a fingerprint file. The identification of fingerprints, on the other hand, is performed not by pattern interpretation but by comparing ridge minutiae.

Inexperienced technicians sometimes tend to call patterns questionable when they are unusual in formation but still can be assigned to a pattern group. So it is important to have a thorough knowledge of the rules that determine pattern types. The pattern in Figure 112 is clearly a loop. The only unusual feature is that it flows up instead of down. Yet its interpretation as a loop poses no problem for the skilled technician, nor does ridge counting. Figure 113 is clearly a plain loop, even though it somewhat resembles a central pocket loop, because it lacks a sufficiently smooth second recurve below the core. In Figure 114, the pattern appears to be a loop. Yet close study of the ridge detail reveals it to be a tented arch: no unspoiled recurving ridges pass between the apparent core

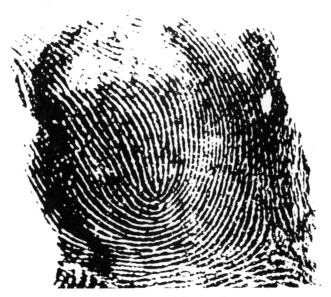

Figure 112. Upward-flowing loop.

Figure 113. Plain loop.

Figure 114. Tented arch.

and the apparent delta. Figure 115 also shows a plain loop: no un-spoiled second recurve appears below the core, which is a charac-teristic of a central loop. A truly questionable pattern is shown in Figure 116. It might be interpreted as a double loop or as an acci-dental whorl. Figure 117 is highly unusual in that a small second loop appears below the pattern area. For that reason, it would be interpreted as a double loop, yet the pattern deserves a plain loop reference, too, because it looks more like a plain loop. Figure 118 should be interpreted as a tented arch because it does not fulfill any of the requirements of other patterns. Yet, because the break in the almost circular core ridge might be the fault of faulty recording, the pattern should be referenced as a plain whorl. Indeed, if the break in the innermost ridge were not present and if the centermost ridge formed an oval, the pattern would satisfy the minimum require-ments for interpretation as a plain whorl.

An endless variety of questionable and unusual patterns could be shown. While such oddities are uncommon in view of the untold millions of fingerprints preserved in the fingerprint files of the world, thousands of odd and questionable patterns have been ob-served. For a number of years, the *FBI Law Enforcement Bulletin*

Figure 115. Plain loop.

Figure 116. Questionable pattern.

Figure 117. Double and plain loop.

Figure 118. Tented arch and plain whorl.

has printed a questionable or unusual fingerprint pattern on its back cover each month. Similarly, but for many more years, *Finger Print and Identification Magazine* has regularly printed odd and questionable patterns. Both periodicals comment on the interpretation of such patterns.

Chapter 4

Latent Prints

A criminal's most treacherous tools are his own hands and feet. On his way to and from the scene of a crime, he leaves foot or shoe impressions in soil, dust and mud, and even on carpets. At or around the scene of the crime, he leaves his personal calling card wherever he touches a smooth surface. The friction skin of the hands, fingers and feet is dotted with pores, which serve as ducts for the release of perspiration formed in the corium. Perspiration acts as a natural lubricant to prevent the skin from cracking, but it also leaves a true reproduction of the friction ridge design of the skin on any smooth surface it comes in contact with. These impressions are often invisible to the naked eye. They are the so-called latent fingerprints, and special techniques are required to make them visible.

FINGER PERSPIRATION

Under unusual circumstances, the composition of perspiration can vary slightly as a result of bodily conditions. The composition of perspiration is also greatly influenced by the nervous system. The quantity secreted depends on climate and on the physical condition of the subject, and it too can vary greatly. It is known that the lactic acid content of perspiration increases with bodily exertions and that special nutritional and pathological influences change its composition. There are reasons to assume that the amino acids in perspiration are hydrolytic products of dermal proteins, so amino acid output is probably dependent on sweat gland activity as well as on the resistance of the skin to keratin solubility. The effects of impuri-
102

ties on the skin's surface as well as evaporation or decomposition also contribute to the variability of the composition of perspiration. The well-known fact of the individual odor of perspiration must be attributed to individual composition. The slight but chemically important differences in procedural techniques for developing latent prints have grown out of the need to cope with the various compositions of perspiration.

Some authorities say that the finger pressure necessary to produce a legible fingerprint is at least one pound. But that is hypothetical and should be dismissed as inaccurate. Finger pressure is of little importance. Of far greater consequence is the bodily condition of the subject at the time he touches a surface. A person committing an act for which he fears detection perspires more than usual. The subject's age is also an important factor here. Young people, having a better lubricated skin, usually perspire more freely than older people.

The prints of young people are easily distinguishable as such because they lack ridge patterns carved with the creases that result from age, but it is almost impossible to determine sex from a latent fingerprint. Some men have small hands with fine ridges, which are most often characteristic of females. Conversely, some women have large hands with heavy ridges that leave prints easily mistaken for those of males.

THE NATURE OF LATENT PRINTS

The word "latent" is derived from the Latin *latere,* which meant "to lie hidden," and the Latin came from a Greek verb meaning "to escape notice." In the language of fingerprinting, all traces made by friction skin and found at or near the scene of a crime are referred to as latent prints. Most of the ridge traces discovered at crime scenes are made by human fingers and thumbs. However, friction ridge prints discovered at the scene of a crime could have been made by the palms or by the soles of bare feet: there is no basic physiological difference between the skin covering the inside of the fingers and thumbs and that covering the palms and soles. It is up to the fingerprint technician to interpret latent prints correctly, but the fingerprint searcher can eliminate some possibilities by describing the scene of the crime and where the prints were found (a latent print discovered on a doorknob in the winter would more than likely not be a soleprint). Regardless of the initial uncertainty concerning the friction-skin origin of latent prints, identical procedures are used in searching for, developing, transporting and preserving evidence bearing all types of latents.

Latent prints are divided into three categories: visible prints, those made by skin smeared with colored substances such as wet paint, blood, ink or mud; invisible prints, those left through the contact of the clean friction skin with a smooth surface and consisting only of a perspiration impression; and molded or plastic prints, those left in soft substances such as putty, grease, wax, paraffin, soap, asphalt or pitch, and those left in dust. In the first two categories, latents are true reproductions of the ridge patterns in an apparently two-dimensional image; in the third category, latents are impressed into the soft substance, and the grooves of the latent image represent the actual, three-dimensional friction ridge patterns of the skin.

Police officers have been heard to declare that, since most criminals nowadays know of the danger of leaving fingerprints at a crime scene and wear gloves, searching for latent prints is a waste of time. To check the validity of such a statement, many departments have conducted surveys to determine how many identifications were made from latent impressions discovered at crime scenes. By comparing the results of various surveys, it has been found that the practical use of searches for latent fingerprints depends largely on the efforts put forth by each department. The more time spent searching for latent impressions, the greater the positive results in identifying criminals. At most crime scenes a tremendous number of latents are discovered, most of which cannot be used for identification because they are blurred, superimposed or of insufficient ridge detail, the very existence of which indicates that most criminals still do not wear gloves when committing a crime. But there is a more practical reason why criminals leave fingerprints. When working, as a criminal usually does, in the dark and in unfamiliar surroundings, a person bent on unlawful enterprise must rely to a large extent on his sense of touch. Wearing gloves, the criminal soon discovers that he is seriously handicapped. Attempting to open a jewelry box lock while wearing gloves should convince anyone that only the naked hand can be successful at such a delicate operation. Nor can a person with gloves on easily feel his way around a pitch-black room; his covered fingers cannot distinguish the textures of objects, cannot inform the criminal what he is touching.

Latent impressions are indeed being found at crime scenes, and departments that seriously search crime scenes report continued success in identifying criminals by the prints they leave behind. In at least one case on record, a burglar left so many impressions at a crime scene that fingerprints for all ten fingers could be pieced together from the latents. In another case, a person who used rubber gloves and discarded them at the crime scene before leaving was identified from a fingerprint developed from a latent left on the inside of one of the rubber gloves.

SEARCHING FOR LATENT PRINTS

When a fingerprint technician learns that a crime has been committed and that he is to examine the location for latent impressions, he should immediately take all possible precautions to avoid any disturbance of the locale. He should also attempt to secure the recorded fingerprints of all persons who regularly use the premises, as well as those of officers initially investigating the crime who might accidentally have left their own impressions. As a rule, a search for latent impressions starts where a criminal gained entrance to the premises and ends where he left. The fingerprint technician examines all surfaces that the criminal might have touched. Since a number of methods exist for developing latent impressions, it is important for a technician to determine which method will give the best results on each surface he encounters. The general method used in developing latent impressions consists of applying powders to surfaces suspected of having been touched, directing fumes or vapors toward them, or applying chemical solutions to them. Whenever a technician isn't certain which method will yield the best result on a particular surface, he can first test the surface by pressing his own fingers on it or a similar surface and trying various techniques. But of course even before he decides which method to use, the technician must conduct a preliminary examination to find out if any latent impressions exist on a surface. Most invisible latent prints show up under oblique light, reflected or transmitted light, or ultraviolet or infrared rays; many show up when simply breathed on. None of these methods destroys the evidence; most save considerable time in locating latent impressions.

There are two methods for developing latent fingerprints: physical, or mechanical, and chemical. Physical means are based on the fact that perspiration retains certain substances without fusion. Examples of physical development are powder dusting and iodine fuming. Chemical techniques affect the components of perspiration directly, causing a reaction that results in discoloration. Ninhydrin, osmium tetroxide and silver nitrate are among the chemicals used.

POWDER DEVELOPMENT

If the powdering technique is preferred, it is not theoretically important which powder is used as long as it is fine grained and of a color that contrasts with the background. A fingerprint technician's field kit usually contains black, gray, silver, red and gold fingerprint powders.

Powders

Early fingerprint technicians had to prepare their own powder formulas or select single-ingredient powders from a variety of readily obtainable substances. Originally, lampblack or finely ground charcoal was used on light surfaces, lead powder or cigar ash was found useful for dark surfaces. But it was soon discovered that single-ingredient substances available from chemical houses or drug stores did not perform well under a variety of conditions. Special formulas were needed. Today, reputable fingerprint supply houses sell excellent fingerprint powders of all kinds. Most powders come in a great variety of colors that are sold under brand names and their exact composition is a trade secret. The cost of powders is so low that do-it-yourself, combination powders are no longer justified. For black powders, the principal ingredients used are lampblack, graphite, black carbon and charcoal. The most popular gray powder is an aluminum dust. It has the advantages of being extremely fine and of having tremendous adhesion. As a matter of fact, its adhesive qualities are such that it may become a disadvantage because it tends to stick to the background as well as to the hands and clothes of the user. It also is so light that it tends to blow away in a light draft; for that reason, commercially available gray powders with an aluminum base include other ingredients to minimize disadvantages. For those who attempt to experiment with making fingerprint powders, a good black powder might consist of two ounces of powdered black carbon or charcoal, one ounce of lampblack, and one-fourth ounce of aluminum dust or powdered white lead as a base.

A good, white fingerprint powder originally consisted of two ounces of white lead and one-half ounce of powdered French chalk. The use of lead, however, can cause lead poisoning because of its absorption into the system. For that reason, powders containing a lead base are seldom used in professionally prepared fingerprint powders. Another white powder that produces excellent results but suffers from the same disadvantages as the lead-content one consists of mercury and chalk—hydrargyrum-cum-creta, a developing medium recommended by the fingerprint pioneer Henry as far back as 1905. Although the powder is excellent, the disease it can cause has resulted in the total abandonment of mercury for fingerprint powders. Mercury vaporizes at room temperature, and vapors are highly poisonous. Poisoning can also occur by inhaling finely powdered mercury. The toxic effects of constant exposure to a gray fingerprint powder composed of mercury and chalk are considered to be a hazard if exposure approaches or exceeds two hundred and fifty hours a year. Prolonged exposure to the powder is capable of producing mercury poisoning. Seven men out of a group of thirty two in an English police department using mercury powder developed symptoms of chronic mercury poisoning.

A red powder that is considered to be one of the essential products in the fingerprint kit is "dragon's blood." It is a finely powdered red resin from the fruit of a palm that is used in the manufacture of zinc engravings. When a latent print is developed with dragon's blood and heat is applied to it, it will stand considerable usage without losing its image.

Among the substances used as single-ingredient fingerprint powders, or in combination with one another, are the following: anthracene (a fluorescent powder), antimony sulphide, argentorat, ashes, barium sulfate, black lead, bone black, bronze, calcium sulfite, calomel, chalk, charcoal, cobalt oxide, cupric oxide (also called copper monoxide), dragon's blood, ferric oxide, gold dust, graphite, hydrargyrum-cum-creta, kaolin, lampblack, lead carbonate, lead iodide, lead sulfate, lycopodium, magnesium carbonate, magnesium oxide, manganese dioxide, mercurous nitrate, methylene blue, potassium acid tertrate, red lead, red sulfide of mercury, Sherolite, silver chloride, silver protoinate, Sudan red, sulfur, talcum, titanium dioxide, uranyl phosphate, vermilion, white lead and zinc oxide.

When fingerprints have to be developed on multicolored surfaces, such as tin can labels, cereal boxes or magazine covers, using powders for one color may not always be satisfactory because of a lack of contrast in part of the latent. For that reason, such prints are developed with fluorescent powders. After a latent image has been developed with a fluorescent substance in the same manner as it would have been with an ordinary powder, the object bearing the latent print is removed to a dark room and exposed to ultraviolet light. A latent impression glows under ultraviolet rays and can be photographed in the dark so that the colored background of the object does not show.

Most fingerprint powders are available in one- and two-ounce jars. Since the early 1960s, manufacturers have offered aerosol as a propellant for fine fingerprint powders, but spray cans are still not widely used because serious disadvantages have been noted. Powder cannot be applied as precisely as with a fingerprint brush, and the spray process is more expensive yet does not improve the quality of obtainable latents.

Powdering Instruments

A variety of instruments is available for the purpose of developing latents, the most popular being a camel's hair brush with bristles at least two inches long—three is better—for the good resiliency necessary in high-quality dusting and developing. Shorter bristles can destroy latent ridges. Brushes are also made of horse hair, feathers, fiberglass filaments, and other soft materials (see Figure 119).

Powder is applied to a surface either by dipping a dusting brush into a powder jar and tapping powder onto the surface or by using an ear syringe, an atomizer or a spray can. Experts in the identification section of the Tokyo National Police Agency developed a dusting apparatus in 1959 that works like a vacuum cleaner. The instrument contains a small motor that simultaneously blows powder out onto surfaces and recovers excess powder. But the expensive apparatus has never been widely used because its results are not significantly superior to those of the common brush method.

Powdering Techniques

Powder a suspected surface lightly. As powder is brushed over an area containing a latent print, particles adhere to moisture deposits. Only ridge patterns stand out from the contrasting background. Good results in powdering latents are obtained only when powder

Figure 119. Six different powdering instruments. Left to right: a feather duster, three camel's hair brushes, a Zephyr fiberglass duster and a horsehair brush.

is applied sparingly. Too much powder usually causes blurring because the grooves between the ridges fill up with powder. Brush strokes must be gentle. Once the outline of a friction ridge pattern appears, better results can be obtained if the sweeping motion of the brush follows the flow of the ridges. Obtaining consistently good results can be expected only after considerable practice.

When the object bearing an impression is small and can be easily moved, brush development isn't needed. After powder is sprinkled on a suspected surface, the object should be alternatively tilted toward all sides so that the powder slides freely over the surface. Once an outline of a ridge pattern appears, tilting should be directed toward keeping enough powder sliding over the latent impression until the desired intensity is obtained. Then remove excess powder by turning the object upside down. Latents developed by the sliding method are sometimes clearer than brushed ones (see Figure 120).

Lifting Powdered Prints

Whenever fingerprints are found on a surface that cannot be readily transported or photographed, they have to be lifted from that surface for comparison. Various techniques are available for lifting powdered latent prints. The media most commonly used are

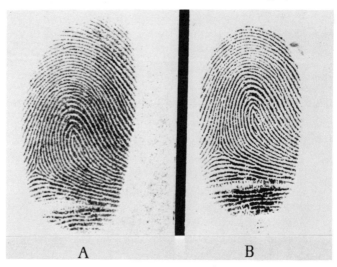

Figure 120. The latent print in A was developed by the powder and brush method. In B, the print was developed by sliding powder over the latent-bearing surface. The print developed by the sliding method is noticeably clearer and resembles an inked impression.

transparent lifting tape, individual transparent lifters, and opaque rubber lifters. Transparent fingerprint lifting tape comes in rolls resembling adhesive tape, but it is wider, free from impurities, and manufactured under more exacting conditions. Lifting tape is available in clear and matte finishes. Individual lifters, consisting of a small piece of lifting tape with or without a backing sheet but having a tab on the lifter, come in sizes of from about two-and-a-half inches square to four inches square. Opaque rubber lifters come in sheets of black or white flexible rubber that are four-by-nine-and-a-half inches and resemble tire patch. Rubber lifters, however, cannot be used when latent impressions are developed with mercurized white or chalk powders because both preparations blend into the rubber and darken it.

After a print has been developed with powder and excess powder has been carefully brushed away from the surface adjacent to the print, a piece of lifting medium (cut to size in the case of tape or rubber sheets) should be applied to the powdered print by pressing the adhesive side down firmly, with the fingernail over the print to remove air bubbles. If tape or individual cellophane lifters are used, the lifting medium should be peeled slowly off the print and transferred to a special latent print transfer card.

Most latent print transfer cards are three-by-five cards provided with a one-and-a-half inch blank square to which the lifted print is applied. There are two different kinds. On one, the blank square is white to receive black powdered lifts. On the other, the square is black and serves as a contrasting background for gray and white powdered latent lifts. The rest of the card contains spaces for recording appropriate data concerning the location from which the latent was lifted, the date of processing, the name of the technician, and so on (see Figure 121). Because a powdered surface shows through the tape on the lifter, the image as viewed through the tape appears exactly as it was seen on the object that contained the chance impression from which it was taken. Incidentally, tape also protects latent images from accidental destruction.

If opaque rubber lifters are used, the image of the latent print cannot be seen directly through the tape; the image on the lifter is a reverse reflection of the original. So a loop sloping toward the left will appear to slope toward the right. To obtain the correct appearance of the latent, the image on the rubber lifter must be photographed and the negative printed upside down: that is, with the emulsion side away from the emulsion of the photographic paper.

Latent fingerprints on paper or cardboard cannot be lifted by any of the methods so far described because peeling adhesive tape or an

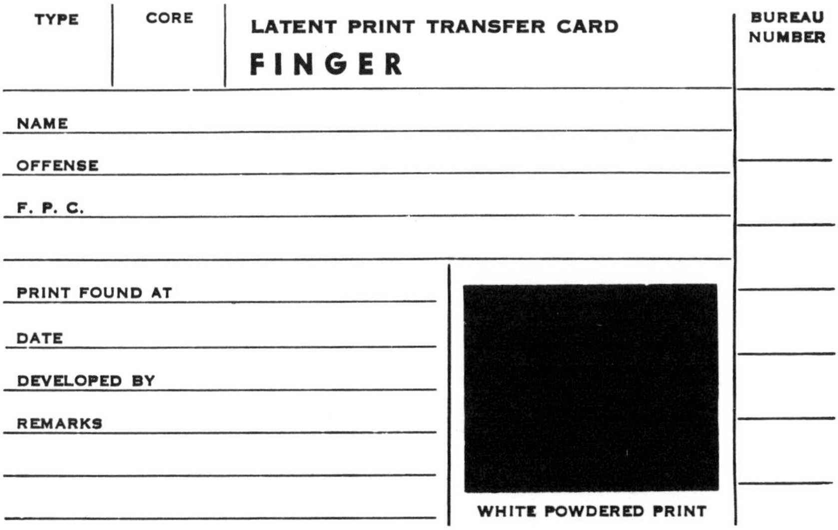

TYPE	CORE	LATENT PRINT TRANSFER CARD FINGER	BUREAU NUMBER
NAME			
OFFENSE			
F. P. C.			
PRINT FOUND AT			
DATE			
DEVELOPED BY			
REMARKS		WHITE POWDERED PRINT	

Figure 121. Sample of a latent fingerprint transfer card.

individual lifter form paper causes the fibers to stick to the tape. But most paper and cardboard surfaces can be easily transported, so lifting prints from them is unnecessary. Latent impressions on such surfaces can be protected from damage merely by being covered with transparent lifting tape, which should not be peeled off. The same is true of latent prints on small movable objects.

Before any fingerprint is lifted, high- and medium-contrast photographs should be taken. Should the lift become torn or the print destroyed accidentally during the lifting process, the evidence will not be lost and a comparison will be possible from a photographic reproduction. Once a fingerprint has been developed and lifted, sufficient sweat deposits remain to permit renewed powdering and lifting. Under ideal circumstances, a series of up to eight lifts can be made from one latent impression. The second lift of a fresh print sometimes shows more contrast than the first lift because the excess perspiration present before powdering occurred causes the powder to adhere too freely to the impression, resulting in blurring on the lifting tape. After the first powdered image is removed, the second one, though slightly fainter, shows clearer detail.

Remember that powdered fingerprints should not be lifted from any object or surface that can be transported to the courtroom. If it becomes necessary to lift a print, the latent should be photographed while still on the object and in the presence of witnesses so that where the lifted print came from can be clearly established in court. Good practice requires that lifting be witnessed by two other persons, who initial the latent print transfer card with an annotation pertaining to the origin of the lifted fingerprint.

MAGNA BRUSH DEVELOPMENT

Although essentially a powder and brush method, the Magna Brush requires special mention. Although the "brush" has no bristles, because the metallic base powder itself is suspended magnetically from the apparatus to produce a bristlelike character, the method of developing latents with the Magna Brush is essentially the same as that used with ordinary fingerprint powders and the camel's hair brush. The Magna Brush was developed by the noted criminologist Herbert L. MacDonell in 1962 and constitutes one of the most important advances in powder development of latent impressions ever (see Figure 122).

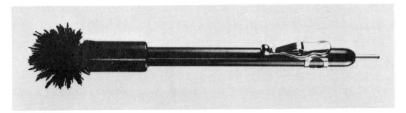

Figure 122. The Magna Brush developed by the criminologist Herbert L. Mac-Donell. (Courtesy: MacDonell Associates.)

The method is quick and inexpensive, and it allows the development of latent prints on porous surfaces such as raw wood (see Figure 123), leather, paper and even cleaning tissue (see Figure 124). Because of the absence of bristles, there is less danger of acciden-

Figure 123. Latent fingerprints developed on an unpainted, porous, wooden hammer handle with the Magna Brush. (Courtesy: MacDonell Associates.)

Figure 124. A latent fingerprint developed on a Kleenex tissue with the Magna Brush. (Courtesy: MacDonell Associates.)

tally destroying latent images through overly vigorous brushing. Almost no experience is required to use the Magna Brush in an expert fashion. It is the ideal instrument for the underside of tables and for desks, walls, ceilings and surfaces to which it is difficult to apply ordinary powders, because powder cannot fall off the Magna Brush without intentional shaking. One disadvantage is that, since specially manufactured powders are suspended magnetically from the apparatus, less than satisfactory results are obtained in the development of latents on metallic objects, where conventional powders and brushes work better. Nevertheless, the Magna Brush has come to constitute an indispensable item in the technician's field kit as well as in the crime laboratory. The versatility of the powders supplied by the manufacturer of the apparatus is much greater than that of any other powder: Magna silver powder, for instance, when lifted and transferred to a clear surface shows up black and can therefore be used as a positive projection print.

IODINE DEVELOPMENT

The iodine method is probably the oldest process of developing latent impressions on porous surfaces. Advocated by Pierre Aubert in Paris in 1876, it has been, until very recently, a favorite method for use on papers and cardboard. Basically, iodine development of latent impressions is achieved when the small fatty or oily deposits of a latent physically absorb the iodine fumes. It is therefore a mechanical or physical union between iodine and a latent print. Iodine is used in the form of resublimed, hot or cold iodine crystals.

In cold form, half a teaspoonful of crystals is placed in a small glass dish at the bottom of an empty glass container, such as an aquarium, of sufficient size to hold the object being examined. Above the dish, the object or document is suspended or propped up with the side suspected of bearing latents facing the iodine crystals. The container is then closed off with a sheet of glass to keep the slowly produced iodine fumes from dispersing throughout the room. Since iodine crystals evaporate at room temperature, vapors cause latent images to become visible as brownish orange prints. Depending on the age of the latent prints, the temperature in the room and the number of crystals used, latent images develop within ten to sixty minutes. Too long an exposure to the fumes darkens the document completely, obliterating detail.

Iodine is dangerous in other ways, too. Because its vapors are poisonous, care must be taken not to breathe them. Iodine tarnishes metal objects and instruments and slowly "burns" through many other substances, so only glass implements should be used to contain it. Crystals should be stored in glass jars with glass stoppers.

Several variations on the iodine technique have been reported. One that has proved particularly effective consists of covering an area suspected of bearing latent prints with a paper towel. Iodine crystals are then sprinkled on the towel and covered with a piece of glass. After a few minutes, the latent prints appear, and when the desired density is obtained quick photography is indicated. Better results can be obtained by placing fewer crystals in the same glass dish on a tripod. A low-flame alcohol burner is placed under the tripod to heat the crystals. The resulting fumes are more intense and latents develop almost immediately.

A technique called Porous Glass Iodine Fuming was developed by MacDonell, inventor of the Magna Brush. It consists of a powder made from ground, porous glass that has been saturated with iodine. The powder is a dry form of iodine, which MacDonell named Driodine. He described porous glass as chemically inert (96 percent silica), optically transparent, rigid, thermally stable, and having pore diameters of about four millimicrons. The powder is placed on an object being examined for latents and the impregnated iodine releases its vapors at a controlled rate. Porous glass in the form of a slab, rather than ground into powder, can be placed over the object to provide localized vaporization while eliminating the need for a fuming cabinet.

The iodine process is useful for recently placed latents and it usually fails when applied to extremely porous or coarse paper, such as newsprint. Damaged areas of paper (as by erasure) and areas subjected to excessive pressure attract more iodine fumes and therefore appear as brown blurs. A major disadvantage in the use of iodine fumes is that they make latent images fugitive. As soon as an object containing latents is removed from a fuming cabinet, the prints begin to fade. There are ways of fixing iodine-fumed prints to retard fading, but it is nevertheless imperative that prints be photographed immediately. This disadvantage can, in some instances, become an advantage, as when it is necessary to conceal the fact that a document has been examined for latent impressions or when a document must be preserved without marring or staining. Since developed prints sooner or later disappear, a document ultimately regains its previous, unmarked appearance. If traces of iodine discoloration persist, they can be removed by exposing the document to ammonia fumes. But after fingerprint images have faded, they can be revitalized an indefinite number of times and prints developed from them with powder.

Iodine Fuming Pipe

It would be difficult to make practical use of iodine fuming outside the laboratory in any of the methods so far described because each requires a fuming cabinet. To overcome this handicap, the iodine fuming pipe has been developed. Basically, the instrument consists of a straight glass tube about four inches long and one-half inch in diameter that has a rubber stopper at each end. Inside is a quantity of anhydrous calcium chloride crystals that fills the tube but is separated from the rubber stoppers by Pyrex glass wool. A hole one-eighth inch in diameter is drilled through the rubber stopper at each end of the tube. The narrow end of a thistle tube is inserted through one of the holes and the other through a small glass connecting tube. A small quantity of iodine crystals is placed in the cup of the thistle tube and held in place by glass wool. The connecting glass tube in the rubber stopper at the other end of the instrument is inserted into a sixteen inch length of three-sixteenth inch rubber hose (see Figure 125).

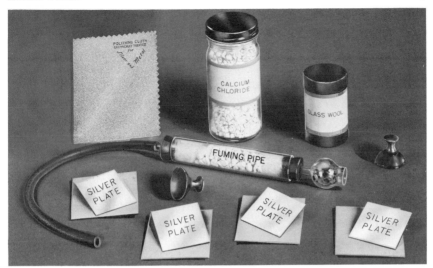

Figure 125. An iodine fuming pipe and equipment used to transfer iodine-fumed latent prints onto sterling silver plates. (Courtesy: Institute of Applied Science.)

Holding the tube containing calcium chloride crystals in one hand, the technician holds the cup of the thistle close to the surface to be examined for latent impressions, and blows through the rubber hose. His breath passes through the calcium chloride crystals, which dehydrate and warm it. Continuing through the apparatus, the breath causes the heated crystals to give off fumes, which develop the latent prints. The thistle tube should be moved in a circular motion over the examined surface in order to develop the latent images evenly. The method is faster than the cold iodine process, though slower than heating iodine crystals over an alcohol burner inside a fuming cabinet. But the fuming pipe is easy to move to and use at the crime scenes. Care must be taken, when using the apparatus, not to inhale through the rubber tube because iodine fumes can injure the throat membranes.

In 1956, Detective Chief Inspector Kenneth Ross of Renfrew and Bute Constabulary in England invented an iodine fuming instrument that is similar in principle to the conventional fuming pipe but dispenses with oral operation. It vaporizes iodine crystals by direct heat from an electric lamp and ejects fumes by a preheated current of pressurized air from a rubber bulb. In operation, the technician simply plugs the electric cord into a wall socket, switches on the lamp, and waits about three minutes to give the lamp time to heat up. Then, by depressing the rubber air bulb, he directs the fumes onto the object to be examined.

The disadvantage of the iodine fuming pipe is that its storage, or simply lapse of time, causes the rubber stoppers and the hose to become "cured" or "vulcanized" through the chemical action of the iodine fumes. MacDonell has eliminated this objection to the standard instrument by eliminating the rubber stoppers, adding a ground glass stopper to the thistle tube to avoid continuous slow leakage of iodine fumes during storage, and inserting a glass stopcock at the other end of the main tube that prevents the iodine vapors from coming in contact with the rubber tubing when it is closed. He has also added potassium bromide crystals to his fumer to retard the fading of fumed fingerprints.

Fixing Iodine-Fumed Prints

As already explained, the rapid disappearance of iodine fumed latent prints is sometimes an advantage. More often than not, however, it is a nuisance to the technician, who must have his photographic equipment ready so that he can immediately reproduce the faint yellow-orange-brown ridges on film. For that reason, much effort has been expended toward finding a suitable means of rendering the iodine-fumed latent image permanent.

No one method has been totally successful in fixing iodine-fumed prints. Around 1930, European criminologists advocated the use of starch solutions. Other technicians in the United States experimented with submerging the iodine print in a solution of soluble starch, without satisfactory results, and refined this method by applying starch solution to the iodine print with an artist's spray atomizer under about ten pounds of pressure. They found that the finer the spray, the more even the solution could be distributed without wetting the document and the better the result.

In 1962, Larsen of Toronto advocated a new method using starch powder and steam. Instead of a starch solution and spray, Larsen used finely ground starch powder, which he applied to the iodine-fumed print with a camel's hair brush. After blowing excess starch powder off the print, he quickly exposed the print to a gentle steam from a kettle, which fixed the print in one or two seconds as a permanent blue-black. The iodine-developed ridges caught a fine layer of starch powder without the iodine reacting to it because of the dry condition. As soon as microscopically small drops of water moistened the powder on the ridges, a microsolution formed that reacted with the iodine and formed the dark blue complex in which under normal conditions, iodine is captured for a long time. Because most paper contains starch gained during the sizing process of paper making, Larsen's method can be duplicated in a somewhat cruder manner simply by breathing on an iodine-fumed print. Moisture in breath acts the same way as steam from a kettle. If an iodine fuming pipe is used in the development of prints, adding potassium bromide crystals to the iodine crystals, as done by MacDonell, promotes the starch-iodine breath fixation of fumed prints. But it has been found in practice that fading is not usually rapid enough to make print fixation absolutely necessary. Without undergoing a fixing process, iodine-fumed prints have remained on documents for as long as twenty-four hours, which is ample time for photographically recording ridge detail.

Silver Transfer Lifting

While developed prints should be photographed immediately, a method exists by which images can be permanently preserved that is much like the lifting tape method described in the powdering processes. To lift and preserve iodine-fumed prints, use is made of a two-inch square flat sterling silver plate (see again Figure 125). After a fumed print has reached desired intensity, one plate is placed on the print with an even motion to avoid sliding. After leaving it on the fumed print for approximately two seconds, lift the plate straight up and hold it before a 500 watt photoflood lamp for one or two seconds. This process "develops" the image on the silver, causing ridge patterns to appear in dark brown. The image thus obtained is relatively stable if the plate is kept in a dark envelope at all times except for the purpose of photographing it. Continued exposure to daylight causes the image to become overexposed through a general darkening of the plate, with a resulting loss of ridge detail. Silver plates can be cleaned with a polishing cloth and used again for different sets of transfers.

Another method of lifting iodine-fumed prints was developed at the Rhode Island State Crime Laboratory. A completely exposed and developed negative is moistened either by being dipped in water or by being breathed on until it becomes slightly adhesive, in which condition the film is pressed against the iodine-fumed print and then dipped into a mixture of chrome alum and nitric acid, which dissolves the silver background that is not protected by silver iodide and leaves a fingerprint outline. The result is a positive fingerprint that can be used for direct comparison or enlarged photographically.

As far back as 1935, Dr. Wagenaar of Rotterdam used specially prepared paper with a sensitized coating made from 1 gr. rice starch, 20 cc water, 2 grams potassium iodide, and 0.3 gram thymol, which he pressed against an iodine-fumed print to obtain a transfer in much the same way as an opaque rubber lifter. The solution must be freshly prepared and applied to the special paper with a paint brush. The paper is applied to the print just before it is dry.

Silver Nitrate Development

Developing fingerprints on paper, cardboard or wood by means of a silver nitrate solution is as old as the use of powders and the iodine method. As long ago as 1877, the French physician Aubert used the silver nitrate method in connection with his studies of skin diseases and the glandular excretions they cause.

Silver nitrate development is particularly useful for paper, cardboard and even unpainted wood. Prints can be raised that are up to two years old. The developed image is of high contrast and long durability, although photographic reproduction within a day or so is still advisable. In most instances, though, no observable obliteration or fading of the developed image can be noticed beyond what may occur during the first week. The composition of the paper is of little importance; excellent prints have been raised by this method even on coarse newsprint.

A major disadvantage of the silver nitrate method is that it fails with impressions stored under very high humidity. When Aubert experimented with silver nitrate solutions in 1877, he found that as silver nitrate comes in contact with sodium chloride deposits in perspiration a reaction results in the form of silver chloride which is light-sensitive: when exposed to light silver chloride is reduced to silver, which shows up almost black and sometimes reddish brown. When prints have been stored in highly humid places, the migration of chloride ions contained in perspiration prevents the successful use of this method.

There are various ways of using the silver nitrate process. The most popular one employs a silver nitrate solution of from three to five percent. To prepare the solution dissolve 20 grams of silver nitrate crystals in 400 cc of distilled water. Then add three or four cubic centimeters of concentrated nitric acid, being careful to add the acid to the water, rather than vice versa. The resulting solution is suitable for the development of latent impressions.

It should be poured into a porcelain developing tray and the document to be treated floated on top of the solution with both sides exposed equally. The length of time is not critical; all that is required is that the document be thoroughly soaked. Silver nitrate solution can also be applied with cotton or with a dentist's spray. Since the solution stains whatever it touches, rubber gloves must be worn in handling it. After the solution has been applied to a document, it should be airdried. Excess moisture can be removed by blotting the document with unused photographic blotting paper. The entire process of soaking and drying should preferably be done in subdued lighting.

After the document is thoroughly dry it should be exposed to a light source with a high concentration of ultraviolet rays, such as a photoflood lamp or an ultraviolet lamp without a filter. Remove document from under the light when the latent prints are sufficiently developed or when the entire surface darkens. The document must then be stored in total darkness, except for the short periods required to photograph developed latents. If the paper is sealed in a lightproof wrapper, the prints will remain for many years.

The reagent prepared for the development of latent images can be stored in a brown bottle in a dark location. After extended storage, experiment with your own latent impressions to see if the solution is still usable before applying it to evidence. Deteriorated solutions discolor paper without developing the latents. Silver nitrate stains can be removed by dipping the document in a two percent solution of mercuric nitrate. Another stain remover is composed of equal parts by volume of five percent bichloride of mercury (five grams of mercuric chloride in 100cc of distilled water) and five percent ammonium chloride (five grams of ammonium chloride in 100cc distilled water). The stain remover is stable and can be used repeatedly until exhausted. Images developed by silver nitrate can be fixed in a regular, photographic hypo bath.

NINHYDRIN DEVELOPMENT

The ninhydrin method of developing latent prints is fairly recent. In 1954, an article titled "Detection of Fingerprints by the Ninhydrin Reaction" appeared in the British scientific journal *Nature*. Authored by the Swedish scientists Svante Oden and Bengt Von Hostem, both of Uppsala, it described the development of latent fingerprints on paper using a well-known test for amino acids frequently used in paper chromatography. The application was discovered by accident when the two scientists were analyzing paper: the fingerprints of everyone who had touched the documents developed before their eyes.

An advantage of the ninhydrin method over any other is that it reveals the presence of very old prints—prints that cannot possibly be brought out in any other way. Also, the ridge detail is sharply defined, clearer even than by the silver nitrate method. The substances that react to ninhydrin are subject to considerably less migration than, for example, chloride ions. In experiments, the author developed several identifiable latent impressions in a college textbook that he had not used or touched for at least nine years. The image was stable, too.

According to Noller's *Chemistry of Organic Compounds,* ninhydrin oxidizes the alpha-amino acids in perspiration whereby the resulting amino acids break down into ammonia, carbon dioxide and the corresponding aldehyde. Ninhydrin is thereby reduced to diketchyndrol. In a second stage, ninhydrin and the ammonia with diketchydrindol formed in the first stage are condensed into a usually blue-violet molecule. This reaction also takes place with proteins, polypeptides and peptides, which contain a free carboxyl and alpha-amino group.

Various ways of using ninhydrin in the development of latent fingerprints have been suggested. All involve the use of a solution of 1, 2, 3, triketohydrindene hydrate powder or ninhydrin, in a volatile substance such as acetone, ether or ethyl alcohol. When ninhydrin powder is thus dissolved, it can be applied to the document or the surface to be examined by spraying, immersion or painting. A dentist's spray is effective and handles easily. The document can also be immersed in ninhydrin solution in a developing tray. Painting the solution on a document or other surface with a brush, or swabbing it with a cotton ball, accomplishes the same result. It is recommended that rubber gloves and protective clothing be worn and that document spraying be performed in a fuming hood so that toxic vapors can be carried away in the exhaust. Ninhydrin is not poisonous, but its solvents are.

By reacting to the amino acids in human perspiration, ninhydrin causes stains to appear that range from pink to purple-reddish brown. When latent impressions are present on a surface, ninhydrin stains the trace patterns and renders latent images visible. When especially heavy imprints are on a surface, ninhydrin development can cause the touched area to stain to such an extent that latent friction ridges cannot be distinguished from background coloring.

Various proportions for diluting the substances have been recommended. Early writing on ninhydrin development suggested a 0.4% solution. Some authors advocate a 3–5% solution. Probably the most frequently used is 1.5% which means that 1.5 grams of ninhydrin are dissolved in 100 cc of ethyl alcohol or acetone. The use of a 1.5% solution hastens reaction time. Prints can be expected to appear within three to five hours after application of the developing reagent, but they will continue to appear for about twenty-four hours. After treatment, the document must still be handled carefully with tongs and placed in a protective cover because it remains sensitive. Touching it may cause additional prints to develop. It is therefore imperative that contamination be avoided.

A longer reaction time is required when a 0.4% solution is used. The development of the image can be hastened by placing a treated document in an oven heated to 130–150°F for approximately twenty minutes. Whenever possible, however, the "slow cure" at room temperature is preferable. Prints have appeared or intensified as late as ten days after the application of ninhydrin solution to a document.

A disadvantage of ninhydrin is its sensitivity to temperature and humidity. In dry climates, ninhydrin performs poorly. Excessively humid conditions are not much better. The best results are obtained in a relative humidity of about seventy. In periods of dry weather, a steaming kettle of water placed in the same room where spraying is done can help get better results, although it is admittedly a poor substitute for controlled humidity.

Another factor that must be considered when using ninhydrin is its effect on latent prints of various ages. While it is usually agreed that ninhydrin works best on old prints, sometimes a fresh print appears almost immediately when treated with ninhydrin. As a rule, prints placed on a document a short time before applying the reagent develop more slowly. In some experiments it was found that recently placed latents did not respond to ninhydrin but did reveal their presence when the document was subjected to the silver nitrate solution process.

A danger in handling documents with ninhydrin, to some extent shared by the silver nitrate process, is that it may destroy minute details of the text or at least render such details useless for examination by a document examiner. As a rule, photographs are made of any document prior to processing. However, no matter how carefully made and faithfully reproduced, a photograph cannot depict all of the minute details of the original. In fact, photographs in certain instances conceal important documentary evidence. A vehicle registration card that was forged by tracing may serve as illustration. A conventional photograph often shows a traced line as a solid line, although it is actually separated ever so minutely from the original, written line. When such a document is processed for fingerprints using the ninhydrin method, the ink of both lines is temporarily dissolved. Upon drying, the two lines—one genuine, the other forged—become fused and can no longer be distinguished. When the mutilated document is later compared with a photograph of it taken before the ninhydrin treatment was performed, it is nearly impossible to determine that the apparently solid line in fact represents two separate and distinct lines.

Even sparing the use of ninhydrin solution does not always prevent fusion. It creates quite a problem inasmuch as many documents examined for fingerprints also contain questionable writing that must be examined by a document specialist. Another characteristic of carelessly processed papers on which ninhydrin has been used is oversaturation, which causes paper fibers to swell, obliterating indentures as well as certain striations which to a document examiner can be highly revealing. When the ink "bleeds" as a result of ninhydrin saturation, it can become impossible for a document examiner to distinguish such minute details as intersections, pen lifts and overwriting. It must be observed that the diffusion of writing traces is not limited to ballpoint writings and certain fountain pen inks; it occurs in typewriting and printed copy as well.

To reduce ink running which cannot be completely controlled

the reagent can be applied through filter paper placed on top of the document in question, but the results so far have been only marginally better than those produced by ordinary spraying. In order to preserve invaluable written details without ink running, documents can be sprayed after the critical written portions are covered with a plastic mask. In the identification laboratories of the United States Postal Inspection Service, less ink running has been noticed when a 0.75% solution that uses ethyl alcohol as a solvent for ninhydrin is employed; the solution must be throughly mixed with petroleum ether and the heavy darker solution drained off from the bottom of the mixture..

Ninhydrin solutions must be prepared by technicians; they do not come already packaged. The solution is generally stable and can be stored until completely used or until a blue discoloration indicates that no ninhydrin remains. In 1955, the Swedish scientist Svante Oden took out patent number 2,715,571 at the United States Patent Office for the ninhydrin process of developing latent fingerprints, and under that patent a firm also developed an aerosol can for ninhydrin labeled NIN-Spray. The validity of the patent can be questioned, though, because the use of ninhydrin solutions for spraying amino acids onto paper chromatograms dates back to papers published in 1944. Even earlier biochemists used the product as an amino acid color indicator and advised care in using this technique to avoid developing one's own fingerprints.

As a process, ninhydrin must be employed before silver nitrate. The correct sequence for searching for latent fingerprints on a document is a visual examination under normal light or under ultraviolet or infrared radiations, followed by iodine fuming, the ninhydrin process and finally the silver nitrate method. But after the silver nitrate method has been applied, no observable reactions can be obtained by using ninhydrin.

It is sometimes advanced that, because ninhydrin proves to be such a sensitive reagent, use of the silver nitrate method should be rare, but that claim is a fallacy. Ninhydrin reaction has failed in cases for which iodine and silver nitrate have given identifiable results. Even if the prints develop under the ninhydrin method, that does not mean every latent impression on the document has been included. It is impossible to determine in advance from which components of perspiration the latent image was made, so all methods must be tried. Prints should be photographed between each step. In a few cases, prints developed on paper with ninhydrin might be redeveloped with silver nitrate, while in other cases silver nitrate can obliterate ninhydrin prints.

OTHER LATENT PRINT METHODS

Over the years, researchers have advocated the use of a great many more techniques for the development of latent impressions. Some are chemical; others more properly belong among those already discussed. But let's here consider briefly some of the best known.

Variations on the Powdering Method

In xerography an image is transferred through a lens onto a selenium-coated drum that has an electrical resistance that varies according to the intensity of light. In conjunction with this process, the Xerox Corporation uses a fine powder, called Xerox toner, consisting partially of thermo plastic. When toner is applied to a surface and heat is directed toward it, it fuses with that surface. A few experts have used Xerox toner powders to develop latents on porous surfaces. The technique of applying powder varies somewhat from traditional brushing methods in that powder must be shaken gently onto a surface and the excess blown off. The remaining toner adheres to any latent print present. After latents have been so developed, the object that carries them is subjected to heat, which fuses the prints onto the surface and results in permanent latent images that can withstand rough handling. Advocates of this system refer to it as the fused print method.

Another system of developing latents is called the flame process. Here the developing medium is the soot produced by igniting certain materials. The originators recommend the use of camphor because of its ready availability, ease of ignition, complete combustion and jet-black soot deposits. A spoonful of camphor in a Pyrex dish is ignited and any solid object suspected of bearing latent prints is passed repeatedly through the apex of the flame until it is thoroughly coated with soot, most of which is brushed off with a feather duster to reveal a sooty outline for each latent fingerprint. Further clarification of the impressions can be obtained by gently washing the object under slowly moving cold water. Prints developed by this method can be lifted the same way as ordinary powdered prints, and the process can be repeated several times on the same latent. Soot-producing substances other than camphor that can be used are pine chips and resin, among others.

A process known as vacuum metallization involves volatizing a mixture of specially chosen metallic powders over a surface suspected of bearing latent prints. Rather than adhering to sweat deposits on the friction ridges, dust particles settle into the spaces between the ridges, giving a chromatically reversed image in which ridges show up white and grooves black. Volatization occurs in an evaporator ordinarily used in electron microscopy, the document being placed in a bell jar. The technique was developed in 1967 by French scientists and described in the April, 1968, issue of the *International Criminal Police Review*.

Osmic Acid Fuming Method

This method is useful in developing invisible, oily prints. When such latents are exposed to the vapors of osmic acid, oxidation of sebaceous matter occurs, causing the reduction of osmic acid to dark gray, metallic osmium. The method, using osmium tetroxide, a yellow inorganic crystalline chemical derived from osmium, was first suggested by the French criminologist Rene Forgeot in 1891. The chemical is expensive and dangerous, and osmium tetroxide fumes must be handled under laboratory conditions. Chemical preparation is as follows: three grams of osmic acid are dissolved in 100 cc of carbon tetrachloride, phosphorus oxychloride, ether, or ethyl alcohol. Osmic tetroxide crystals are stable when kept in a sealed glass ampule, but deteriorate after the ampule is broken. The solution is not stable.

A drop or two of the solution and the document to be tested are placed in a small evaporating disk at the bottom of a glass container similar to the one used for fuming prints by the hot or cold iodine method. The solution turns into fumes at normal room temperature. Development of the prints is slow, taking from one to twelve hours depending on the age of the latents and other factors. The latent image developed is stable and sharp in outline. Care should be taken to avoid breathing the fumes because they are penetrating, can be poisonous, and can cause blindness. It is believed that the osmic acid fuming method does not affect the subsequent treatment of a document by other processes.

Leuco-Malachite Green

This light brown powdered dye is valuable for determining whether or not bloody latents are present. One gram of leuco-malachite green is dissolved in 7cc of ether. Ten drops of glacial acetic acid are added to this solution. A working reagent is obtained by adding a few drops of fresh, 20-volume hydrogen peroxide to part of the solution, which is allowed to flow over the area suspected of bearing prints immediately after being mixed, while a source of forced air or heat, or both, is used simultaneously to assist the rapid evaporation. Prints in blood may appear in green, but the entire surface of the treated document will be stained light green.

Benzidine Free Base

This white, yellow or pink organic powder must be handled with the greatest care because it is absorbed rapidly through the skin and may be carcinogenic. Latents that have faded and are made by bloody fingers on either absorbent or nonabsorbent surfaces can be developed by using this technique. It involves making a fresh solution by saturating benzidine free base in 70-percent by weight ethanol and then letting the solution stand for one hour to insure that proper saturation is achieved. After the waiting period, an equal volume of 70-percent ethyl alcohol is added. Immediately before application, one part of 20-volume hydrogen peroxide is thoroughly mixed with three parts by volume of benzidine solution.

If used on hard surfaces, it is necessary to fix prints before treatment by running 70-percent ethanol over the surface. The solution can be sprayed on or poured over the surface, evidence can be dipped into it. After the prints turn deep blue, the evidence is immediately washed with cold water and air dried. If a blue latent print appears, the print might have been made in blood. The entire surface of the treated evidence will be stained light brown. The benzidine free base technique can be used after the leuco-malachite green method, after iodine fuming, and after the ninhydrin and silver nitrate methods. It cannot precede the silver nitrate method. If the latter method is used, only an alcoholic solution of silver nitrate should be used before a print is processed with benzidine.

Hydrofluoric Acid

This is a colorless, mobile, volatile and fuming liquid that is very corrosive and has a sharp, suffocating odor. When not in solution, it is also known as hydrogen fluoride. As with many sophisticated methods of fingerprint development, the use of hydrofluoric acid vapors for developing chance impressions was first suggested by Forgeot in 1891. The chemical must be handled with great care since it can cause extremely painful burns that heal very slowly. When glass is suspected of bearing latent impressions, prints can be developed by exposing the glass surface to hydrofluoric acid vapors, which erode the glass except under grease deposits left by the friction ridges that made the impressions.

Autoelectronography

This method of developing latent fingerprints on human skin was first reported in 1965. The noted criminologist Herbert L. MacDonell states that the principle behind this method is the autoelectronographic reproduction of a latent fingerprint that has been dusted with finely divided lead powder and is then subjected to filtered X rays in a manner that permits backscattering into a photographic emulsion. MacDonell states that, in practice, X rays (200 kv @ 20 ma) are passed through a one-centimeter thick copper filter to remove any soft X rays that would fog the film, then through two millimeters of aluminum, a piece of cleared film, the photographic film itself, and finally onto the dusted fingerprint. Each filter removes secondary X-ray emissions produced by the previous filter. In this manner, the photographic film is not fogged and responds only to backscattered, secondary X rays from the lead powder in fingerprint detail. The equipment necessary is expensive, which alone would be a considerable drawback to the general use of autoelectronography. Further, while experimenters have succeeded in developing a latent print on human skin under ideal conditions, other researchers doubt the practicality of revealing latent prints on skin by any method known today.

Autoradiography

This method was first used by Dr. Toyosaburo Takeuchi in 1958 to develop old latent prints, the secretions of which had dried, and to develop impressions made on absorbent surfaces or on multicolored backgrounds. In detecting latent impressions by means of autoradiography, one or more mechanisms may be involved: the chemical reaction of radioactive compounds or elements with the substance contained in the secretion left on materials, the absorption or sorption of radioactive compounds or elements into substances in the secretion, the exchange of atoms of the substances in the secretion with radioactive atoms, or the activation of atoms of substances in the secretion from radioactive atoms by irradiation with neutrons or other suitable energetic particles. The method is confined to use in highly specialized laboratories.

Electronautography

This method uses soft X rays to develop latent fingerprints by using finely divided lead powder to create an opaque X-ray mask in the friction ridge patterns. It, too, has little practical usage.

LATENT PRINT AGE AND DURATION

It is not possible to determine accurately how long a latent impression will remain on an object or how old an impression is. Latent print duration is affected by many factors. The surface itself is a primary factor. Latent prints last longer on smooth surfaces, provided they are protected from smearing and smudging, than on absorbent or porous surfaces. Other important factors are relative humidity, temperature, and other outside influences. But just as important is the physical condition of the individual who made the impression. Different individuals perspire at different volumes at varying times of the day. When a person is engaged in strenuous work, perspiration flows more freely. The same is true when one works under tension or with the nervousness associated with an alarming task, as is often the case of burglars or other persons engaged in criminal activities. On the other hand, some individuals secrete little perspiration and are therefore less likely to leave abundant chance impressions.

The water content of perspiration evaporates rather quickly. Powder developer can adhere to the moisture in perspiration and to the dry deposits of organic and inorganic matter. Yet powder development is practical only for fresh latent prints and is of limited use anytime after ten to twenty-five days, depending on temperature and humidity. It has been noted that when objects suspected of bearing latent impressions are placed in a cool area for twenty-four hours and then are powder developed at 45°F in a relative humidity of 55% latent prints gain in intensity and powder adheres to them better. The microscopic analysis of powdered prints developed at cool temperatures shows that, when compared with latent prints on similar objects developed at higher temperatures, the former show a slightly thicker coating of powder on the ridge lines. Condensation of water vapor also seems to improve the cohesion of friction ridge lines in latent impressions when powder developers are used.

The approximate age of latent impressions can be determined circumstantially by the use of chemical developing techniques. After all of the water in perspiration has evaporated, enough solid deposit remains to make chemical development possible for an indefinite period of time. Theoretically, such latent print deposits remain on a surface permanently. Practically, though, present developing techniques limit the usable time span for processing. The ninhydrin method can reveal prints up to ten, possibly fifteen, years old. The Swedish scientists who brought the ninhydrin method to the attention of the identification profession claim to have used it to develop a thirty-year old latent impression. Silver nitrate development normally acts only on impressions that are at most two years old. The iodine method can be expected to yield identifiable results for impressions no older than six months. A good latent impression with enough solid deposits can be approximately dated by using all three techniques in succession. It must be remembered, however, that the age of latent impressions can never be established with complete accuracy. At best, print age is the studied opinion of an expert based on the extent of his own experience and investigation. It is sometimes also possible to date a latent impression other than by physical examination. In one such instance, it was possible to state that a latent impression found on a counter top in a bar was less than twenty-four hours old because the bartender remembered that he had thoroughly washed the counter top where the print was found on the evening before it was discovered.

In order to be valuable as evidence, latent prints discovered at crime scenes must be inconsistent with innocence. When prints are discovered on the inside of a transom over a door or in a place that is generally inaccessible to the public, determining print age may be rather immaterial. The same is true when prints are discovered in someone's home and it can be established that the person who left them never had legitimate access to the premises. But when prints are discovered in an area where the defendant in a criminal case might have had innocent access at some time or another, it must be established that the particular latent prints could have been made only at the time the offense was committed.

Another factor that could influence how long a print can last on a given surface is the amount of finger pressure exerted to make the impression. In 1932, Edward C. Walker performed experiments to determine the effect on powder development of varying degrees of pressure. For his investigation, he cleaned glass microscope slides with alcohol and distilled water and then quickly dried them in a stream of warm air. He made three impressions of the same finger on one side of each slide. The impression was made with eight-ounce pressure, as measured by a spring scale. The second impression was made with a two-pound pressure and the third with a five-pound pressure. Walker reported that the eight-ounce impression was much fainter on the glass slide than the other two, but was perfectly clear and able to be photographed.

Walker also experimented with heavier pressures and found that impressions made with a 10-pound pressure are still perfectly clear and sharp, but at fifteen pounds of pressure, which is about all a person can comfortably press with an index finger, the ridges start to smudge, although some portions remain identifiable. It is almost impossible to exert twenty-five pounds of pressure without outside assistance. That amount results in impressions which are generally too blurred to be identified. Yet such pressure could be exerted if a person carrying a heavy object allowed his laden hands to touch a surface. Walker prepared several hundred of his slides and then subjected them to further tests. Some were left exposed to ordinary room temperature and conditions. A few were turned upside down, a few were put on edge, and some were protected from any exposure by a plain sheet of glass. Afterward he developed the latent impressions with powder and found that they could all be developed just as easily at the end of each five-day interval for a month as when they were fresh, showing that normal change in temperature and humidity as well as light and dust had no apparent effect on the latent impressions for thirty days.

A different experiment was conducted in 1959 by Richard J. Blum and Walter J. Lougheed of the Flint, Michigan, Police Department under conditions in which latent fingerprints were preserved and processed in a laboratory and were not subjected to unusual conditions, contamination or the influences of wind, dust or sunlight. The purpose of the Flint experiment was to determine under artificially induced circumstances what results time, temperature and humidity can have on latent fingerprints developed by powders. The Flint experts conducted dusting tests and photomicrographic analyses on numerous latent fingerprints made on clear glass by four male subjects, ages 21, 24, 28, and 34. The processing was done immediately after the impressions were made on the glass, as well as at intervals of 24, 48 and 72 hours. Processing conditions varied from 40° F at 55% relative humidity to 70° F at 25% relative humidity and at 82° F at 23% relative humidity. The conclusions were that "the reaction of the secretion matter at high relative humidity range(s) is exactly opposite to the reaction of the secretion matter [at] high temperatures and low relative humidity range(s) wherein the moisture content of secretion material is absorbed into the surrounding atmosphere."

No meaningful studies have been made on the degree of deterioration after longer periods of time in order to determine the effectiveness of chemical developers on latent impressions placed months or years earlier. The author has begun a study along these lines that will require an additional four or five years to complete.

CHOICE OF DEVELOPING METHOD

Confronted by an array of methods—powders, vapors, chemicals—the technician must make a selection. Which system will produce the best results? In some instances, mentioned throughout the text, several methods can be used in succession, but in many cases a technician has only one try. Most technicians have acquired, through experience, a sound knowledge about which methods work best under which conditions. But no claim is made that only the recommended methods will work. In fact, the particular dexterity a technician may have acquired in working with one process may allow him to obtain excellent results with that method on surfaces which would normally call for the use of a different process. Also, the choice of developing process for a particular purpose may be greatly influenced by the suspected age of the latent impressions or by the sheer practicality of its use. Difficulties are especially encountered in examining ceilings, the undersides of heavy tables, desks and permanently fastened shelves.

As a merely general indication, then, the following methods of development are recommended for these surfaces:

Paper and Wood

Powder (for fresh latents), iodine, ninhydrin or silver nitrate. For paper toweling, cleansing tissue and cardboard use Magna black, Xerox toner (fused prints), ninhydrin or silver nitrate.

Metal

Dragon's Blood.

Glass and Mirrors

Powder or iodine. If latents are found on both sides of a glass panel, they should be developed separately. A recommended technique involves treating one side with a white powder and photographing it by holding it in front of a dark background. Developed prints can be darkened by being exposed for a few minutes to the vapors of ammonium sulfide. Then the second side is again developed using white powders. When photographing the second side, the previously blackened latents on the other side will be invisible.

Leather

Magna silver or Xerox toner.

Rubber

Dragon's Blood.

Cloth

Latent prints on shirts, collars, cuffs, handkerchiefs, sheets and pillow cases are difficult to detect. Usable results have been obtained by spraying with a ten-percent silver nitrate solution to which a small percentage of acetic acid was added. The cloth must be dried in a darkroom; when completely dry, it is exposed to ultraviolet radiation and then photographed. Afterward, prints can be fixed by being treated with a five-percent solution of ammonium hydrosulfide and washed in running water for an hour. Fingerprints on black satin have been developed with calcium sulfide powder after the material was stretched on a frame.

Blood

Leuco-malachite green or benzidine free base.

Skin

Limited experimental success has been achieved with electronautography and autoelectronography.

Regardless of the type of surface, the conditions of the surface sometimes indicate that special procedures should be followed, particularly when latent prints are found on greasy surface or in dust, powder or flour. An impression's ridge structure in flour, powder or dust is often clearly visible, but any attempt to powder or further develop it would destroy the fine ridge detail. Photography with grazing light is usually sufficient to record the impression. Sometimes a casting can be made directly from a print. The most popular method uses a commercial product called Moulage, a synthetic rubberlike substance that can be melted with moderate heat and poured on an impression after a "dam" has been made around it to hold the liquid until it hardens. A liquid solution of white gypsum or plaster of paris is also used. Another method requires the use of the metallic alloy known as Woods metal, which melts at sixty-eight degrees and dries almost immediately. Considerable experience in working with these materials is required in order not to destroy the fine ridge structure.

Latent prints on greasy surfaces can usually be photographed quite legibly under oblique light. Another method is recommended by the San Francisco fingerprint experts Palla and Wiebe. In a darkroom, an unexposed sheet of high-contrast photographic paper is immersed in warm water; prints are fumed with an iodine fuming pipe; after the photographic paper is blotted to remove excessive water, the dampened paper is held firmly against the print for about one minute, but not so firmly as to flatten the oily pattern. The paper is then placed in a paper developer for from fifteen to twenty seconds under the safelight to permit thorough soaking. Next the paper is exposed to normal room light so that the paper begins to fog. The places on the paper that were subjected to the iodine-fumed prints will fog more slowly. When the desired contrast is achieved, light development is stopped by immersing the photographic paper in a fixing solution (hypo) for about fifteen minutes, following which it is washed and dried in the same manner as photographic prints. A positive can be obtained by making a photostatic copy of this reversed (or negative) print.

In summary, then, powders adhere to moisture and to solid matters, iodine fuming acts on the fatty or oily deposits of perspiration by mechanical absorption, osmic acid reacts to fatty deposits, ninhydrin reacts to amino acids, and silver nitrate reacts to sodium chloride in perspiration. If a sequence of developing methods is employed, it is essential to remember that iodine fuming has no harmful effect on subsequent methods, ninhydrin development must precede silver nitrate development, and silver nitrate must be used in alcoholic solution if it is used before leuco-malachite green or benzidine free base. Fingerprint powders should not ordinarily be used in conjunction with chemical techniques.

HANDLING FINGERPRINT EVIDENCE

To search for crime-scene fingerprints, it is preferable to transport all objects that are not too bulky to the crime laboratory for examination, but it must be emphasized that no object should be removed from a crime scene before it has been photographed exactly as and where it was found. One of the most important objectives is to preserve the evidence by preventing contamination. Therefore, when a case warrants the attention, fingerprints on walls, doors, windowpanes or furniture should be protected by being covered with transparent cellophane tape and furniture should be taken apart, wall panels and windowpanes cut and doors removed for transportation to the crime laboratory and storage in the evidence vault. Transported objects should not be wrapped in paper or cloth. Guns should be lifted by inserting a pencil through the trigger guard and then suspended in a box. Papers or small objects, depending on size and weight, should be picked up with tweezers or tongs and gently deposited in boxes of sufficient size. Special rubber stoppers attached to a screwdriver handle make it easy to pick up bottles without touching the glass surface. Field kits usually include several pieces of pegboard, to which objects of many sizes can be tied before being placed in boxes.

To handle objects that bear latent fingerprints requires common sense and ingenuity. No special rules exist, although specially manufactured carrying aids can be bought. In most instances, the fingerprint technician must design and make his own devices for moving objects that might become important evidence in a criminal case.

Chapter 5

Recording Prints

If practical use is to be made of fingerprint patterns, then procedures to record and reproduce the pattern images are an absolute necessity. It is not surprising that a great many techniques have been developed to record prints permanently as well as to reproduce all or part of the recorded prints for illustrative purposes and for court exhibits. These various means are designed specifically to obtain the best results for the specific purposes intended. On one hand, techniques are necessary to initially record the fingerprints of persons placed under arrest; on the other hand, special procedures must be used to record the fingerprints of cadavers, some of which may be in advanced stages of decomposition. Recording footprints of newborn infants presents special problems too, as does photographing inked and latent impressions.

INKED IMPRESSIONS

The standard method of recording the fingerprints of arrestees involves inking the fingers and rolling and placing them on a fingerprint card. It is a method which has remained essentially unchanged since the 1890s, when Galton advocated the use of printer's ink as the medium for recording finger impressions. A few variations have been devised, some of which will be discussed in this chapter.

Recording Equipment

The equipment necessary to record fingerprints consists of a slab, fingerprint ink, an ink roller, a card holder, fingerprint cards and

137

cleaning supplies. The slab most frequently used today is made of ¼–⅜-inch-thick glass measuring approximately four by twelve inches with beveled edges to avoid injury during use. Some early fingerprint pioneers suggested using a copper slab, but chemicals used to clean the copper plate pit its surface and render it unsuitable for further printing. For a long time, Galton's advocation of printer's ink was followed, and it is indeed possible to obtain clear and legible prints with printer's ink. Inks most used in police departments today, however, are specially prepared, often according to protected formulas, to give consistently better results than printer's ink.

The ink roller is usually a rubber roller 2½ to 4 inches wide of the type used to smooth photographic prints on a ferrotype plate in the darkroom. It is used to smooth the ink on the slab before inking the fingers. A fingerprint card holder is an instrument used during the recording process. It consists of a wooden or metal base on which is mounted a steel frame hinge for holding and folding cards while recording fingerprints.

The fingerprint card in standard use in the United States today measures eight by eight inches and is printed on sturdy stock. It provides spaces for the subject's name, alias, bureau number, color, sex, fingerprint and reference classifications, and rolled and plain impressions of both hands, as well as places to note any amputations and for the signatures of the subject and the recording official. On the back of the card, space is usually provided for a photograph and for the criminal history of the subject. The size of fingerprint record cards varies from country to country. Initially, fingerprint "slips" were printed on sheets of paper that measured 8½ x 13 inches and were filed horizontally in drawers or pigeonhole cabinets. In January of 1905, Captain Michael P. Evans, head of the identification bureau of the Chicago Police Department, introduced eight by eight inch cards and suggested filing them vertically. The card found favor in the United States and has been generally adopted here. Several other countries also use it and the vertical filing method. But many countries use fingerprint cards of varying sizes, from 3½ x 8½ inches (in Argentina) to 8½ x 14 inches in (Sweden). The fingerprint slip utilized for male arrestees in Belgium is 8½ x 13¼ inches and it is printed in black ink. Slips used to fingerprint female arrestees are printed in red ink.

Necessary in the fingerprint recording process is a supply of cleaning materials, generally including cotton or rags and a cleaning fluid such as carbon tetrachloride, acetone, turpentine or paint thinner. Some departments use soap and water to remove ink from fingers. The fingerprinting equipment also has to be cleaned to prevent the ink from hardening on the slab and ink roller.

Recording Procedure

The first step in recording fingerprints is to ink the slab by putting a few dabs of fingerprint ink on the slab and rolling it out smoothly with the roller until the slab is covered with a thin, even layer of ink. Then the fingers are rolled from nail to nail over the inked slab, taking care to ink the complete ridge pattern of the end joint along with a small area of the second joint below the flexure crease. After the right hand is inked, the fingers are rolled in the appropriate square for the right-hand fingers on the fingerprint card so that an inked impression of the ridge patterns of all the fingers appears on the card. In order to avoid smudging, rolling must be done in a smooth fashion, with equal pressure on all portions of the fingers. After the fingers of the right hand are printed, the ink on the slab is rolled smooth and the procedure is repeated for the left hand, after which the ink is again rolled smooth and the plain impressions of the four fingers of each hand are made. The same is done for the thumbs. Rolled prints are taken because they show the full pattern area, including deltas, and all ridge characteristics. Plain prints are taken because they more closely represent chance impressions found at crime scenes and because they check the correctness of the sequence of rolled prints. See Figures 126A–H for characteristics of improper recording, and note especially in Figures 126G and H that the absence of the portion below the flexure crease may result in difficulties in tracing whorls and that showing too much of the middle phalanx of a finger may interfere with recording fingerprints in adjoining squares. Figure 127 shows a set of fingerprints in which the rolled prints are inadvertently switched. Studying the plain prints reveals that the rolled prints of the right hand are printed in the spaces reserved for those of the left hand, and vice versa. Plain prints must be made simultaneously to insure that they, too, are recorded in correct sequence and that they can be used to cross check the accuracy of the recording sequence for rolled prints. Figure 128A shows an example of properly recorded, simultaneously taken, left-hand plain fingerprints, whereas Figure

Figure 126. Eight examples of improperly recorded impressions.
A. Blotched or weakly printed portions (ink unevenly distributed on roller slab).
B. Smear caused by perspiration or blotch caused by foreign matter on finger (hands not clean).
C. Flattened ridges (excessive finger pressure).
D. Smeared print (fingers unevenly rolled).
E. Delta of loop missing (finger not fully rolled).
F. Print not properly centered in card square.
G. Absent print area below flexure crease.
H. Print overrun into next card square.

128B illustrates improperly placed plain prints taken one after the other.

The importance of fully rolling the fingers from nail to nail cannot be overemphasized. Incomplete rolling can result in failure to record the delta in a loop or a whorl, as in Figure 126E, and it can lead to erroneous pattern interpretation as in Figure 129; on the left, the plain print appears to be a loop, while the fully rolled print on the right clearly shows a double loop pattern.

Abnormal Conditions

Special procedures are called for when the person being fingerprinted has a bandaged finger, open sores or a skin disease. Under no circumstances should infection be risked by applying ink to a wounded finger. A notation of the condition should be made on the card and the finger or fingers affected passed over. The same rule applies for bandaged fingers. If the subject is under arrest, he can be printed at a later time when the wound has healed. If the finger

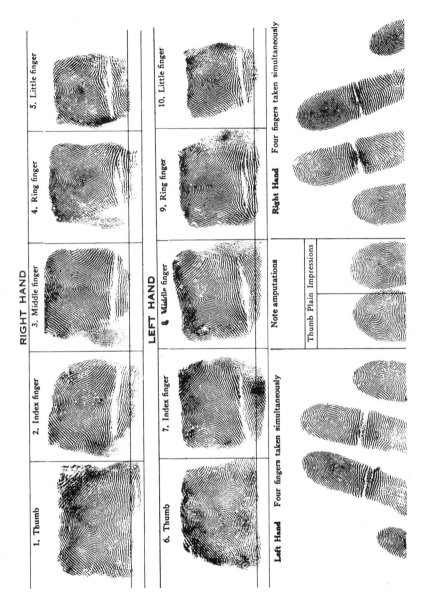

Figure 127. Inadvertently switched rolled prints.

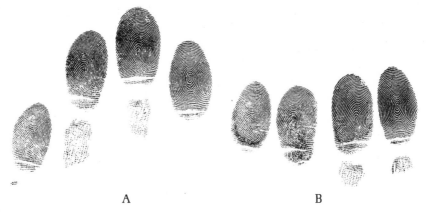

A   B

Figure 128. A. Properly recorded plain impressions (simultaneous).
            B. Improperly recorded plain impressions (not simultaneous).

is not bandaged, the technician taking the print might observe the pattern type of the wounded finger(s) and make the appropriate notation on the card to enable the identification bureau to run a preliminary check through the files.

Under some conditions, ordinary rolling of the fingers is rather difficult and for that reason it is impossible to obtain clear impressions. This happens frequently when attempting to fingerprint older persons who suffer from rheumatism or who have arthritic fingers. People suffering from such afflictions frequently cannot bend their fingers. They can be fingerprinted by inking their fingers directly with the roller and by printing the inked fingers on cut out blocks of a fingerprint card, either holding the paper in the palm of the

Figure 129. The importance of properly rolled prints.

hand or using postmortem paddles or spoons, which will be described soon. A similar problem can occur with subjects suffering from ankylosis, a pathological condition in which an abnormal union of bones results in the stiffening of a joint. When it affects a finger, the finger is either permanently fixed in a straight position and cannot be bent or it is bent and cannot be straightened out. Here, too, fingerprinting may be accomplished by inking the finger directly with the roller and printing on cut out blocks.

Other Recording Methods

Over the years a number of recording methods have been developed that obviate the conventional inked slab and roller routine. Some of them are so-called inkless methods based on a chemical reaction that occurs when a finger touches specially prepared paper or after the finger has been rolled on a special pad containing an invisible chemical catalyst that reacts to the chemically treated paper. Some of these methods have had a degree of success, especially in hospitals for footprinting babies, but by and large they have not been adopted in law enforcement agencies because of the lack of clarity and durability of the prints they produce.

In the early 1960s, a special inking pad was introduced which needs no re-inking or roller. The heart of the pad, marketed as the Ace Porelon Pad, is porelon, a microreticulate, thermoplastic resin that acts as a reservoir for specially prepared ink made of carbon and dyes that dries in approximately three seconds and is not toxic. Although difficulties were experienced with the early models, the pads now appear to measure up to their claimed performance of producing a minimum of 50,000 fingerprints without re-inking. The pad is mounted in a high-grade steel case and measures $5\frac{1}{4}$ x $2\frac{3}{4}$ x $\frac{1}{2}$ inches, making it easy to carry for field use.

Among the other modern methods for recording fingerprints are several photographic reproduction techniques, all of which make use of an apparatus upon which the fingers are placed so as to permit a direct photograph of the ridges of the fingers. Because of the cost involved, as well as other performance limitations, no such apparatus has ever gained practical acceptance. It is possible, however, that sometime in the future electronic and computerized applications to fingerprinting might revive interest in such methods.

The National Police Agency of Tokyo, Japan, developed an electronic fingerprinting method that uses specially prepared paper and the powder toners used in xerography. The advantages of this method, according to its developers, are increased clarity in ridge detail and avoiding of any staining of the fingers with fingerprint ink. The system does not seem to have any significant acceptance.

RECORDING PALM AND SOLEPRINTS

Recording the palmprints and soleprints of adults is essentially the same as recording fingerprints. The main differences are the ink is rolled onto the feet and hands, and high-gloss paper is used to insure clear ridge impressions. Special sized recording slips or cards are used, although many departments use standard eight by eight inch cards for palmprints as well as for fingerprints. A special apparatus has been developed for recording palmprints. It consists of a slightly convex surface over which a palmprint slip is placed.

Baby Footprinting

Since the early days of fingerprinting, the concept has been advanced that footprinting infants in maternity wards is an excellent means to make sure that the right baby is sent home with each new mother. Since there is no biological, physiological or physical difference between the friction skin on the fingers and that on the palms and soles, the premise is undoubtedly true. Identification can be as easily made from the palms and feet as from the fingers. Accordingly, footprinting of newborn babies in hospitals has been practiced for over half a century. Many critics have called footprinting a waste of time and expense because of the small percentage of identifiable prints obtained from babies' feet. A 1966 medical study involving the footprints of fifty-one babies revealed that only twenty percent of the prints were identifiable. And in my own experience, three cases in which I was asked to identify young children on the basis of hospital footprints taken at birth proved to be impossible: the inked footprints presented nothing more than big blobs of ink lacking all identifiable ridge detail. But to condemn a method of identification because of poor practices and inexperienced application does not seem to be a valid premise.

It is true that the ridge detail on the feet of the newly born is extremely tiny and fragile and requires careful preparation. It is also true that nurses who are asked to perform the task of footprinting in the delivery room are under pressure and do not generally have the training or the time to take legible footprints. On the other hand, a 1957 study in Los Angeles involving 491 babies showed that the rate of identification was directly proportional to the type of equipment and the degree of care used by the nurses. For the different types of equipment used in four separate test areas of the experiment, identifiable footprints, registered 14, 30, 35 and 84 percent. The conclusion of the researchers was that footprinting infants at birth can be extremely valuable for proving identity if the proper methods and materials are used.

Generally speaking, the best results are obtained with dry-plate methods (chemical reactions), several of which are commercially marketed under various trade names and sold directly to hospitals. The dry plate is inserted in a holder about the size of an ordinary stamp pad that fits comfortably in a nurse's hand. The plate is pressed gently against an infant's foot and the foot is then pressed gently against a sheet of glossy, coated paper. Results so obtained are much better than those gotten by the conventional ink and roller method. Much less smudging is noted and the baby's foot is not so soiled.

POSTMORTEM FINGERPRINTING

As long as sufficient friction ridge detail remains, it is possible to identify individuals. Decomposition and certain other conditions such as burning ultimately destroy all skin. Yet we have only to recall the preserved, many centuries old body of the Grauballe Man found in a Danish peat bog in 1952 to realize the feasibility of fingerprinting the dead. In fact, it has become one of the primary methods of identification for victims of natural and human disasters, including casualties of conventional warfare. The FBI's Disaster Squad has identified numerous human remains recovered from airplane, boat and train wrecks, and the FBI's fingerprint files have been used to establish the identity of thousands of deceased people whose prints are sent to Washington by state and local law enforcement agencies. Figure 130 illustrates how difficult the task of identifying human remains can sometimes be.

Technicians have by necessity invented special tools to assist them in attempting to record the impressions of cadavers. The most essential instrument holds strips of paper upon which prints are made. Since fingers of even the recently dead are not pliable once

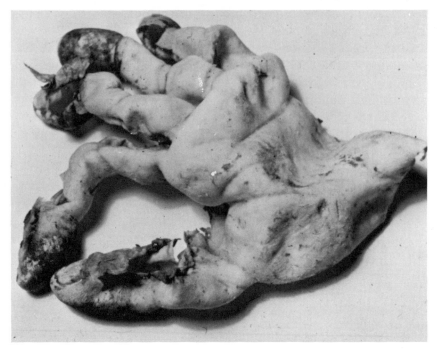

Figure 130.

rigor mortis has set in, the fingers must be inked directly with a roller, provided the friction skin is not damaged. After a finger is inked, a special postmortem spoon or shoehorn instrument is employed to accommodate the so-called fingerprint strips that are rolled over the inked finger to make a print (see Figure 131). A number of other instruments, including special rollers and finger clamps to straighten fingers, have been devised by inventive technicians.

Friction skin severely damaged by decomposition or by exposure to water, sun, fire or explosion must be cleaned and restored before an attempt can be made to secure fingerprints from it. Hands so damaged should be immersed in running water or gently washed with soap, 90% alcohol, benzine or xylene. For the procedure, the technician should of course wear rubber gloves. If it is necessary to amputate fingers for the purpose of identification, the receptacles should be labeled with the name of the digit and state and local laws should be checked to see if any legal restrictions exist on amputating or mutilating human remains for identification.

Shrunken or shriveled fingers can be restored to normal size by

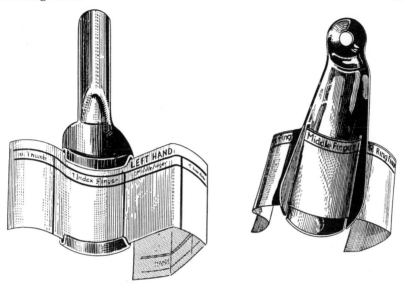

Figure 131. Postmortem spoon and shoehorn. (Courtesy: Institute of Applied Science.)

blowing air into the bulb of each finger with a hypodermic syringe. Inflation of the finger with approximately 1–1½ cc of air causes the wrinkles to recede as long as the skin is sufficiently intact to seal the air inside. Massaging the needle opening usually causes the skin opening made by the syringe needle to close. If the skin is damaged to the extent that the bulb of the finger will not hold air, the finger can in some instances be restored to proper size by the injection of a solution of one part hot gelatine and seven parts glycerin with a hypodermic syringe equipped with a larger needle than that used to blow air into the finger. Again, after injection of the hot solution, the finger opening made by the needle must be massaged to prevent leakage of the solution. When the finger has been restored to normal size by one of these procedures, it can then be inked with a roller and impressions can be taken from it with a postmortem spoon, shoehorn instrument or other paddles designed especially for the purpose.

Epidermal Gloves

In some cases of advanced decomposition, the epidermis detaches itself from the dermis (again see Figure 130). Obviously, such hands and fingers must be carefully handled. After they are cleansed, fingerprinting can sometimes be performed in the way used for live subjects by fitting the putrefied epidermis onto the technician's own fingers (wearing rubber gloves, of course) much like a finger glove. If the epidermis is too soft and unmanageable, the skin can be hardened somewhat by being submerged for twenty-four hours in a solution made of 12 parts of 40% formaldehyde, 68 parts of alcohol, and 20 parts of glacial acetic acid. Soaking skin in this solution can preserve it indefinitely, but causes it to swell somewhat.

Dermal Surface Impressions

If the epidermis is totally absent or unusable for purposes of identification, friction ridge designs may still be noted on the dermis. Although most inking processes of dermal patterns are doomed to failure, it is often possible to obtain a legible ridge pattern by directly photographing the finger (see Figure 132) or by X-ray tech-

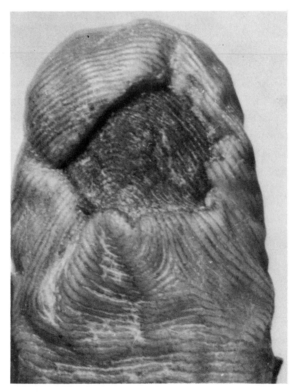

Figure 132. (Courtesy: Ohio State Bureau of Criminal Identification and Investigation.)

niques. The well-known expert Felino Padron suggests that the technician prepare the fingers for X-ray procedure by mixing 20 parts of carbonate of lead and 100 parts of melted paraffin in a glass container and applying it evenly on each finger, after which radiographs are made. As an alternative, it has been suggested that lanolin and carbonate of bismuth can be used to prepare dead fingers and palms for X-raying. As with all postmortem techniques, the technician must precede any finger preparation or restoration by carefully cleansing the skin.

Other methods for obtaining dermal impressions include making a cast of the skin, which means that it must first be submerged for a few hours in glacial acetic acid, to be swelled, then rinsed in running water. After such a cast has been obtained, graphite is sprinkled over the print until the powder sets in the depressions. The excess is then wiped off with a cloth moistened with silicone. Since the grooves in the cast actually represent the ridges of the dermal surface, a photograph of them will yield an image in which the original ridges are black and the grooves are white.

Macerated Fingers

Partially rotten and saponified to the extent that the end joints have hardened and wrinkled after excessive submersion in water, macerated fingers can be restored for identification by being softened in a solution of four parts of concentrated ammonium hydroxide and one part of glycerin. The amputated fingers should remain in the solution for from thirty-six to forty-eight hours. When the desired degree of softness is obtained, the fingers should be washed in warm water and then dried by being dipped in acetone. The smooth ridge patterns on the fingertips can be removed with a scalpel and placed between glass microscope slides, where they can be exposed directly in an enlarger without a negative. The Royal Canadian Mounted Police cites cases in which a solution of lactic acid, phenol, glycerin and distilled water softened the skin on the fingertips of a drowned man enough to enable fingerprints to be taken.

Mummified Fingers

Usually hard and shrunken mummified fingers can be restored and the skin made pliable by being soaked in a 1–3% solution of potassium hydroxide (caustic potash). After they have swelled to normal proportions, they are dried, inked and fingerprinted in the conventional manner. During submersion in the caustic potash, which may be as long as thirty-six hours, the progress of the swelling must be watched to avoid bursting or disintegrating from over-exposure. Placing the digits in a 5% solution of Formalin checks the action of the potash. Other techniques used when the skin tissue is dehydrated by extreme heat or mummified include submersion of the digits in differently graded solutions of alcohol. The Russian criminologist Dr. Zakonov suggests soaking the mummified hand for several hours in warm water containing an antiseptic and, if necessary, other chemicals to facilitate the absorption of water by the dried tissues. He then injects warm paraffin under the skin to remove wrinkles. His method, he suggests, would make it possible to record the fingerprints of ancient Egyptian pharaohs or Inca chiefs, if the skin were not altogether destroyed.

Because of the many varied circumstances under which unidentified bodies have been discovered, fingerprint technicians have had to use great ingenuity in dealing with problems not previously encountered. Accordingly, the technical literature abounds with descriptions of various postmortem techniques. Essentially, however, all experts agree that the three basic steps in dealing with cadavers involve cleaning the skin tissue, restoring the tissue and fingerprinting the ridge patterns. It might be added that photographing ridge patterns should be attempted at various stages while preparing the skin tissue of the dead for printing. Since photography is a harmless means of recording ridge detail, it sometimes preserves identifiable images of friction skin that because of subsequent improper handling is rendered useless for fingerprinting.

FINGERPRINT PHOTOGRAPHY

The reproduction of inked or latent impressions by photographic means does not present any special problem to one skilled in the principles of photography, one who is thoroughly knowledgeable of darkroom techniques, light-sensitive emulsions, and various types of cameras, enlargers, accessories and lighting equipment. Inked impressions are usually easy to photograph because it is essentially a straight copying job that can be performed with any type of camera equipped with a ground glass viewing screen for accurate focusing. The same is true for reproducing latent impressions. The camera most widely used for identification photography is the 4 x 5 inch press type because of its versatility: it permits the use of glass plate holders, sheet film holders, roll film adapters, film pack holders and even Polaroid adapters and ground glass focusing. The double-extension bellows of most models allow direct photomacrographic work—close-up photography without the use of a microscope. The large negative makes it easy to handle and, when fine grain photography is required, permits virtually unlimited enlargement with high resolution and sharpness.

Actually, any type of camera that has accessories for close-up work can be used in fingerprint photography. Many 35 mm cameras on the market have through-the-lens ground glass viewing and come with 1:1 close-up reproduction accessories. They have come into considerably increased use in identification work in the past ten years, although large press or view cameras are still the most widely used. The only disadvantage of all such cameras is the long set-up time. The camera must be mounted on a tripod in front of the fingerprint evidence, lights must be installed and the image must be focused on the ground glass. But special fingerprint cameras have been designed which eliminate those preliminary preparations. Self-contained, with a lens, shutter and diaphragm, lighting system and batteries, viewing panel and hood, these special cameras need no outside lighting, no focusing and no setting up (see Figure 133). The camera is placed directly against the evidence bearing either inked or latent fingerprints, with the sheet film holder in place and the dark slide removed. When the shutter is pressed, the self-contained light source illuminates the object evenly during exposure.

Various models of fingerprint cameras are manufactured by fingerprint supply houses such as Faurot, Burke & James (the Watson-Holmes Fingerprint Camera) and Sirchie. Most models take film sizes 2¼ x 3¼ inches and photograph "same size," or 1:1, although some models come equipped to hold up to 4 x 5 inch film. Some models have a standard AC adapter cord, although nearly all are used with the self-contained power source that is furnished by flashlight cells or batteries. Most models also have coated, anastigmatic lenses with between-the-lens shutters affording flexibility in exposure time, as well as iris diaphragms to stop the lens down to f:22. Because the fingerprint camera is always ready for use at a moment's notice, it is an instrument that is particularly suited for crime-scene use, although most fingerprint technicians use it in the laboratory as well.

Efforts have been made to adapt ordinary cameras for fingerprint

Figure 133. The Faurot Fingerprint Camera with carrying case and film holder.

photography by the use of new accessories. One that is particularly valuable for fingerprint work is the Faurot Foto Focuser, which is attached to the lens mount of a 4 x 5 inch Speed Graphic or Crown Graphic and which, when the bellows are pulled to a preset distance, converts the press camera into a fingerprint camera. The adapter is placed directly on the surface being photographed and it produces a 1:1 negative (see Figure 134). Lighting for the reproduction can be provided by holding a flash gun toward the area being recorded on film. The advantage of this method is that the 4 x 5 inch negative permits large areas containing latent prints to be photographed on one negative and in natural size. On the other hand, considerable experimentation to obtain correct exposures is necessary because the distance between the flash and the surface being photographed is not fixed. Some set-up time is still required.

Special Hints on Latent Print Photography

Essentially, the object of photographic reproduction is both to preserve and record evidence and to improve the detail of latent images, all of which can be accomplished by the judicious use of filters, different types of lighting (oblique, transmitted and ultraviolet, for example) and different photographic emulsions. Photographic

Figure 134. The Faurot Foto Focuser mounted on a 4 x 5 inch press camera.

reproduction works especially well when latent prints are discovered on colored and multicolored surfaces.

When a surface is colored and the photographer wishes it to appear white in the photograph, he can use a filter of the same color as the surface. If a latent print is developed with black powder on a blue surface, little contrast will be shown in a photograph taken with panchromatic film, which records all of the colors of the visible spectrum in varying shades of gray. Ridges in such a photograph would not stand out well against the background. But if the photograph is made with a blue filter, the filter will lighten the background enough to make it appear white in the photograph, thus affording an excellent contrast for the black powdered ridges of the latent print.

Polarized light can also greatly enhance the ridge detail in a latent print. Light can be polarized with special polarizing filters. In Figure 135A, a latent print found on an old Delft dinner plate that was badly cracked shows little detail or contrast when photographed with ordinary illumination. When the plate was photographed with polarized light, however, as shown in Figure 135B, the latent image was brought out quite distinctly.

Latent prints on glass surfaces can present special problems. In

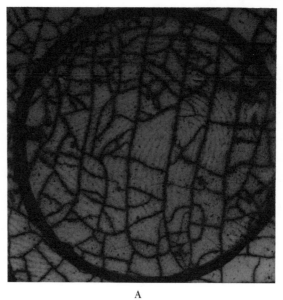

A

B

Figure 135. The value of photographing latent prints under polarized light. (Courtesy: Technical Bureau, Civic Guard Headquarters, Dublin, Ireland.)

most cases, the problems can be solved by experimenting with different lighting techniques. Lighting placed at an oblique angle to the surface, or even transmitted through the glass, provides a good outline of the ridge structure when the image is viewed on the ground glass of the camera. White powdered latents on transparent glass can be photographed by placing black paper behind the glass; black powdered latents can be photographed by using a white sheet of paper. Bottles or glasses can be filled with an opaque substance of contrasting color to the latent print. Thus a black powdered latent on a drinking glass will stand out clearly if the glass is filled with milk, while a gray or white powdered print on a bottle may show good contrast when the bottle is filled with black ink. Reflections in the glass produced by the light source can be eliminated by adjusting the angle of the lights.

Reflections cause the greatest difficulties with highly polished surfaces such as chromium, silver, nickel and mirrors. Stray lighting can often be avoided and reflections eliminated by using indirect lighting obtained by directing the light source onto a white surface, such as a sheet of paper, away from the polished surface, but reflecting it toward the latter (see Figure 136). On mirrors,

Figure 136. A fingerprint photographed under indirect light.

reflections can be avoided by scraping the silver from the rear of the mirror. If the mirror is too valuable or if other circumstances prohibit such procedure, white powdered prints can be covered by a photographic ground glass placed with the rough side of the glass toward the impressions. This will eliminate ghost images but a lower contrast will result. By varying the position of the lights, white powdered ridges can be made to appear either black or white in the photograph. The ground glass can also be made a little more translucent by rubbing the ground surface with a drop of light machine oil. If this procedure is used, it is of course necessary to carefully clean the surface of the glass so that the oil cannot damage the latent image. Photographs of latent prints on opaque glass can sometimes be made by shining light through the glass. Good reproductions of black powdered latent prints discovered on a light bulb have been made by simply screwing the bulb into a socket and using the bulb itself as the light source.

Whenever plastic or relief impressions are discovered in soft substances, development by powders is not possible. The only way to record these impressions is by direct photography, usually with a grazing (oblique) light which causes the elevations in the soft substance (which correspond to the grooves of the finger) to cast dark shadows into the grooves of the soft substance (which in turn correspond to the friction ridges of the skin). The dark shadows will show up dark in the photograph, thus giving a black-on-white ridge pattern of the impression.

Whenever white or gray powdered latents appearing on a dark surface are photographed, the friction ridges in the photograph will appear as white lines on a dark background. In comparing these ridges with the inked impressions of a suspect, care must be taken to match the white lines of the latent to the black lines of the inked print. In order to avoid this background discrepancy, it is possible to make a reversal negative of the latent impression. This is done by making a contact print of the original negative used to photograph the latent impression onto another sheet of film. In this manner, a reversal negative can be obtained. By this procedure, it is possible to obtain a tone and/or a position reversal negative.

Some technicians try to have all of their court exhibits show latent and inked print comparisons in the same color, so as not to confuse the jury by asking them to look at white lines in the latent print and compare them with black lines in the inked impressions.

Most experienced fingerprint men, however, seem to prefer avoiding this extra step to prevent additional confusion by explaining the reversal process and presenting evidence in color as it actually appears on the object bearing the latent print.

The photography of fingerprinting is really not a specialty because it requires only a sound knowledge of general photographic work coupled with some ingenuity to solve particular problems. In the final analysis, fingerprint photography is straight copy or reproduction work.

Chapter 6

Fingerprint Classification in the United States

The classification system used in the United States consists of the basic Henry system, as modified and extended by the Federal Bureau of Investigation. Henry's original system was designed to accommodate files of up to one hundred thousand sets of prints and was soon found to be inadequate for large accumulations of fingerprints. The classification formula consists of letters and numerals arranged in the form of a fraction with a numerator and denominator; it determines at what place within a fingerprint file a particular set of fingerprints will be located. The formula is based on a study of the ten fingerprints of an individual.

Before a technician can proceed with devising the classification formula for a set of fingerprints, he must first interpret each individual pattern and mark the results of his interpretation on the fingerprint card. The procedure of assigning the pattern interpretation symbols to a set of prints is referred to as "blocking out."

There are two steps in blocking out a set of prints. The first consists of placing the symbols for the patterns under the rolled impressions on the fingerprint card. Ulnar loops are represented by a slanted line to the right (\) for those appearing on right-hand fingers (Figure 137, under the patterns of the right middle, ring and little fingers) and to the left (/) for those ulnar loops appearing on left-hand fingers (Figure 137, under the left middle finger pattern). Radial loops are represented by a capital R if they appear on index fingers (Figure 137, right index) and by a small letter r if they appear on any other finger (Figure 137, left little finger).

Arches and tented arches appearing on the index fingers are rep-

158

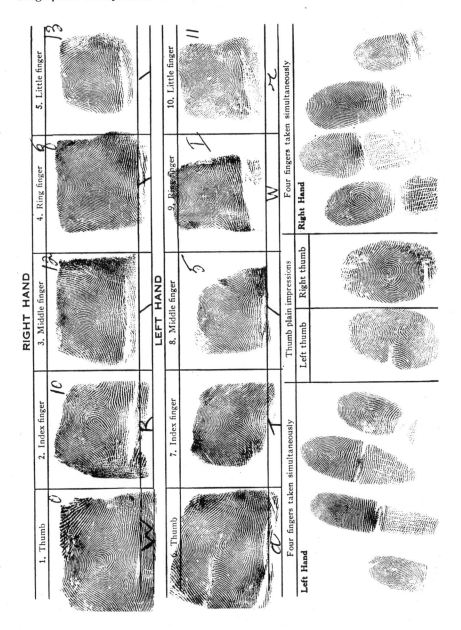

Figure 137.

Classification:

$$\frac{10 \quad 1 \quad\quad R \quad\quad (OOI) \quad 13}{18 \quad aT--r \quad (-II) \quad 11}$$

resented by the capital letters A and T, respectively, and by the small letters a and t if they appear on any finger other than the index finger. All four whorl patterns are represented by the capital W only, regardless of the finger on which they appear.

The second step in blocking out consists of recording, in the upper-right hand corner of every rolled pattern block, the ridge trace of each whorl and the ridge count of each loop. Approximating patterns are blocked out first by their primary interpretation and then by their reference interpretation; the two symbols are separated by a question mark. Examples: W?/ or /?t or M?O or 7?9. (A fully blocked out set of prints is shown in Figure 137.) After all of the pattern symbols have been marked on the set of prints, the classifier has all the data he requires to arrive at a classification formula for that set of prints.

The classification formula is a series of letters and numerals arranged in the form of a fraction and consisting of different sections or steps that are derived and used one after another. In logical order, these different steps are called: primary classification, secondary classification, subsecondary classification, major division, final classification and key.

Primary Classification

To arrive at a primary classification, patterns are first divided into numerical and nonnumerical patterns, and secondly are paired off according to odd- and even-numbered fingers. Whorl patterns are numerical patterns; all other patterns (arches, tented arches and loops) are nonnumerical patterns. Numerical patterns are assigned a numerical value that varies according to the finger upon which they appear after the set has been paired off. On a fingerprint card, the rolled impressions are numbered from one to ten, as may be seen in Figure 137. The order is: 1—right thumb; 2—right index; 3—right middle finger; 4—right ring finger; 5—right little finger; 6—left thumb; 7—left index; 8—left middle finger; 9—left ring finger; and 10—left little finger. In pairing off the patterns for the purpose of classification, the sequence of the patterns is altered. All even-numbered fingers are placed in the numerator and all odd-numbered fingers make up the denominator. Thus we obtain the following paired-off sequence:

2.R.Index	4.R.Ring	6.L.Thumb	8.L.Middle	10.L.Little
1.R.Thumb	3.R.Middle	5.R.Little	7.L.Index	9.L.Ring

All numerical patterns (whorls) are assigned the following values: when they appear on fingers one and two of the paired-off sequence, a value of 16; on fingers three and four, a value of 8; on fingers five and six, a value of 4; on fingers seven and eight, a value of 2; and on fingers nine and ten, a value of 1. All nonnumerical patterns are assigned a value of 0 (zero). To obtain the primary classification, all values in the denominator are totaled and 1 is added; all values in the numerator are also totaled and 1 is added. The fraction thus obtained constitutes the primary classification. The reason for adding 1 to both numerator and denominator is to obtain a formula consisting of at least 1-over-1, rather than 0-over-0.

The practice may be made clearer by the following examples:

Set of Prints Original Sequence	Set of Prints Paired-off Sequence	Values	Primary Classification
W R W W a / a W r W U	R W A R U / W W A W W	0 8 0 0 0 / 16 8 0 2 1 $+\frac{1}{1}=$	$\frac{9}{28}$
W W W W W / W W W W W	W W W W W / W W W W W	16 8 4 2 1 / 16 8 4 2 1 $+\frac{1}{1}=$	$\frac{32}{32}$
W T W U W / U W t U W	T U U T W / W W W W U	0 0 0 0 1 / 16 8 4 2 0 $+\frac{1}{1}=$	$\frac{2}{31}$
a U U U U / U R t U U	U U U T U / A U U R U	0 0 0 0 0 / 0 0 0 0 0 $+\frac{1}{1}=$	$\frac{1}{1}$
r W U W U / t W W W W	W W T W W / R U U W W	16 8 0 2 1 / 0 0 0 2 1 $+\frac{1}{1}=$	$\frac{28}{4}$

The practice of pairing off odd-numbered and even-numbered fingers to arrive at the primary classification is cumbersome and seems impractical. It could be legitimately asked why the right-hand patterns are not selected for the numerator, and the left-hand patterns for the denominator. The reason for the awkward method of calculating the primary classification is based on fingerprint history.

Before Henry devised his numerical primary, what feeble attempts as had been made to classify fingerprints had resulted in dividing all patterns into two groups, L and W. The L group was comprised of loops, arches and tented arches. The W group included plain whorls and all composite patterns. To file fingerprints, a set of ten fingers was divided into five pairs of patterns, which gave each pair these four possible combinations:

$$\frac{L}{L} \qquad \frac{L}{W} \qquad \frac{W}{L} \qquad \frac{W}{W}$$

With four possible variations for each pair of prints and five pairs per set, the early workers in the field realized that there could be 1,024 possible combinations, the product of $4 \times 4 \times 4 \times 4 \times 4$. They envisioned a filing cabinet consisting of 1,024 pigeonholes, 32 compartments across and 32 compartments down (see Figure 138). To file a set of prints, the cabinet was divided and subdivided five times so that the correct pigeonhole could be located for the particular primary classification at hand. A number of sets of prints were so classified and filed—the start of the tremendous collections of fingerprints of the future.

Henry wanted to use the existing 1,024-hole cabinet as well as devise a numerical primary that would result in a set of fingerprints being filed in the same pigeonhole, regardless of whether his new system or the old one by the L and W scheme was used. To accomplish this result, he assigned numerical values—16, 8, 4, 2 and 1—to whorl patterns and worked out the pairing off method. The combination of pairing off and assigning numerical values to whorls accomplished the desired result and a set of prints could be filed in the same pigeonhole by either method.

By the time American fingerprint men decided that Henry's primary classification scheme was unnecessarily involved, too many fingerprints were already on file across the country to warrant the tremendous expenditure that would be needed to fund a conversion to a simpler primary system.

Not all identification bureaus in the United States employ the Henry primary. At least one bureau, the New York State Division of Identification in Albany, now part of the New York State Intelligence and Identification System (NYSIIS), employs what is called the American system. When the New York bureau adopted fingerprinting to replace Bertillon's anthropometry in the early years of this century, Captain James H. Parke decided that the Henry system's complications in arriving at a primary could be avoided by simply assigning numerical values on the basis of the natural sequence of patterns in a fingerprint card, that is, right-hand fingers make up the numerator, and left-hand fingers the denominator. The

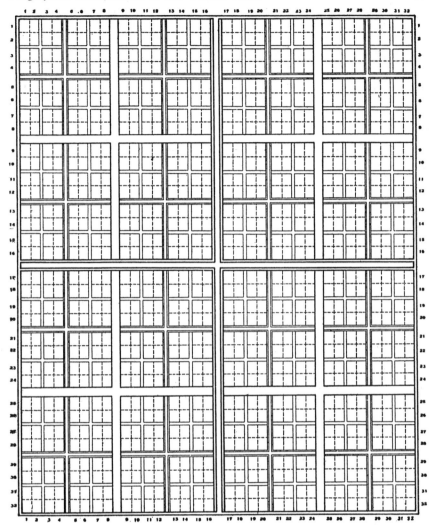

Figure 138. The pigeon hole filing cabinet that led to the development of the Henry primary classification.

American system also has 1,024 primaries, but with the exception of all-nonnumerical sets of prints (1-over-1 primary) and all-whorl sets of prints (32-over-32 primary) a set of prints would have a different primary classification in the American system from what it has in the Henry method. For example, the set

$$\frac{\text{W} \quad \text{A} \quad \text{T} \quad \text{W} \quad \text{U}}{\text{W} \quad \text{W} \quad \text{U} \quad \text{U} \quad \text{W}}$$

would have a Henry primary of 14-over-19 and an American system primary of 19-over-26.

The overwhelming majority of American identification bureaus, including the Federal Bureau of Investigation's Identification Division with its gigantic collections utilize the Henry system. By now so many millions of sets of prints are classified and filed under the Henry primary system that the time in manpower that would be required to convert to an easier primary system is prohibitive. Until such time as our present system of classifying fingerprints is totally abandoned in favor of an electronic, computerized system of interpreting and filing along lines totally different from present concepts, we cannot expect a change toward the use of the American system.

SECONDARY CLASSIFICATION

The secondary classification subdivides large groups of fingerprint sets having the same primary classification. In the primary classification, the fingers are paired off in order to obtain a numerator consisting of all the even-numbered fingers and a denominator consisting of all the odd-numbered fingers. The process of pairing off is utilized only for the purpose of obtaining the primary classification. For all subsequent subdivisions, including the secondary classification, the sets of prints are studied in their natural sequence. This means that all the right-hand fingers make up the secondary numerator, while all the left-hand fingers make up the secondary denominator.

The secondary classification consists of capital letter symbols for the patterns on the two index fingers, with the right index finger symbol appearing in the numerator and the left index symbol in the denominator. The five basic pattern types that can appear on either index finger are: arch (A) tented arch (T), radial loop (R); ulnar loop (U) and whorl (W). For the purpose of classification, central pocket loops, double loops and accidentals are classified the same as plain whorls under the symbol W. Since any of the five pattern types may be encountered on the index fingers, there are twenty-five possible combinations of secondary classifications:

$$\frac{A}{A} \quad \frac{T}{A} \quad \frac{R}{A} \quad \frac{U}{A} \quad \frac{W}{A} \qquad \frac{A}{T} \quad \frac{T}{T} \quad \frac{R}{T} \quad \frac{U}{T} \quad \frac{W}{T} \qquad \frac{A}{R} \quad \frac{T}{R} \quad \frac{R}{R} \quad \frac{U}{R} \quad \frac{W}{R}$$

$$\frac{A}{U} \quad \frac{T}{U} \quad \frac{R}{U} \quad \frac{U}{U} \quad \frac{W}{U} \qquad \frac{A}{W} \quad \frac{T}{W} \quad \frac{R}{W} \quad \frac{U}{W} \quad \frac{W}{W}$$

In addition to the capital letter symbols representing the types of patterns occurring on the index fingers, secondary classification also includes small letters for arches (a), tented arches (t) and radial loops (r) that appear on fingers other than the index fingers. If one of these patterns occurs on a thumb, the corresponding small letter precedes the capital letter representing the index finger. Thus if the right thumb is a plain arch and the right index is a radial loop, the secondary numerator is aR. When an arch, tented arch or radial loop appears on the middle finger, the respective lower case letter follows the capital letter of the secondary. Thus if the right thumb is a tented arch, the right index an ulnar loop and the right middle finger a radial loop, the secondary numerator is tUr. If the left index is a whorl and the left middle finger an arch, the secondary denominator is Wa.

If an arch, tented arch or radial loop appears on either a ring or a little finger, the same lower case letters are placed to the right of the index finger symbol, with appropriate dashes inserted between the index symbol and the small-letter symbol to indicate the absence of small-letter patterns on intervening fingers. Thus, if the right index is an ulnar loop, the right middle a whorl, the right ring finger an ulnar loop and the right little finger an arch, the secondary numerator for that set would be U– –a. Or if the left thumb is an arch, the left index a whorl, the left middle and left little fingers ulnar loops, but the left ring finger a tented arch, the secondary denominator for that set is aW-t. When two or more small letters or the same type follow each other immediately, as in aa, ttt, or rr, they would instead be written as 2a, 3t, and 2r, respectively.

Examples of primary and secondary classifications are:

Sets of Prints Original Sequence	Primary and Secondary Classifications	
W T U U U	1	T
A R U W U	18	aR
U W W W W	32	W
W W W W W	16	W
W A R U W	2	Ar
T U U R W	21	tU–r
A A A A A	1	aA3a
A A T R R	1	aAt2r
U U U U T	5	U– –t
W R A U U	1	Ra

As may be observed, in the classification formula the secondary appears to the right of the primary classification.

SUBSECONDARY CLASSIFICATION

The subsecondary classification further subdivides large groups having the same primary and secondary classifications. As for all subdivisions, fingers are not paired off for the subsecondary. Right-hand fingers make up the numerator; left-hand fingers the denominator. The subsecondary classification is represented by symbols that may be I, M or O. These symbols are derived from the ridge traces of whorls appearing on the index, middle and ring fingers, or from the ridge counts of loops on those fingers. Whorls may be I (inner), M (meeting) or O (outer). Loops are grouped into inner loops (symbol I) or outer loops (symbol O), depending on their ridge count. Loops are "inner" when the ridge count is from 1 to 9 on index fingers, from 1 to 10 on middle fingers and from 1 to 13 on ring fingers. Loops are "outer" when the ridge count is 10 or higher on index fingers, 11 or higher on middle fingers, and 14 or higher on ring fingers. When an index, middle or ring finger has an arch or a tented arch on it, a dash is brought up into the subsecondary classification in the appropriate place, as was done in the small-letter group under secondary classification. Whenever small-letter secondaries exist, a subsecondary is usually not required because small-letter secondaries provide enough breakdown for the files. In the classification formula, the subsecondary is placed to the right of the secondary.

Examples of primary, secondary and subsecondary classifications are:

Set of Prints Original Sequence	Primary, Secondary and Subsecondary Classifications
O M O U W W W W	32 W OMO
W W W W W I I I	16 W III
7 12 13 U U U U U	1 U IOI
U R U U U 11 10 17	1 R OIO

	Set of Prints Original Sequence				Primary, Secondary and Subsecondary Classifications		
I	8	M					
W	W	U	W	U	26	W	IIM
U	R	U	W	W	18	R	OII
	14	10	I				
		9	13				
W	T	U	U	U	2	T	–II
U	R	U	U	W	17	R	OII
	10	10	10				

MAJOR DIVISION

The major division is derived from the patterns on the thumbs of both hands. In the classification formula, the major division is placed immediately to the left of the primary classification. Whorls on thumbs are represented in the major division by their ridge traces as I (inner), M (meeting) or O (outer). For loops on the thumbs, the division is by S (small), M (medium) or L (large) according to the following tables:

1. Loops on the left thumb:

        Ridge count of 1 to 11   S (small)

        Ridge count of 12 to 16   M (medium)

        Ridge count of 17 or higher   L (large)

2. When the left thumb is represented by S (a ridge count of 1 to 11, inclusive) or M (ridge count of 12 to 16, inclusive), the right thumb is:

        Ridge count of 1 to 11   S (small)

        Ridge count of 12 to 16   M (medium)

        Ridge count of 17 or higher   L (large)

3. When the left thumb is represented by L (a ridge count of 17 or higher), the right thumb is:

        Ridge count of 1 to 17   S (small)

        Ridge count of 18 to 22   M (medium)

        Ridge count of 23 or higher   L (large)

When an arch, a tented arch or a radial loop appears on one or both thumbs, there is no major division for that set of prints.

Examples of primary, secondary and subsecondary classifications as well as the major division are:

```
9   7   12  13
U   U   U   U   U          S   1   U   IOI

U   R   U   U   U          S   1   R   OIO
12  11  10  17

O   I   8   M
W   W   U   W   U              0   26  W   IIM

U   R   U   W   W          L   18  R   OII
18  14  10  I
```

FINAL CLASSIFICATION

The final classification is derived from the patterns on the little fingers of both hands. The right little finger symbol is placed in the numerator to the far right of the fraction; the left little finger symbol in the denominator to the far right of the fraction. If both little fingers are loops, the final classification is the ridge count of both loops, as in

$$\frac{\overset{7}{U\ U\ U\ U\ U}}{\underset{13}{U\ R\ W\ W\ U}}$$

where final classification is $\dfrac{7}{13}$

If only one of the little fingers is a loop, then the final classification of that set of prints consists of the ridge count of that loop, in the numerator if the right little finger is a loop, in the denominator if the left little finger is a loop. Any finger that lacks a loop is ignored for final classification purposes, whether a whorl, an arch or a tented arch. If the patterns on both little fingers are arches, tented arches or an arch and a tented arch, then there is no final classification for the set of prints.

If both little fingers are whorls, a ridge count of the whorl on the right little finger may be used for the final classification (in the numerator of the formula) if such a breakdown is required. The technique for obtaining a ridge count in a whorl is similar to that used in counting loops: the count is made from the left delta to the apparent core of the whorl. Ordinarily, a ridge count for whorls is required only in the most voluminous files, and even then usually only for a few sections of the file, notably the all-whorl sets with a primary of 32-over-32.

KEY

The key is the last part of the FBI classification formula, although it is placed in the numerator to the far left of the formula. It is the ridge count of the first loop in a set of fingerprints beginning with the right thumb but not utilizing the ridge counts of loops on little fingers (which are used for final classification only). If there is no loop in a set of prints or if the only loops in a set are those on the little fingers, then there is no key for that set of prints. The key always appears in the numerator of the classification formula, even if it is derived from a left-hand digit.

Here are some examples of completely worked out FBI classification formulas:

$$\frac{\begin{array}{ccccc} 14 & I & M & 12 & 10 \\ U & W & W & U & U \end{array}}{\begin{array}{ccccc} W & W & U & U & U \\ I & O & 10 & 16 & 18 \end{array}}$$

$$\frac{\begin{array}{ccccc} 14 & M & 21 & W & IMI & 10 \\ I & & 11 & W & OIO & 18 \end{array}}{}$$

$$\frac{\begin{array}{ccccc} I & O & M & I & I/12 \\ W & W & W & W & W \end{array}}{\begin{array}{ccccc} W & W & W & W & W \\ M & M & I & O & O \end{array}}$$

$$\frac{\begin{array}{cccc} I & 32 & W & OMI & 12 \\ M & 32 & W & MIO \end{array}}{}$$

$$\frac{\begin{array}{cccc} M & 11 & 12 & 4 \\ W & R & U & A & U \end{array}}{\begin{array}{ccccc} T & U & U & W & W \\ & 10 & 11 & M & I \end{array}}$$

$$\frac{\begin{array}{cccc} 11 & 2 & R{-}a & 4 \\ & 18 & tU & \end{array}}{}$$

$$\frac{\begin{array}{ccccc} O & & I & M & 9 \\ W & A & W & W & U \end{array}}{\begin{array}{ccccc} A & T & U & U & U \\ & & 12 & 17 & 18 \end{array}}$$

$$\frac{\begin{array}{cccc} 12 & 9 & A & IM & 9 \\ & 25 & aT & OO & 18 \end{array}}{}$$

FBI EXTENSION SYSTEMS

The fact that the unaltered Henry system of fingerprint classification would work only with files of up to 100,000 sets of prints prompted the development of the modifications by the FBI which we have just reviewed. Yet these divisions too were found to be inadequate in certain portions of the enormous FBI Identification Division files where the standard FBI system still left accumulations of large groups of fingerprint cards having the same classification formula. So FBI technicians devised further extensions for the classification system that were to be used in certain portions of the files only. The three extensions still in use are the SML extension, the numerical extension and the WCDX extension.

SML Extension

The SML extension is used in certain portions of the file where the six fingers used in subsecondary classification are loops (index, middle and ring fingers of both hands). SML extensions are derived from the ridge counts for those six loops according to this table:

On index fingers:	1 to 5 ridges	S (small)
	6 to 12 ridges	M (medium)
	13 or more ridges	L (large)
On middle fingers:	1 to 8 ridges	S (small)
	9 to 14 ridges	M (medium)
	15 or more ridges	L (large)
On ring fingers:	1 to 10 ridges	S (small)
	11 to 18 ridges	M (medium)
	19 or more ridges	L (large)

The SML extension, like the main parts of a classification formula, is written in the form of a fraction, with the numerator making up the symbols for the right index, right middle and right ring fingers, and the denominator representing the left index, left middle and left ring fingers. The SML extension is used in addition to the normal subsecondary and is placed in the formula immediately above the subsecondary. Here is an example of a set of prints fully classified, including SML extension:

Set of Prints	*Full Classification*
	MMM
	MML
18 10 10 15 13	
U U U U U	18 L 1 U OIO 13
U R U U U	M 1 R IOO 15
12 9 14 19 15	

The SML extension is also employed in a few sections of the FBI file where whorls appear on one or both index fingers, in which case only five or four SML extension symbols appear above subsecondary, since whorls are not included in this extension.

Numerical Extension

The numerical extension provides additional classifying symbols for all-ulnar-loop sets, the l-over-l, U-over-U group primarily. When used, it replaces the SML extension. Only one or the other of the extensions is used. The numerical extension is also derived from the ridge counts for both index, both middle and both ring fingers in a set of prints. As with the SML extension, it is used in addition to the subsecondary classification and is placed in fraction form above subsecondary symbols. Here the symbols are numerals, rather than letters, and are determined according to this table:

Ridge counts of 1 through 4	Numerical Symbol 1
Ridge counts of 5 through 8	Numerical Symbol 2
Ridge counts of 9 through 12	Numerical Symbol 3
Ridge counts of 13 through 16	Numerical Symbol 4
Ridge counts of 17 through 20	Numerical Symbol 5
Ridge counts of 21 through 24	Numerical Symbol 6
Ridge counts of 25 or higher	Numerical Symbol 7

An example of a set of prints fully classified, including numerical extension, is:

Set of Prints	Full Classification
	215
16 8 3 18 15	324
U U U U U	16 S 1 U IIO 15
U U U U U	L 1 U OIO 12
18 10 5 14 12	

WCDX Extension

The WCDX extension is used in those sections of a file containing many whorls, as in the all-whorl primary (32-over-32) and the 31-over-28 primary group. It can be used in any primary group where whorls predominate. The WCDX extension uses all ten digits in a set, not just the six fingers of the subsecondary classification. Basically, it consists of splitting a whorl group, which for other classification purposes has been symbolized by a W only, into four groups:

plain whorls, symbols W and w; central pocket loops, symbols C and c; double loops, symbols D and d; accidentals, symbols X and x. Capital letters (W, C, D and X) are used for index fingers and lower case letters (w, c, d and x) are used for whorls on all other fingers.

In order to prepare a card for WCDX extensions, an extra step is required during the blocking out stage of preparing a set of prints. During blocking out, you will remember, ridge counts and ridge traces for all loops and whorls are placed in the upper right-hand corners of the rolled impression blocks on the cards. At the same time, when the use of the WCDX extension is contemplated, the symbols for whorls are written in the upper left-hand corners of the same blocks. In arriving at the WCDX extension, the symbols for whorls are brought up in fraction form in the same way as for the other extensions and are placed immediately above the subsecondary. Capital letters are used for index fingers, and small letters are placed either in front of or immediately following the capital letter representing the index finger, depending on which finger is symbolized (thumbs to the left of the index finger symbol, all other fingers to the right). The small letter w, for plain whorl, is used in WCDX extension only when a plain whorl appears between the index finger symbol and other whorls or when a plain whorl appears between two central pocket loops, two double loops or two accidentals. The purpose of recording a small w, then, is merely to indicate the exact location of c, d, and x patterns in relation to the index finger. Since there is no need for such indication when plain whorls appear on thumbs, no small w symbol is used to the left of the index finger symbol.

These series of sets of prints illustrate the application of the rules pertaining to WCDX extensions:

Sets of Prints					*Full Classification Formula*				
							Wwd		
w O	W I	w I	d I	w 16			cXwwc		
W	W	W	W	W	O	32 W	III	16
c I	X I	w M	w O	c I	I	32 W	IMO	
W	W	W	W	W				
							Wcxc		
w O	W I	c O	x O	c 17			dDwcd		
W	W	W	W	W	O	32 W	IOO	17
d I	D O	w I	c I	d M	I	32 W	OII	
W	W	W	W	W				

	Sets of Prints					Full Classification Formula				
								W		
w M	W I	w I	w O	w 12				W		
W	W	W	W	W		M	32 W	IIO	12	
w O	W O	w M	w I	w I		O	32 W	OMI		
W	W	W	W	W						
								X		
w I	X O	w M	w M	w 13				xWdcc		
W	W	W	W	W		I	32 W	OMM	13	
x M	W I	d O	c I	c I		M	32 W	IOI		
W	W	W	W	W						

Chapter 7

Five-Finger Classification

The millions of sets of fingerprints housed in the files of large identification bureaus are of limited use when it comes to searching for crime-scene prints. We have already seen in the last chapter how fingerprint sets are filed according to a classification formula obtained from studying the ten patterns on the digits of one person, but we have also noted that crime-scene searches more often than not yield only one latent print. Clearly, then, to make use of the ten-finger file, the prints of every finger of an individual are needed so that a classification formula for that set of prints can be developed to determine if an individual's prints are on file and then to conduct a search in the appropriate place.

While it is next to impossible to identify a single crime-scene print by using the ten-finger file, if a person has been previously arrested and fingerprinted it is usually possible to discover the classification of the full set of his fingerprints by looking through the name-index file and pulling the ten-finger set of that suspect to compare his prints with the unknown latent print found at the scene of the crime. So unless investigation reveals the names of possible suspects in a crime, the main fingerprint file cannot be used to identify a crime-scene print.

In order to remedy such a serious defect in the usefulness of fingerprinting for establishing criminal identity, researchers have devised systems by which each finger can be separately printed, interpreted, classified and filed on a special fingerprint card about the size of the latent print transfer card illustrated in Figure 121. But since each fingerprint card has to be printed, interpreted, clas-
174

sified and filed, the task can become gargantuan in time and man-power. The value of single-print files, however, is directly proportional to the number of fingerprints on file: the more single prints in the file, the more likely that a crime-scene latent print can be identified. Yet searching is usually a hopeless impracticality, and additional cards mean more classification extensions in order to maintain a relatively fine breakdown in the number of prints that can be found within any one subdivision of the file. As a result of all this complexity, the usefulness of single-print systems in metropolitan areas has been seriously questioned, and the means of searching for crime-scene latent prints has been shifted to a special five-finger system in the past few decades. The adoption of the five-finger system heralds the eventual demise of single-print systems, just as progress in computerizing fingerprint files will no doubt eventually mean the abandonment of all traditional five- and ten-finger classification systems.

Instead of using special fingerprint cards for each finger, the five-finger classification system uses two cards, one for right-hand rolled prints, the other for left-hand prints. Since most bureaus design their own cards, no standard size is being used, but most are from three to five inches high and eight inches wide. A typical five-finger card, in slightly reduced size, is illustrated in Figure 139. It measures four by eight inches.

Five-finger classification is relatively simple and fast. Its pattern

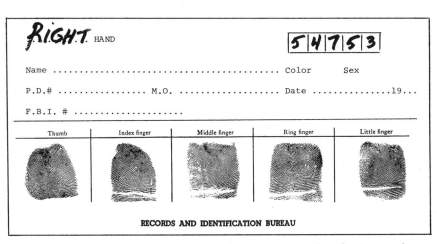

Figure 139. Sample of a typical five-finger classification record card. The actual size is 4 x 8 inches.

names are those used in the Henry system and answer to the rules for pattern interpretation used in that ten-finger system. The various pattern types are assigned numerical symbols, according to this table:

Amputated finger	0.
Arch	1
Tented arch	2
Right slope loop	3
Left slope loop	4
Plain whorl and central pocket loop	5
Double loop	6
Accidental	7
Scarred or mutilated pattern	8

The only difference in pattern names between the five-finger system and the Henry-FBI, ten-digit system involves loops. In the ten-finger system, loops are divided into ulnar and radial loops. Since it may be impossible to determine from a single latent print discovered at a crime scene whether it is a right- or left-hand impression—which is necessary to determine whether the loop is radial or ulnar—the five-finger system divides loops into right-slope and left-slope loops. The numerical symbols for the patterns are placed on end in a five-digit formula and provide the classification for the set of prints. Left-hand prints are filed separately from right-hand prints. The classification for the set of prints illustrated in Figure 139 is 54753.

The filing sequence for each hand is from 00000, 00001, 00002, and so on to 88888. Wherever large accumulations of cards occur, as in the all-loop sections (33333 in the right-hand file and 44444 in the left-hand file), the all-whorl section (55555) and others, subdivision can be made by ridge count or ridge trace.

To start a five-finger file is a relatively easy process. After determining whose prints should be included in the file, the ten-finger cards for those individuals are photographed, the right- and left-hand rolled prints cut out and mounted on 4 x 8 inch cards. To continue feeding cards of new arrestees into the five-finger file without using special size cards, some departments utilize 8 x 8 inch cards with two five-finger strips, as shown in Figure 140. At the time the regular ten-finger card is recorded, an extra set of rolled prints is made on the double five-finger card. After recording, the double

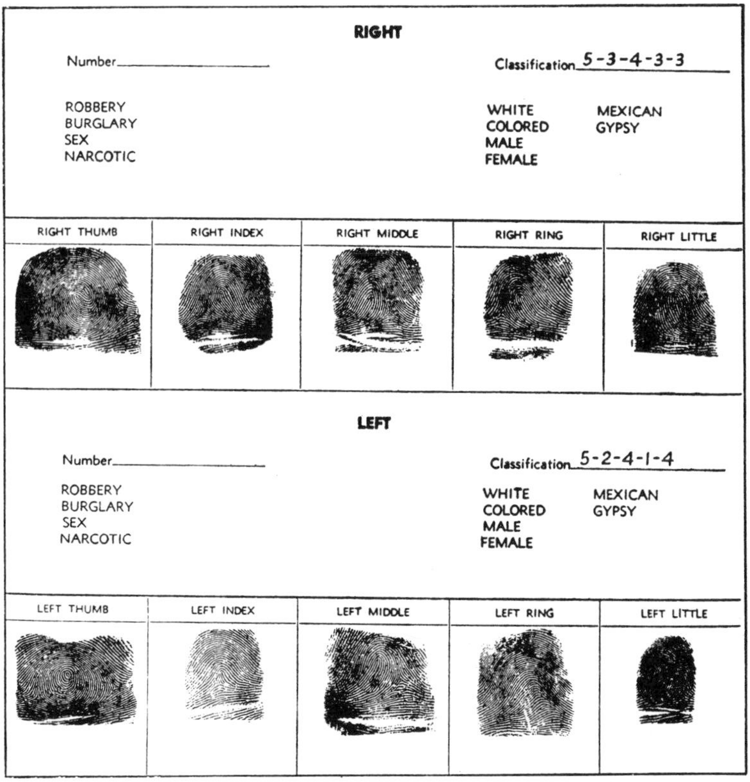

RIGHT

Number__________ Classification 5-3-4-3-3

ROBBERY
BURGLARY
SEX
NARCOTIC

WHITE
COLORED
MALE
FEMALE

MEXICAN
GYPSY

RIGHT THUMB	RIGHT INDEX	RIGHT MIDDLE	RIGHT RING	RIGHT LITTLE

LEFT

Number__________ Classification 5-2-4-1-4

ROBBERY
BURGLARY
SEX
NARCOTIC

WHITE
COLORED
MALE
FEMALE

MEXICAN
GYPSY

LEFT THUMB	LEFT INDEX	LEFT MIDDLE	LEFT RING	LEFT LITTLE

Figure 140. A double five-finger form. The actual size is 8 x 8 inches. (Courtesy: Police Department, Indianapolis, Indiana.)

card is cut in half and each section is filed among the sets for the appropriate hand. The Indianapolis, Indiana, Police Department uses such cards for its five-finger files of persons arrested for robbery, burglary, sex crimes (exposing person, all degrees of rape, peeping tomism and sodomy) and narcotics violations; all persons of Mexican nationality and all Gypsies are also so recorded.

Subdivisions are used in the all-loop sections according to the FBI extension method:

Right-hand classification, 33333;
left-hand classification, 44444

Index

Ridge counts 1 to 5 are given the value of S
Ridge counts 6 to 12 are given the value of M
Ridge counts 13 and higher are given the value of L

Middle finger

Ridge counts 1 to 8 are given the value of S
Ridge counts 9 to 14 are given the value of M
Ridge counts 15 and higher are given the value of L

Ring finger

Ridge counts 1 to 10 are given the value of S
Ridge counts 11 to 18 are given the value of M
Ridge counts 19 and higher are given the value of L

THE TEN-ONE FILE

The Orange County, California, Sheriff's office developed a manual punch card system in 1957 adapted to five-finger and single-print files. Although it contains all ten fingerprints, it is called the Ten-One file because it permits searching for a single fingerprint. It was the result of an attempt to eliminate the arduous reference searches required under the old system when only one fingerprint was found.

The cards used for the Ten-One file are 8 x 5 inches, contain the ten rolled fingerprints, and are manufactured by Unisort and Keysort. Holes are punched all around the edges of the cards. The five-finger classification is punched manually at the edges in such a way that, by passing a sorting needle through a mass of cards, the ones that do not match in classification are separated from the ones that have been notched for the desired information (see Figure 141).

Some of the advantages of this filing system are that only one card is necessary for each subject. Since cards are not individually handled, sorting is rapid. The pattern types, ridge counts and ridge traces of the Henry system are available from the 8 x 8 inch card and are coded directly onto the Ten-One file cards without recourse to any other system of classification. A minimum of equipment is needed: a sorting needle, a hand-slotting punch and a supply of cards. Filing is simple because the cards need not be maintained in any particular sequence. Sufficient edge space is available on each card for coding other desirable information. Reference searches are also eliminated because after a proper sorting search the only cards that remain contain patterns similar to that of the latent print.

The fingerprint code used in the Ten-One file is as follows:

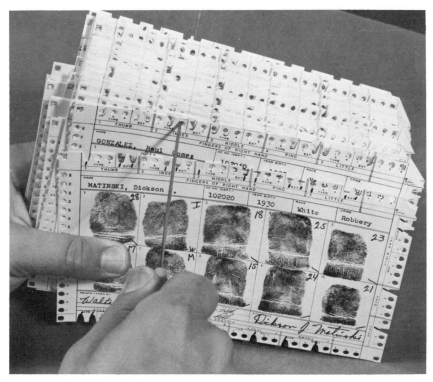

Figure 141. Key-sorting the Ten-One File. (Courtesy: Sheriff's Department, Orange County, California.)

Fingerprint Type

0—Amputations
1—Right-slope loops
    Extensions: 0—1 to 6 ridge count
                 1—7 to 12 ridge count
                 2—13 to 18 ridge count
                 3—19 or over ridge count
2—Left-slope loops
    Extensions same as for right-slope loops
3—Arches and tented arches
4—Plain whorls and central pocket loops
    Extensions: 0—meeting trace
                 1—inner trace
                 2—outer trace

Fingerprint Type

5—Double loops and accidentals
   Extensions same as for plain whorls and central pocket loops
6—Scarred and mutilated patterns

Race Code

1—White or Caucasian
2—Spanish or Spanish appearing
3—Negro
4—All others

Crime Code

1—Burglary
2—Robbery
3—Narcotics
4—Theft
5—Grand theft auto

Five-Finger Extensions and Automated Search

In order to provide both a faster search capability and a greater breakdown by special subdivisions, Alex Russak of Miami adapted the five-finger system to electronic searching. His primary classification deviates slightly from that used in the original five-finger system in that numerical symbol 6 is assigned to twinned loops, while 7 is assigned to accidentals, composites and lateral pocket loops. Patterns that are mutilated beyond recognition are assigned the primary 9. Russak left the primary 8 open for future use.

The Russak method uses special filing cards of 4 x 8 inches, but no fingerprints are recorded on them. Instead, an extra 8 x 8 inch standard fingerprint card is cut into three sections, one strip with the right-hand rolled prints, one with the left-hand rolled prints, and the bottom of the card containing the plain impressions. Each of these three sections is stapled to the special 4 x 8 inch Russak cards, as shown in Figure 142. The top two cards, which hold the right-hand prints and the left-hand prints respectively, are filed according to five-finger primary classification. The bottom card, containing the plain impressions, serves as an alphabetical index-card system and contains both primary classifications for right and left hands.

In order to make electronic searching possible when only one latent print is discovered at a crime scene, Russak further subdivides

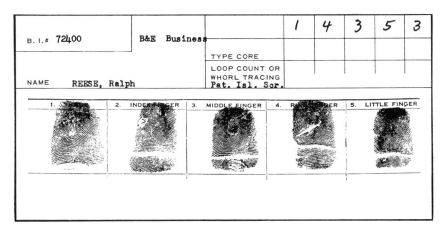

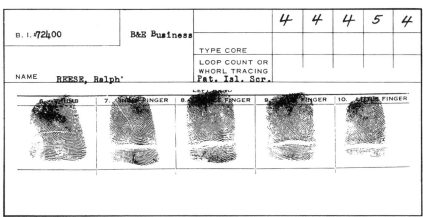

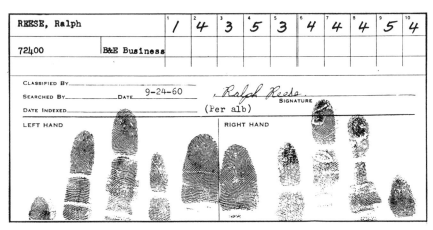

Figure 142. The rolled and plain prints on a standard 8 x 8 inch fingerprint card are cut into three strips and affixed to the cards designed for the Russak system. (Courtesy: Police Department, Miami, Florida.)

the five-finger cards and punches all relevant information onto a standard IBM punch card composed of eighty columns and ten rows.

Russak's subdivisions are based somewhat on the Battley single-print system (to be discussed in the next chapter), from which Russak borrowed the special reticle (illustrated in Figure 143). It consists of seven concentric circles with radii of 3 mm, 5 mm, 7 mm, 9 mm, 11 mm, 13 mm and 15 mm. Amputated digits (primary 0) and arches (primary 1) are not subclassified.

Tented arches are subdivided by placing the center spot of the reticle on the core of the pattern after determining within which circle the platform ridge falls. If it falls within the center circle, the pattern is assigned a subdivision of 1 for the core; if in the second circle, 2; and so on. A subdivision of 9 is assigned when the platform ridge is damaged. A further subdivision proceeds according to the slope of the tented arch: if the pattern has no recognizable slope, a value of 1 is given; a left slope is given a value of 2; a right slope, 3. When the tented arch has unusual peculiarities, it is given a value of 4.

The two final breakdowns for tented arches also apply to loops, whorls and dual loops. The first one is known as the island breakdown and consists of recording the number of "islands" that fall within the center circle of the reticle. A value of 1 is assigned when there is one island in the center circle, a value of 2 is given when there are two islands, and a value of 3 is given if there be three or more. The second breakdown is concerned with the appearance of

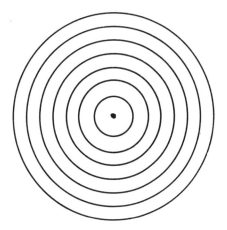

Figure 143. The Battley reticle used in the Russak system has seven concentric circles with radii of 3 mm, 5 mm, 7 mm, 9 mm, 11 mm, 13 mm and 15 mm.

scars in the pattern. If there is a scar in the center circle, a value of 1 is assigned. If the scar is outside the center circle and shows at about 12:00 o'clock, a value of 2 is assigned. If the scar appears at about 3:00 o'clock, a value of 3 is given; if at about 6:00 o'clock, 4; and if at about 9:00 o'clock, 5. When the scar appears directly outside a delta, 6 is assigned as its value.

For loops, the primary classification is arrived at by determining the slope, either a 3 (right-slope) or a 4 (left-slope). The first subdivision for loops proceeds according to the modified Battley core formation illustrated in Figure 144, which provides nine subclasses. The second subdivision is the circle reading of the delta, performed strictly according to the Battley method: it is arrived at by placing the center dot of the reticle on the special core and observing within which circle the delta appears. The third subdivision is by actual ridge count. The fourth subdivision allows for five subclasses on the basis of the general loop, as follows: 1 for tented arch loops, 2 for a converging loops, 3 for loops bordering on the central pocket loop, 4 for nutant loops, and 5 for unusual loops. The final two steps in subdividing loops involve recording islands and scars, as was done for tented arches.

Whorls are first subdivided according to the eight types of cores devised by Russak and illustrated in the bottom row of Figure 144. The second subdivision is the circle reading of the left delta. The third subdivision calls for ridge tracing and gives a value of 1 to an inner trace, 2 to a meeting trace, 3 to an outer whorl, 4 when no trace can be obtained because of a scar, and 9 when both deltas are damaged. The fourth subdivision is the circle reading of the right delta. The fifth subdivision is concerned with the general shape of the whorl according to these values: 1 for whorls that approximate dual loops, 2 for whorls that look like central pocket loops, 3 for spiral whorls, 4 for elongated whorls, 5 for elliptical whorls, 6 for unusual types, 7 for whorls that have a type 1 or 2 core with a left-hand twist, 8 for whorls that have a type 1 or 2 core and a right-hand twist. The final two subdivisions again involve islands and scars.

Dual loops (primary value 6) correspond to the twin loops of the original Henry system—double loop patterns in which the loops exit on opposite sides. The first subdivision types the core of the ascending loop, as in Figure 144. The second, third and fourth subdivisions involve, respectively, the left delta reading, the ridge trace

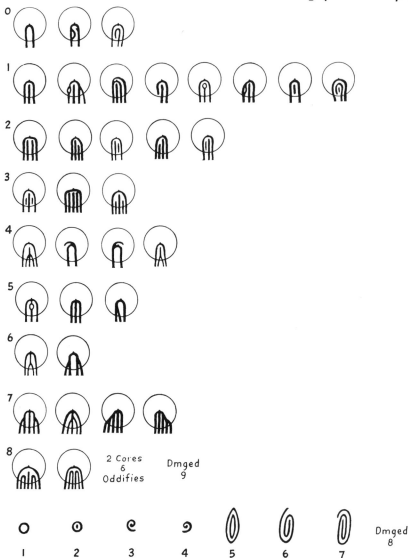

Figure 144. The core formation subdivision designed by Russak and based on the Battley system for loops (nine top rows) and whorls (bottom row). (Courtesy: Police Department, Miami, Florida.)

and the right delta reading (as was done for whorls). The fifth subdivision assigns a value of 1 when the ascending loop slopes upward toward the right, or a value of 2 when the ascending loop slopes upward toward the left. The sixth and seventh subdivisions are again concerned with islands and scars.

Only one breakdown is provided for class 7 primary patterns (accidentals, composites and lateral pocket loops), namely by pattern types: 1 for lateral pocket loops, 2 for accidentals, and 3 for composites (using the original Henry definitions of all these patterns).

Other rules that Russak devised give numerical preference in case of doubt. A pattern that could fall within either a 2 or a 3 subgroup is given a value of 2. Only thumbs, index, middle and ring fingers are subdivided. Little fingers, the prints of which are rarely found at crime scenes, are not subclassified.

When latent prints are discovered at a crime scene, the prints are classified according to Russak's method as far as can be done. Then the search board of the IBM sorter is wired to correspond with the data, taking into account reference interpretations for doubtful details, and the punch cards are fed through the sorter. Cards that are thrown out are searched in the name-index file (bearing the plain prints) for visual comparison with the latent prints.

Chapter 8

Other Classification Systems

When an identifiable latent print is discovered at a crime scene, it has most likely been left there by someone having legitimate access to the premises. So it is most important to compare the latent print with the recorded prints of the victim, people who normally occupy or work at the location, and everyone who has had recent access, including police who might have touched the surface upon which the latent print has been discovered. If the latent print remains unidentified after this process of elimination, it can then be handled as a questioned print that may have been left by the criminal.

In order to locate an unknown criminal by searching for a latent print in fingerprint files, single-print systems were devised. In these systems, each fingerprint is filed on a separate card and is indexed and classified apart from all others. It would not be feasible to convert a ten-finger file to a single-print system because it would require ten cards for each individual, so a single-print file usually contains the fingerprints of certain classes of criminals only, notably burglars, forgers, auto thieves, bank robbers and others who are likely to leave latent prints during the commission of their crimes.

A great number of single-print systems have been developed over the years. The pioneers were Oloriz from Spain and Stockis from Belgium, although their systems proved inefficient and cumbersome. Good systems developed later included the Jorgensen system in Denmark (1921) and the Collins system in England, used there until it was replaced by the better and now widely used Battley system. Other single-print systems have been those of Crosskey, Larsen, Wentworth, Neben, Barlow, Taylor, Gasti, Giraud, Born,

Jaycox, Sagredo, Borgerhoff, Basu, Cataldo, Snell and Moran. A few were referred to by the name of the place where they were used, such as the Lyons (France) system, or by the terminology used in describing them, such as ZIMOX. In the United States, the most widely used single-print system is that devised by Sir Harry Battley of New Scotland Yard.

Special-purpose classification systems, a few of which will also be discussed in this chapter, include those devised to classify and file palmprints and footprints or to further subdivide certain sections of the ten-finger file according to middle phalanx characteristics, ridge edges, and the like. While many ten-finger classification schemes are used around the world—Boolsen lists thirty-three foreign systems—it should be observed that many are merely modifications of other methods. The only two ten-finger classification systems we shall discuss here are the Canadian and Vucetich systems.

THE CANADIAN FINGERPRINT SYSTEM

The Canadian system as used by the Royal Canadian Mounted Police is basically the Henry system with extensions. The Canadian Police divide all fingerprints into two types: nonnumerical and numerical patterns. Nonnumerical patterns are the following: (1) arch (symbol A), (2) tented arch (symbol T), (3) radial loop (symbol R), and (4) ulnar loop (symbol U). Numerical patterns are: (5) whorl (symbol W), (6) central pocket loop (symbol C), (7) twin loop (symbol D), (8) lateral pocket loop (symbol D), (9) composite (symbol X), and (10) accidental (symbol X).

The interpretation of patterns is substantially the same as in the Henry system except for double loops, which are interpreted as twin loops and lateral pocket loops, and accidental whorls, which are called composites. The system also adopts the special type of accidental, which does not exist in the United States. In blocking out, capital letters are placed under all patterns except ulnar loops, which have a slanted line according to the slope of the loop. Ridge tracing and counting is conducted as in the United States.

There is no difference from the basic Henry system with respect to primary classification. Capital letter symbols representing the patterns on the index fingers (A, T, R, U, W, C, D, X—in this sequence) are used for secondary classification. Although sixty-four combinations in the secondary classification are possible, only sixteen are available under any primary classification. Secondary classification also lists small letters for arches (a), tented arches (t), and radial loops (r) in the same manner as American extensions and modifications of the Henry system, but the Canadian Police also include in the small-letter secondary classification the symbols for twin and lateral loops (d) and for composites and accidentals (x). No dashes are used to indicate the finger on which these patterns occur, as is done in the United States.

Subsecondary classification is arrived at by counting ridges on loops and tracing ridges on whorls exactly as in the American system. The same is true for major division, which is arrived at according to the same procedures as those used by the FBI; but contrary to FBI practices, major division may also consist of a symbol for one thumb only, if the other thumb contains an arch or a tented arch. Radial loops are also considered for major division. There is no difference between the methods of the Canadian Police and the FBI in determining final classification.

A significant difference between the United States and Canadian systems is that the dashes used in the FBI's small-letter secondary classification system are not used in Canada, where they have been replaced by small numerals in parentheses above the classification to indicate the finger on which the small-letter pattern occurs.

$$\frac{1 \quad \overset{(3)}{Ut} \quad 7}{1 \quad U \quad 9} \quad or \quad \frac{1 \quad \overset{(3)}{\underset{(8)}{Ut}} \quad 7}{1 \quad Ua \quad 9}$$

Such a practice permits the following combinations: (3), (4), (5), over (8), (9), (10), or:

(3) (4) (5) (3) (4) (5) (3) (4) (5)
(8) (8) (8) (9) (9) (9) (10) (10) (10)

The Canadian Police use a "Code," which is the same as the FBI's numerical extension for the all-loop group, or for a few other large primaries, as in $9/1$, $9/2$, $1/17$ and $5/17$. When a numerical pattern appears, the ridge trace would be noted as I, M or O in the Code (for example, 13M, 11O, 12I). The Key subclassification is also determined in the same manner as in the FBI system, but it is not used extensively except in classifications where no final class is present. The Key is placed to the far left of the formula, a little higher than the numerator. The Canadian Police also use a "Trend" subclassification that is applied exclusively to tented arch patterns on one or both index fingers. The Trend is governed by the highest or top ridge within the type ridges and can be N (neutral), R (radial) or U (ulnar). It is placed at the extreme left in front of the major division.

Primary, secondary, small-letter subsecondary and final (if any) classifications are always shown. Other subdivisions are utilized only when needed. Amputations are classified the same way as the pattern on the corresponding finger of the other hand. If the same fingers on both hands are amputated, they are arbitrarily classified as X.

14		3	9	2
U	A	U	U	U
U	A	U	U	U
7		10	15	7

M	1	A		II	2
S	1	A		IO	7

16 (R)		9	14	9
U	T	U	U	U
U	T	U	U	U
17 (N)		11	12	14

R	S	1 T		IO	9
N	L	1 T		OI	14

4			9	
U	A	A	U	T
U	A	R	U	U
12		9	11	7

			(3) (5)
			(8)
S	1	Aat	
M	1	Ar	7

14	10	10	14	9
U	R	U	U	U
T	A	U	U	U
		8	13	12

M	1	R	OIO	9
	1	tA	II	12

19	14	M	O	8
U	U	D	C	U
W	U	U	U	U
M	13	10	13	15

L	13	Udc	OMO	8
M	9	U	OII	15

I	O	8		14
X	W	U	A	U
D	X	C	U	U
I	M	I	9	12

		(4)	
I	23	xWa	OI	14
I	19	dXc	MII	12

The Vucetich Fingerprint System

The oldest system for classifying ten-finger sets of fingerprints in practical use in law enforcement—the Vucetich primary classification system—is lauded by experts the world over as the most workable one. It is much simpler than the Henry system and, had it not been for the chance introduction of fingerprinting in the United States by a Scotland Yard expert visiting the St. Louis World Fair in 1904, identification services in this country might now be using the Vucetich system. Had a comparative study been made of the various primary systems when fingerprinting was still in its infancy, the Vucetich system would more than likely have been chosen over the Henry system.

The Argentine Dr. Juan Vucetich started work on a method of classifying fingerprints in 1891 and in a remarkably short time designed a primary classification scheme that was and remains the basis for the Vucetich system. It was originally used in the La Plata police bureau in Argentina. In many countries today, the Vucetich primary classification is used in conjunction with Henry subclassifications or with locally devised subdivisions.

The Vucetich method is based on four fundamental pattern types: arch, inward loop (loop with a slant to the left), outward loop (loop with a slant to the right) and whorl. (See Figure 145.) It also uses type lines in much the same way as the Henry system. Ridges that lie above the upward-moving typeline are called marginal ridges, those occupying the center of the print between typelines are called nucleus ridges (which correspond to Henry's pattern area), and those lying below the lower typeline are called base ridges.

In arriving at a primary classification, Vucetich assigned a symbol to each pattern type as follows:

Arch	1 and A
Inward Loop	2 and I
Outward Loop	3 and E
Whorl	4 and V
Amputations	0
Accidental designs	X

The letters are used to indicate patterns on the right and left thumbs; the numerals indicate patterns on the other four fingers of each hand. As in the Henry system, the formula thus obtained is written in the form of a fraction in which the symbols above the fraction line represent the right hand and those below the line the left hand. In calculating how many combinations the use of these

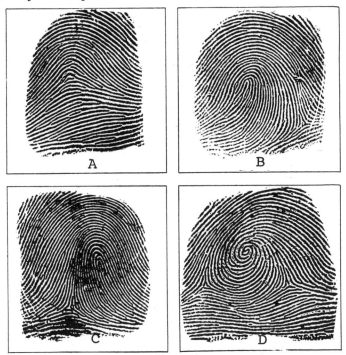

Figure 145. The four basic patterns of the Vucetich system: A for Arch, B for inward loop, C for outward loop and D for whorl.

symbols makes possible, we find 1,048,576 possible primaries in the Vucetich system (as opposed to 1,024 in the Henry system). It must be noted, however, that this total number of possible combinations is largely theoretical, since in all but the largest files many primaries are not represented.

Some primaries are of course found more frequently than others. The experience of fingerprint experts around the world indicates that, because the ulnar loop is the most frequently encountered pattern type, the huge section of a file that contains the 1-over-1 Henry primary classification is also the largest section in a Vucetich file. Ulnar loops on the right hand correspond to Vucetich's external loops, while ulnar loops on the left hand are inward loops in the Vucetich system.

Those sections of the file which are the most crowded in the Henry system are also the most congested in the Vucetich system. They are correlated here:

Henry	Vucetich
1 U	E–3333
1 U	I–2222
1 R	E–2333
1 R	I–3222
1 U	E–3333
1 R	I–3222
1 R	E–2333
1 U	I–2222
1 U	V–3333
17 U	I–2222
32 W	V–4444
32 W	V–4444

The filing sequence in Vucetich's system is as follows: (1) right thumb, (2) other right-hand fingers, (3) left thumb, (4) other left-hand fingers. They are respectively referred to as Fundamental, Division, Subclassification and Subdivision.

When Vucetich devised his primary method, the 1,048,576 possible combinations afforded ample separation of the cards so that no further reduction was necessary. Since the sets of prints accumulated much faster in some sections of the file than in others, he ultimately devised a system of subdivisions. But other bureaus using his basic method had earlier arrived at the same conclusion and devised their own subdivisions or adopted the Henry subclassifications. As a result, Vucetich's primary method is being used today with a great variety or further classification breakdowns. His own subdivisions never acquired the fame and widespread use of his basic system.

THE BATTLEY SINGLE-PRINT SYSTEM

The Battley system for classifying and filing single fingerprints has been found to be the most practical and accurate method of handling single fingerprints. It is still widely used in this country and abroad. The FBI used it for a number of years before abandoning it in favor of its more workable five-finger system.

The definitions used in the Battley system are consistent with those utilized in the Henry ten-finger classification method. Therefore, knowledge of the Henry system is a prerequisite to understanding the terminology of the Battley system. The method outlined here is not identical to the one Harry Battley devised but is slightly modified as used in the United States.

In the Battley system, all prints from one particular finger are filed together, one finger per drawer, on 3 x 5 inch file cards that contain both rolled and plain prints of one finger. Within each drawer, the cards are first subdivided according to general pattern types and are then further subdivided. (See Figure 146.) The apparatus needed for subdividing prints consists of a magnifying glass and a reticle (a sheet of transparent material). In the center of the reticle is a dot, around which seven circles are drawn with radii of 3 mm, 5 mm, 7 mm, 9 mm, 11 mm, 13 mm and 15 mm respectively. The area of each circle is represented by a letter, starting with the center, which is called A, and reading outward. The area outside the circle G is denoted by the letter H. In the United States, Battley's reticles have been modified. They consist of a straight horizontal line printed on the transparent material with the dot in the center of the line. Instead of circles, only semicircles are printed below the horizontal line. The straight line can be used as a guide in ridge counting. (See Figure 147.)

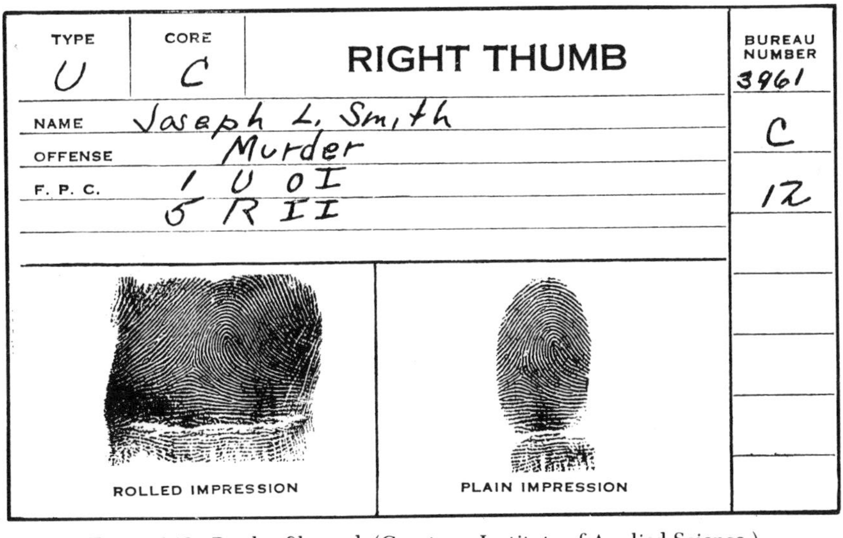

Figure 146. Battley file card. (Courtesy: Institute of Applied Science.)

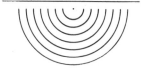

Figure 147. Modified Battley reticle.

In interpreting patterns, the Battley system uses a "special core." In loops and whorls, the special core is located in the center of the summit of the innermost recurving ridge. To obtain circle readings for deltas in loops and whorls, place the center dot of the reticle on the special core and note which circle the delta falls within. (See Figure 148.)

Figure 148. Battley special core in place. (Courtesy: Institute of Applied Science.)

Classification

Rolled and plain prints are made on 3 x 5 inch cards, one print (rolled and plain) of one finger to a card. Each finger is therefore recorded on a separate printed form. All the cards for the same finger—all the right thumbs, all the index fingers of the right hand, and so on—are filed together as a first classification. The first subdivision within each section is made according to the pattern type. The symbols used are A for arches, T for tented arches, R and U for radial and ulnar loops respectively, W for whorls, C for central pocket loops, D for double loops and X for accidental whorls. A special section is reserved for scarred patterns—those in which the scar renders classification by pattern impossible. The letter corresponding to the pattern type is written in the upper left square of the card under the word "type." The next square is labeled "core." All further squares used for subdivisions are arranged vertically along the right edge of the card. Further subdivision depends on pattern type.

Subclassification

Battley devised the following categories:

ARCHES. Since there are no cores in arches and since arches occur rather infrequently, they are not further subdivided. In the upper left-hand square, the type is indicated as A. Under the heading core, "plain" is written.

TENTED ARCHES. The symbol for type is T. Only one subdivision is made. The core symbol is found by taking a circle reading with the center dot of the reticle placed in the center of the summit of the innermost enveloping ridge that makes the crest of the tented arch. The circle reading of the intersection of the first ridge that runs underneath the central area and crest ridges and across the axis of the pattern is recorded by using the letter corresponding to the circle in which that first ridge flows. (See Figure 149.)

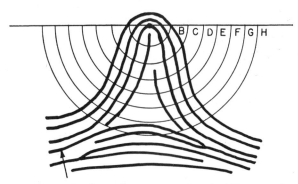

Figure 149. Circle reading on tented arch. (Courtesy: Institute of Applied Science.)

LOOPS. The type symbol is R or U, depending on the slant of the pattern and the finger it appears on. The core subdivision is the next subclassification and provides for eleven subgroups, namely A, B, C, D, E, F, G, H, J, K, and L, according to the core-formation type designed by Battley. The group L (not illustrated) comprises loops that do not fall into any of the ten illustrated subgroups. (See Figure 150.) Each type can be subdivided again by recording the circle reading of the delta, which is obtained by placing the center dot of the reticle on the special core, and then observing within which semicircle the delta falls. The delta reading is recorded on the single fingerprint card to the right, directly under the space reserved for the bureau number. Another division can be made by counting the ridges between the core and the delta. When ridges

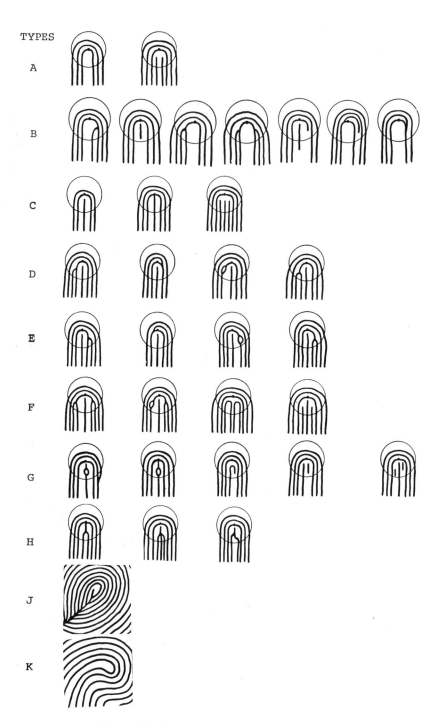

Figure 150. Battley core-formation subgroups.

are counted, the regular core as used in the Henry system must be taken, not the special core.

WHORLS. In the original Battley system, whorls and central pocket loops were grouped together. The FBI's experience proved that it was better to treat them separately. The first subclassification of whorls, recorded under "core," is accomplished by taking the circle reading of the bottom of the first recurving ridge. To achieve that reading, the center dot of the reticle is placed on the summit of the first recurving ridge that forms the special core, then the semicircle letter within which the bottom of the first recurving ridge of the core appears is recorded. This allows for eight subgroups, one for each semicircle of the reticle. (See Figure 151.)

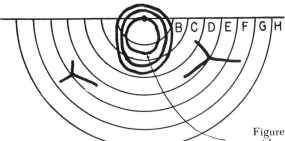

Figure 151. Battley circle reading with reticle.

Whorls with small cores that fall within circle A of the reticle are further subdivided into five divisions according to their core formations, as designed by Battley, and are labeled A-1, A-2, A-3, A-4 or A-5. This subdivision is recorded under "core." (See Figure 152.) The further subdivisions of whorls, recorded along the right edge of the core, are (a) the circle reading of the left delta, found by placing the center dot of the reticle on the special core and ascertaining into which semicircle the delta falls, (b) the ridge trace as used in the Henry system, (c) the circle reading of the right delta, ascertained in the same fashion as that of the left delta, (d) the ridge count from the left delta to the special core, (e) the ridge count from the right delta to the special core.

Figure 152. Further core subdivisions within reticle circle A.

CENTRAL POCKET LOOPS. These patterns are classified exactly like plain whorls, with the exception of the symbol for type, which is C instead of W.

DOUBLE LOOPS. The original Battley system separated double loops into two distinct pattern types: twin and lateral pocket loops. In the United States, no such distinction is recognized; all are designated by the pattern symbol D. The first subdivision (under core) is U or R, depending on the slope of the descending loop ridges. If the open end of the descending loop ridges points toward the direction of the radial bone, the symbol is R; if it points toward the ulnar bone, it is U. (See Figure 153.) The only other subdivision, which is recorded to the right of the card under the bureau number, is the ridge trace as determined in the Henry system.

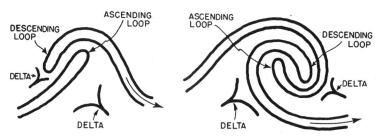

Figure 153. R and U subdivisions for double loops. (Courtesy: Institute of Applied Science.)

ACCIDENTALS. In the original Battley system, a very rare type of pattern was called an accidental. In the American adaptation of the Henry system, it is called a composite. Since Battley's accidental would be classified as a tented arch, a loop or a plain whorl in the American system, it has been dropped altogether from the Battley system as used in this country and replaced by the accidental whorl pattern as it is understood in the United States. Since these patterns are indeed rare, they are indicated merely by X type and can be subdivided, if necessary, according to ridge trace.

SCARRED PATTERNS. If a scar does not interfere with classification, the pattern is classified in the regular way according to pattern type. If the scar interferes with complete classification but the general type of pattern can be ascertained, the pattern is classified according to pattern type as far as possible and is then filed separately behind all other cards for that particular type of pattern and that finger. If the scar obliterates the ridges beyond classification, the pattern is filed behind all other cards for that finger.

THE BROGGER MOLLER PALMPRINT SYSTEM

While palm and soleprints can be just as valuable in establishing identity as fingerprints, palmprints and to an ever greater extent soleprints are not as widely used for identification because few organized collections of such prints exist. Upon arrest, officers generally record only fingerprints. Palmprints and soleprints are obtained only when latent traces for them have been discovered and the need to compare the traces with the friction skin details of known suspects arises. Some departments have a policy to record palmprints along with the fingerprints of certain types of criminals—for example, burglars—but many such bureaus file those palmprints in the criminal history jacket and do not bother to place them in a special file. In time, quite a large number of palmprints may thus be accumulated. Yet the value of such collections of prints remains in doubt as long as they are of use only when a suspect's name is known. It was exactly this state of affairs that led to the development of several palmprint classification systems, among them that devised by Kaj Brogger Moller of the national identification bureau of Denmark in Copenhagen. The Brogger Moller system is among the better known systems and has been adapted for use in several American identification services.

Essentially, in the Brogger Moller system a palmprint is divided into three major zones or areas: hypothenar area, thenar area and base area. The system is based on the principle that a number of widely divergent types of ridge formation can be found within these distinct areas. Such formations can be grouped into certain classes of patterns, which in turn allows us to assign values to these classes, from which a classification formula can be derived. (See Figure 154.) In calculating the classification formula, the areas are used in this sequence: hypothenar, base and thenar. The same sequence is followed in filing. Right-hand palms and left-hand palms are filed in separate cabinets. A special measuring glass is used, on which short lines and three circles are drawn, as illustrated in Figure 155. The diameters of the three concentric circles on the glass are two, four and six centimeters. The distances between the short

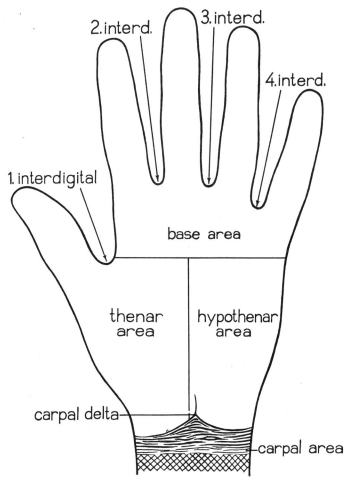

Figure 154. Brogger Moller palmprint zones. (Courtesy: Kaj Brogger Moller, Copenhagen, Denmark.)

lines are three millimeters on the 1–6 scale and four millimeters on the 0–9 scale.

Hypothenar Area

The ridge patterns that appear in the hypothenar area of a palmprint are illustrated along with their primary values in Figure 156. Twenty different designs are shown (lettered a–t) although the primary values range only from 1 to a maximum of 8.

Primary value 1 (design a) includes patterns resembling no given

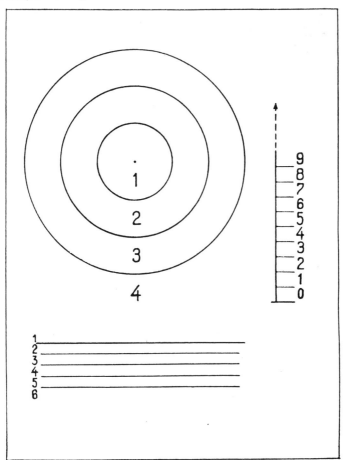

Figure 155. Brogger Moller palmprint values. (Courtesy: Kaj Brogger Moller, Copenhagen, Denmark.)

design except a carpal delta. Secondary classification is obtained by placing the center dot of the special reading glass onto the carpal delta and reading downward to observe the circle within which the lowest ridge of the carpal area falls, as is illustrated in Figure 157, where the lowest papillary ridge of the carpal area falls within circle 3. Palmprints without a carpal delta are arbitrarily assigned a secondary classification of 1. There is no tertiary classification.

Primary value 2 (designs b and c) is assigned to a distal loop opening in the direction of the base area and with a core pointing toward the ulnar side of the palm. Secondary classification is the

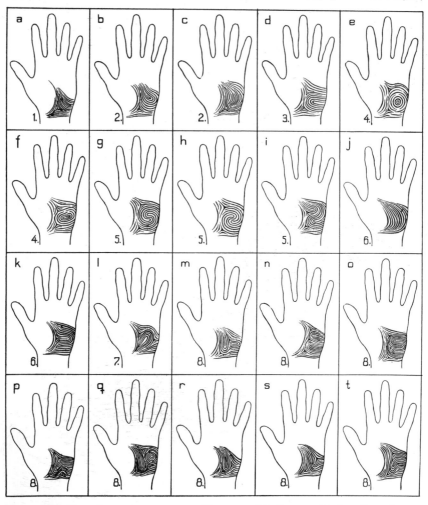

Figure 156. Hypothenar area patterns. (Courtesy: Kaj Brogger Moller, Copenhagen, Denmark.)

distance between the carpal area and the core of the loop, measured on the 0–9 scale. The zero on the scale is placed on the carpal delta and the ladderlike scale is pointed toward the core of the loop to obtain a secondary classification reading of the numbered step of the scale within which the core falls, as is illustrated in Figure 158, where the secondary value of 7 can be noted. When the core of the loop shows a distinct inclination toward either the carpal area or the radial side of the palm, as illustrated in design c, a tertiary classification of 8 is given.

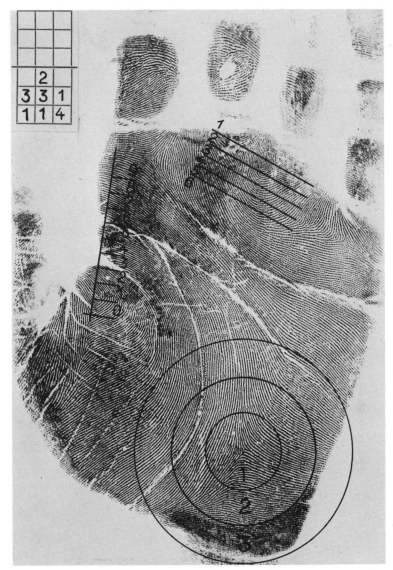

Figure 157. (Courtesy: Kaj Brogger Moller, Copenhagen, Denmark.)

Primary value 3 (design d) is assigned to an outward loop opening in the direction of the ulnar side of the palm and with its core pointing toward the thenar area. If there are two deltas, however, the bottom one is considered to be the carpal delta. Secondary classification is obtained by measuring the distance between the carpal

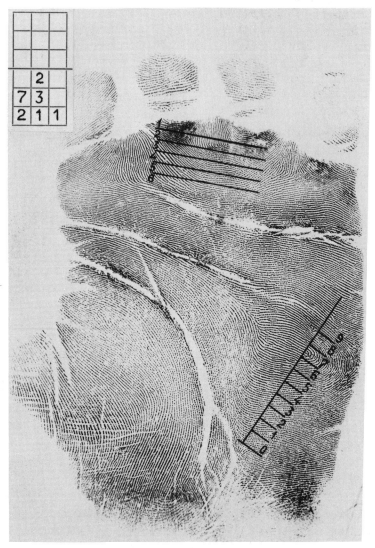

Figure 158. (Courtesy: Kaj Brogger Moller, Copenhagen, Denmark.)

delta and the core of the loop on the 0–9 scale. There is no tertiary classification.

Primary value 4 (designs e and f) is for whorls. Secondary classification is the distance between the carpal delta and the core of the whorl, measured on the 0–9 scale. For elliptical whorls showing two cores, the reading is taken between the carpal delta and the nearest core. There is no tertiary classification.

Primary value 5 (designs g, h and i) is assigned to twin loops. The secondary classification is the distance between the cores of the two loops on the 0–9 scale. There is no tertiary classification.

Primary value 6 (designs j and k) covers arches and tented arches. The base of the pattern adjoins the radial side of the thumb. Arches are given a secondary classification of 1, tented arches 2. There is no tertiary classification.

Primary value 7 (design l) is for proximal loops opening toward the wrist and with cores pointing toward the ulnar side of the palm. Secondary classification is the distance between the core of the loop and the delta above it, measured on the 0–9 scale. There is no tertiary classification.

Primary value 8 (designs m through t) is assigned to the various types of composite patterns. This group is reserved mainly for all patterns that do not fall within the categories covered by primary values 1–7. No secondary or tertiary classification is assigned to patterns falling within this main group.

In marking the classification formula on a palmprint, the primary value of the hypothenar zone is placed first, the secondary value of the hypothenar zone is placed immediately above the primary value, and the tertiary classification, if any, is placed immediately above the secondary value. The primary, secondary and tertiary values for the base area are marked in the same order, immediately to the right of the values given to the hypothenar area; the values of the thenar zone, in the same order, are written immediately to the right of those assigned to the base area. This procedure is illustrated in the little rectangular codes printed in the upper left-hand corner of the palmprints shown in Figures 157 and 158.

Base Area

The ridge patterns that appear in the base area of a palmprint are illustrated along with their primary values in Figure 159. There are ten different designs, lettered a–j, but primary values range only from 1–9 because designs g and h each have a primary value of 7. Pattern form, according to the illustration, determines primary value. Secondary classification is arrived at by considering the position of the patterns in the interdigital area (illustrated in Figure 154). The tertiary classification is derived from the pattern height.

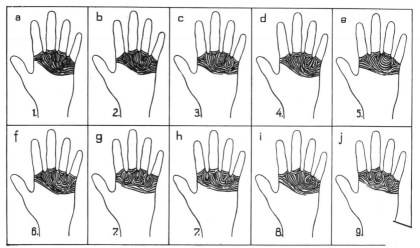

Figure 159. Base area patterns and values. (Courtesy: Kaj Brogger Moller, Copenhagen, Denmark.)

Primary value 1 (design a) is assigned to one loop in the base area. If that one loop occurs in the second interdigital area, a secondary classification of 2 is given; if it occurs in the third interdigital area, it has a secondary value of 3; if it occurs in the fourth interdigital area, it has a secondary value of 4. Determining the height of the loop in order to arrive at a tertiary classification is done by using the 1–6 scale (see Figure 155). Line 1 on the 1–6 scale is lined up with the two deltas that enclose the loop; the tertiary value is the number on the 1–6 scale that corresponds with the core of the loop. Tertiary classification can be from 1–6.

Primary value 2 (design b) is given when one tented arch occurs. If the tented arch is positioned below the index finger, a secondary classification of 1 is given; if below the middle finger, a secondary classification of 2; if below the ring finger, a secondary value of 3; and if below the little finger, a secondary value of 4. In measuring the height of the tented arch in order to obtain the tertiary classification, the first line on the 1–6 scale is positioned so that it touches both the bottom delta of the tented arch and the delta on its ulnar side (or on its radial side if the tented arch occurs under the little finger). The field on the 1–6 scale covering the summit of the tented arch is recorded as the tertiary classification.

Primary value 3 (design c) is assigned when two loops occur in the base area. Secondary classification is assigned according to the position within the second, third or fourth interdigital area. Tertiary classification is assigned according to height of the loop next to the ulnar side of the palm.

Primary value 4 (design d) is assigned when two loops occur within the same interdigital area of the base zone and when tented arches and loops occur in other areas. The position of the two loops within the same interdigital area determines secondary classification. There is no tertiary classification.

Primary value 5 (design e) is assigned to plain arches without proper pattern design. No secondary or tertiary classification is recorded.

Primary value 6 (design f) is for one loop and one tented arch. Secondary and tertiary classifications are assigned according to position and height, respectively, as was done for primary value 1.

Primary value 7 (designs g and h) is assigned to three loops or a combination of three loops and tented arches. If there are three loops, secondary classification is the height of the loop in the fourth interdigital area. If a combination of three loops and tented arches occurs, secondary classification is the height of the pattern, whether loop or tented arch, that is located next to the ulnar side of the palm. There is no tertiary value when only three loops occur; a tertiary value of 2 is assigned when the pattern has three loops and tented arches.

Primary value 8 (design i) is assigned to all combinations that have a long transversal loop below one or several digital deltas. No secondary or tertiary classification is assigned.

Primary value 9 (design j) is assigned when one or several whorls appear alone or in combination with loops and tented arches. Secondary classification is assigned according to the position of the whorl(s) in the same manner as for primary values 1 and 3. There is no tertiary classification.

Thenar Area

Twenty different pattern designs are noted for the thenar area, lettered a–t in Figure 160. Primary values for the twenty patterns range from 1–9.

Primary value 1 (design a) is assigned when no pattern, or a plain arch design, occurs in the thenar area. No secondary or tertiary classification is noted.

Primary value 2 (designs b–g) is assigned to various pattern for-

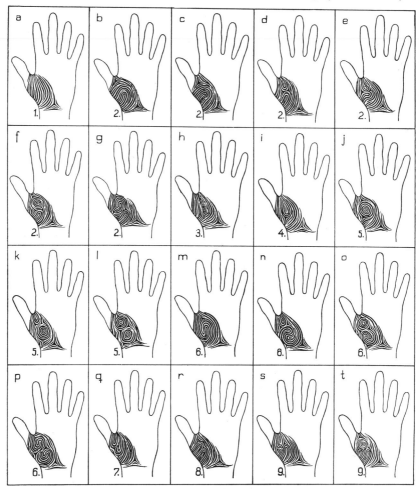

Figure 160. Thenar area patterns and values. (Courtesy: Kaj Brogger Moller, Copenhagen, Denmark.)

mations. If one proximal loop opens toward the radial side of the palm with its core pointing in the direction of the first interdigital area or toward the center of the palm, it is given a secondary classification of 1. Tertiary classification is assigned according to the distance between the core of the pattern and the nearest delta (not the carpal delta) on the 0–9 scale. (See designs b and c.) If one proximal loops occurs in conjunction with a distal loop (one opening in the direction of the first interdigital area with its core pointing downward), a secondary value of 2 is assigned. Tertiary value is again the distance between the core of the proximal loop and the nearest delta (not the carpal delta) on the 0–9 scale. (See designs d and e.) One proximal loop and one whorl (see design f) together have a secondary value of 3 and no tertiary classification. One proximal loop and one twin loop (design g) together have a secondary value of 3 and no tertiary classification.

Primary value 3 is assigned to patterns that cannot be properly classified because of peculiar ridge formations (see design h). There is no secondary or tertiary classification.

Primary value 4 (design i) is assigned to one distal loop opening toward the first interdigital area with its core pointing downward. Secondary classification is the distance between the core of the loop and the delta below (not the carpal delta) on the 0–9 scale. There is no tertiary classification.

Primary value 5 (designs j–l) is assigned to three different pattern formations. When one single whorl occurs (design j), a secondary value of 1 is given; when one whorl and one distal loop occur together (design k), a secondary value of 2 is assigned; when two whorls occur together, a secondary value of 3 is noted. There are no tertiary classifications.

Primary value 6 (designs m–p) is assigned to four different pattern formations. One twin loop alone (design m) receives a secondary value of 1. One twin loop and one distal loop (design n) together receive a secondary classification of 2. One twin loop and one whorl (design o) together are assigned a secondary value of 3. Two twin loop formations (design p) together receive a secondary value of 4. There are no tertiary classifications under primary value 6.

Primary value 7 (design q) is assigned when two collateral distal loops, both opening toward the first interdigital area, occur in the thenar zone. There is no secondary or tertiary classification.

Primary value 8 (design r) is given when two proximal loops occur, both opening either in the direction of the carpal area or one toward the radial side of the palm and the other toward the carpal area. There is no secondary or tertiary classification.

Primary value 9 (designs s and t) is assigned whenever pattern combinations other than those already discussed occur. There is no secondary or tertiary classification.

The Chatterjee Soleprint System

Of the few soleprint classification systems ever developed, the only one to receive any practical application is that developed by Salil Kumar Chatterjee, director of the Central Finger Print Bureau in Calcutta, India. It was recommended by its originator for filing the soleprints of persons who are armless and the soleprints of newborn babies. Chatterjee divided the sole into six zones encompassing the areas shown in Figure 161. Area I is the ball of the pad. Areas II, III and IV are the interspaces among the toes. Area V covers the center of the sole and area VI covers the heel. Essentially, Chatterjee followed the Henry rules for pattern interpretation. In his classification formula, he represented the patterns on the ball of the pad by symbolic letters and the patterns on the inter-toe spaces, center area and heel by symbolic numerals, according to the table on page 212 (also see classified patterns in Figure 162).

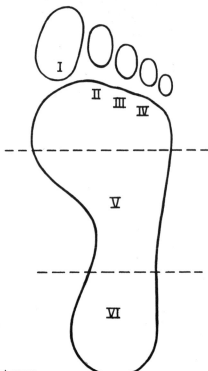

Figure 161. Chatterjee soleprint zones.

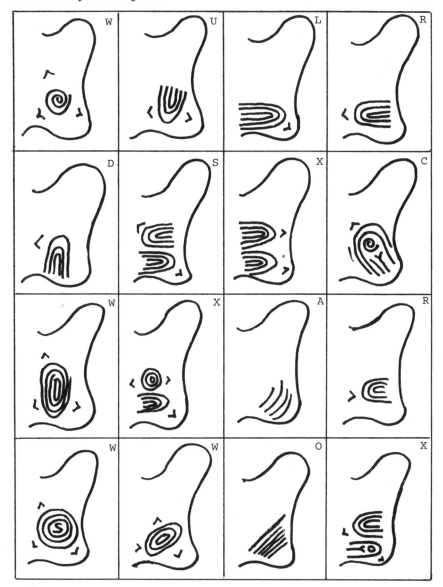

Figure 162. Chatterjee soleprint pattern classifications.

Pattern	Ball Area	Intertoe space, Center and Heel
No pattern	O	0
Arch	A	1
Tented arch	T	2
Right-slope loop	R	3
Loop with upward slope	U	4
Left-slope loop	L	5
Loop with downward slope	D	6
Whorl	W	7
Central pocket loop	C	7
Lateral pocket loop	S	8
Twin loop	S	8
Accidental	X	9

To obtain the formula for a set of soleprints, the primary classification is made up of the patterns on the two ball areas and is shown as a fraction, with the symbol for the right soleprint in the numerator and the symbol for the left soleprint in the denominator. This formula permits 11 x 11 or 121 possible primary combinations. The filing sequence as devised by Chatterjee is: O, A, T, R, U, L, D, W, C, S, X. The denominator is filed before the numerator, as in the Henry filing procedure. Secondary classification consists of a fraction with two five-digit numbers, one for the numerator and one for the denominator, representing the pattern symbols for the intertoe spaces, center area and heel of each foot. The total number of combinations will be from 00000 to 99999 for the numerator and as many for the denominator.

VARIANT FINGERPRINT CLASSIFICATIONS

A number of fingerprint classification systems have been devised that depart from ten-finger, single-print and five-finger classification methods and instead are based on totally different divisions or characteristics of fingerprints. A few are discussed in this section, but it must be emphasized that none of these systems has found widespread use. Most are used only in the identification bureaus where they originated. That the few discussed here are mentioned at all does not in any way signify an endorsement of their individual or comparative values. They are presented merely as recognition of the varied approaches to universal problems of classification that have been attempted over the years.

Three-Finger Classification

This method was devised by the judicial identification bureau of Belgium as an adjunct to the Battley single-print system. As described in the May 1952 issue of *International Criminal Police Review*, the Interpol journal, the three-finger file employs the plain prints of the index, middle and ring fingers of both hands. It was started because identification men discovered that groups of three fingerprints are often found at crime scenes.

Anderson Primary Extension

This method was devised by Captain Wilbur L. Anderson of Topeka, Kansas. Its purpose is to extend the 1-over-1 primary classification of the Henry system, which is of course the most bulky group and the largest among the primary divisions, by subdividing it into an additional 1,024 categories. The Anderson system assigns a numerical value to one-half of all the Henry nonnumerical patterns in order to arrive at a double primary classification, the first one being the Henry primary system and the second one the Anderson extension. Values are assigned to all tented arches, to loops on the thumbs with a ridge count of 16 or less, loops on the index fingers with a ridge count of 9 or less, loops on the middle fingers with a ridge count of 10 or less, loops on the ring fingers with a ridge count of 13 or less, and loops on the little fingers with a ridge count of 8 or less.

Chatterjee Middle Phalanx System

The original Henry system provides no subclassification for arches and tented arches. While only about five percent of all patterns fall within these groups and many of them occur in combination with other pattern types, still a rather sizable group of all-arch cards can be found in today's large identification collections. In a collection of about one million cards, at least five hundred ten-arch cards would be found, which means that all of them would have to be searched through when a ten-arch set of prints is received. Since plain arch patterns are rather featureless, that would be quite a task. It is not surprising, then, that a great number of subclassification systems for plain arches have been devised, based on the most divergent views and concepts. One of the approaches has been to subdivide plain arch sets by studying the ridge patterns on the second phalanx of each digit.

In the middle 1950s, Salil Kumar Chatterjee devised a system to classify middle phalanx prints. According to his system, patterns in the ten-arch group were subdivided on the basis of five groups, as illustrated in Figure 163. The groups were selected from the middle phalanx pattern divisions set up by the scientists Inez Whipple Wilder and Ploetz Radmann, who in earlier works had divided the line designs in four basic and eight combination types of patterns found on the middle phalanges of human fingers. In practice, it was found that the percentage distribution of plain arches in these five middle phalanx subdivisions came to 22.4%, 8.2%, 44.7%, 15.2% and 9.5% respectively. Since almost one-half of all the arch patterns still occurred in the third group, which, of course, would have severely

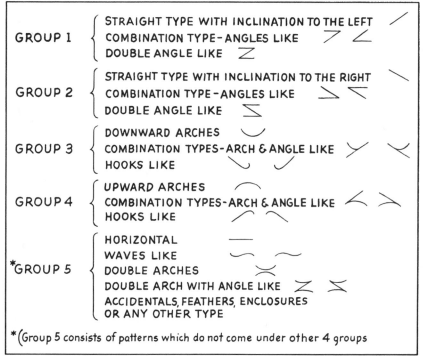

Figure 163. Chatterjee middle phalanx pattern groups. Basic and combination patterns are arranged into these five groups, within which they are assigned classification symbols. (Courtesy: Institute of Applied Science.)

limited the worth of the system, Chatterjee also devised a secondary classification to further subdivide the groups into 15,625 subgroups.

Adoption of the system of middle phalanx classification for the ten-arch group in the Calcutta bureau sparked verbal battles reminiscent of the Faulds-Herschel controversy, with Indian experts publishing articles both in favor of and against the practicality of the system. Its use was abandoned in Calcutta as soon as Chatterjee retired as director of the fingerprint bureau because it was discovered that too many existing files did not show enough of the middle phalanges and that fingerprint slips received from other bureaus often did not show them at all.

Nayar Ten-Arch Subclassification

After Chatterjee's middle phalanx system was dropped, P. S. Nayar, senior fingerprint expert at the Central Finger Print Bureau in Calcutta, publicized the development of a new system within the bureau that attempted to subdivide the ten-arch group by noting enclosures that occur within the central portion of arch patterns. After studying the large arch collection, Nayar noted that the ridge characteristic known as an enclosure is comparatively more frequent in arches than in other patterns and occurs generally near the center of the arch pattern. Out of 1,000 prints examined, it was found that only sixteen of them had enclosures located away from the central portions, and even then there were also enclosures in the centers of the patterns.

Arches were therefore divided into two groups: those having only one or no enclosures, classified as I for inner, and those having more than one enclosure, designated by O. Since the thumbs were considered separately, with the right thumb as the numerator and the left thumb as the denominator, there were four possible subdivisions:

$$\frac{I}{I} \qquad \frac{O}{I} \qquad \frac{I}{O} \qquad \frac{O}{O}$$

By treating these subdivisions as divisions in a major or primary classification, a secondary classification could be made on the basis of a consideration of the index, middle, ring and little fingers, with sixteen possibilities for each hand or a total of 1,024 subdivisions. For subdivisions of about 500 fingerprint cards (as might be expected in a bureau having a total of about one million cards on file), the little fingers could be omitted, since there would still be 256 subdivisions without them. In developing this system in Calcutta, it was found that with it there was no heavy accumulation of cards in any one group.

Chapter 9

Fingerprint Filing and Searching

Fingerprints would be of little practical value without a system which permits us to place a set of fingerprints in a file among millions of others and retrieve the same set from that file at a later date. Filing cards alphabetically by subject names would not be satisfactory because criminals are known to use many aliases and because, across the country, there are many thousands of John Smiths, William Joneses and similarly common names. So fingerprints are not filed alphabetically but rather by classification formula, which is unalterable.

In essence, filing consists of placing a set of fingerprints in the file according to the classification formula that has been worked out for that particular set of prints, a formula that would not vary regardless of how many aliases the subject used. It does not matter what classification system is used in the file, as long as the set of prints is given a formula that corresponds to the filing system used in the particular bureau where it is to be kept. As seen previously, the classification system used most widely throughout the United States is the Henry system modified and extended by the **FBI**. Since the system is based on data extracted from all ten digits on a fingerprint card, it means that we need a complete set of ten fingerprints before we can determine a classification formula for the set. That is why, in the previous chapters, we assigned certain arbitrary symbols to missing fingers in sets containing amputations.

Searching for a set of prints in a file demands that we follow a procedure similar to that used for filing. When a set is received, the classification formula for the filing system used in the bureau is worked out and the file is then searched to find the precise location where that set of prints should be placed. At that location, we should find another set of prints if the subject has been finger-printed previously. Again, the searching procedure implies that we need a full set of ten fingerprints to search the file because we must first work out the classification formula for the set of prints that we want to locate within the file. Therefore, when one or a few iso-lated latent prints are found at a crime scene, it will be impossible to determine from the main file to whom they belong because it will not be possible to arrive at a classification formula. Should we have a sufficient number of latent fingerprints that can be ascribed to one individual—say, seven or eight out of ten—we might be able to use the file by working out a series of reference classifications that account for all of the possible pattern types and subdivisions that might occur on the missing fingers.

The main classification file can be used to search for individual latent prints when the names of suspects are available. Whenever a set of prints is placed in the file, a name card is also filed alphabeti-cally in a separate index file. The name card also contains the classi-fication formula for the fingerprint card. When a latent print is dis-covered at a crime scene and, through the investigative process, detectives can determine that Jonathan Caesar Doakes is suspected of having committed the crime in question, a search of the name-in-dex card of Jonathan Caesar Doakes will also reveal his fingerprint classification. It then becomes relatively simple to pull out Doakes' fingerprint card, assuming he has been arrested and fingerprinted previously, and compare the latent fingerprint with the ten finger-prints on Doakes' card to determine whether or not it matches one of them. Name cards are also made up for all aliases arrestees are known to have used. But unless the names of suspects are known and their fingerprints are already on file, the main fingerprint file will be of little use in searching for single latent prints found at crime scenes. So most bureaus also maintain either five-finger or single-print files of known habitual criminals.

FILING SEQUENCES

To determine the exact location in a file for a particular set of fin-gerprints is a step-by-step process in which the classification for-mula serves as the guide. It can be compared with the filing procedure in a name file, for which the alphabet determines the filing sequence for the last, first and middle names, in that order. The last name could be considered the equivalent of the primary classification in a fingerprint file, and so on. For fingerprint filing, the sequence is determined first by the denominator and secondly by the numerator in each part of the classification. The prime order of search for an FBI classification is: primary denominator, primary numerator, secondary denominator, secondary numerator, subsecondary denominator, subsecondary numerator, major denominator, major numerator, final classification, key.

Primary Filing Sequence

Considering that the primary denominator and numerator may be any number between 1 and 32, it follows that we have 32 x 32 or 1,024 possible primary classifications. In filing a set of prints, then, we would have 1,024 primary divisions, which appear in the form of numerical fractions in which the denominator is filed numerically before the numerator. The sequence then runs from $\frac{1}{1}$ to $\frac{32}{1}$, after which the sequence continues from $\frac{1}{2}$ to $\frac{32}{2}$ and so on until all 1,024 combinations of denominators and numerators are exhausted and the last fraction $\frac{32}{32}$ is reached.

Since some pattern types occur more frequently than others, the distribution of any hypothetical total number of sets of fingerprints will not be equal among the various primaries. We have already seen that about 60–65 percent of all patterns are loops, which means that the greatest concentration of sets of fingerprint cards will be in the lower primaries because loops (as well as arches and tented arches) are nonnumerical patterns. If we were to house a fingerprint collection in one filing cabinet consisting of five double drawers, two of the five drawers would probably be taken up by primaries with 1 in the denominator. Large identification bureaus with files containing millions of sets of prints might need as many as thirty filing cabinets to hold the $\frac{1}{1}$ primary. The 1,024 primary divisions, then, are largely insufficient for dividing fingerprint collections into searchable groups in even small identification bureaus.

Secondary Filing Sequence

All sets having the same primary classification are again divided. Because secondary classification consists of letter divisions (both capital and lower case), an arbitrary order for the letters has been established as follows: A, T, R, U and W. (Letter symbols are never filed alphabetically.) Capital letters, which designate patterns on the index fingers, are filed first by denominator and secondly by numerator, which produces the following twenty-five possible breakdowns:

$$\frac{A\ T\ R\ U\ W}{A\ A\ A\ A\ A} \qquad \frac{A\ T\ R\ U\ W}{T\ T\ T\ T\ T} \qquad \frac{A\ T\ R\ U\ W}{R\ R\ R\ R\ R}$$

$$\frac{A\ T\ R\ U\ W}{U\ U\ U\ U\ U} \qquad \frac{A\ T\ R\ U\ W}{W\ W\ W\ W\ W}$$

Whenever arches, tented arches or radial loops appear on fingers other than index fingers, their small-letter symbols are used. The classification of small-letter secondaries also follows a definite sequence in which the denominator is filed first and the numerator second. The sequence appears in Figure 164, where $\frac{A}{A}$ comes first and is followed by $\frac{aA}{A}\ \frac{tA}{A}\ \frac{ra}{A}\ \frac{Aa}{A}\ \frac{Ar}{A}\ \frac{Ar}{A}\ \frac{aAa}{A}$ through $\frac{rA^3r}{A}.$ At that point, the denominator is changed to aA and we get

$$\frac{A}{aA} \quad \frac{aA}{aA} \quad \frac{tA}{aA} \quad \frac{rA}{aA} \quad \frac{Aa}{aA} \quad \frac{At}{aA} \quad \frac{Ar}{aA} \quad \frac{aAa}{aA} \quad \frac{aAt}{aA}\ \text{through}\ \frac{rA3r}{aA}$$

This procedure is repeated for all possible combinations in the denominator and the numerator until we arrive at rA3r in the numerator over rA3r in the denominator. From A to rA3r there are 160 possible combinations. Since as many combinations are possible in the denominator as in the numerator, 25,600 combinations exist in the $\frac{A}{A}$ to $\frac{rA3r}{rA3r}$ group.

Yet, that takes care only of the A-over-A index combination. Then we move on to the T-over-A section, and again go through all of the possible combinations in the same sequence, beginning with

$$\frac{T}{A} \quad \frac{aT}{A} \quad \frac{tT}{A} \quad \frac{rT}{A} \quad \frac{Ta}{A} \quad \frac{Tt}{A} \quad \frac{Tr}{A} \quad \frac{aTa}{A} \quad \frac{aTt}{A}\ \text{through}\ \frac{rT3r}{rA3r}$$

After the T-over-A combinations have been exhausted, we go on to $\frac{R\ U\ W\ A\ T\ R}{A\ A\ A\ T\ T\ T}$ and so forth until we have exhausted all possible combinations of denominators with numerators, when we will have reached the combination $\frac{rW3r}{rW3r}$. Because of the tremendous number

SMALL-LETTER SEQUENCE

A	tAra	aA2at	tA2tr
aA	tArt	aA2ar	tAtra
tA	tA2r	aAata	tAtrt
rA	rA2a	aAa2t	tAt2r
Aa	rAat	aAatr	tAr2a
At	rAar	aAara	tArat
Ar	rAta	aAart	tArar
aAa	rA2t	aAa2r	tArta
aAt	rAtr	aAt2a	tAr2t
aAr	rAra	aAtat	tArtr
tAa	rArt	aAtar	tA2ra
tAt	rA2r	aA2ta	tA2rt
tAr	A3a	aA3t	tA3r
rAa	A2at	aA2tr	rA3a
rAt	A2ar	aAtra	rA2at
rAr	Aata	aAtrt	rA2ar
A2a	Aa2t	aAt2r	rAata
Aat	Aatr	aAr2a	rAa2t
Aar	Aara	aArat	rAatr
Ata	Aart	aArar	rAara
A2t	Aa2r	aArta	rAart
Atr	At2a	aAr2t	rAa2r
Ara	Atat	aArtr	rAt2a
Art	Atar	aA2ra	rAtat
A2r	A2ta	aA2rt	rAtar
aA2a	A3t	aA3r	rA2ta
aAat	A2tr	tA3a	rA3t
aAar	Atra	tA2at	rA2tr
aAta	Atrt	tA2ar	rAtra
aA2t	At2r	tAata	rAtrt
aAtr	Ar2a	tAa2t	rAt2r
aAra	Arat	tAatr	rAr2a
aArt	Arar	tAara	rArat
aA2r	Arta	tAart	rArar
tA2a	Ar2t	tAa2r	rArta
tAat	Artr	tAt2a	rAr2t
tAar	A2ra	tAtat	rArtr
tAta	A2rt	tAtar	rA2ra
tA2t	A3r	tA2ta	rA2rt
tAtr	aA3a	tA3t	rA3r

Figure 164.

of possible combinations thus afforded, most sections of the file containing small-letter secondaries are not subdivided with a subsecondary classification. In some sections, there will not be any major division, final or key subclassification.

Subsecondary Filing Sequence

Subsecondary combinations are derived from the loop and whorl patterns on the index, middle and ring fingers. The symbols used here are I (for inner loops and inner whorls), M (for meeting whorls) and O (for outer loops and outer whorls), in both denominators and numerators. The possible combinations range, therefore, from $\dfrac{III}{III}$ to $\dfrac{OOO}{OOO}$, as shown in Figure 165.

Major Division Filing Sequence

Major division is shown by the letter symbols S, M and L for loops and by the ridge traces I, M and O for whorls on the thumbs. Four different sequences exist depending on the types of combinations of patterns on the thumbs: two loops, two whorls, a loop and a whorl, and a whorl and a loop. Only one of the four possible sequences can be used in any one primary classification because the appearance of whorl patterns (numerical denominator value of 16 on the right thumb and numerical numerator value of 4 on the left thumb) determines which sequence applies within each primary.

When both thumbs are loops, the major sequence is

$$\frac{S\ M\ L}{S\ S\ S} \qquad \frac{S\ M\ L}{M\ M\ M} \qquad \frac{S\ M\ L}{L\ L\ L}$$

When both thumbs are whorls, the major sequence is

$$\frac{I\ M\ O}{I\ I\ I} \qquad \frac{I\ M\ O}{M\ M\ M} \qquad \frac{I\ M\ O}{O\ O\ O}$$

When the right thumb is a whorl and the left thumb a loop, the sequence is

$$\frac{I\ M\ O}{S\ S\ S} \qquad \frac{I\ M\ O}{M\ M\ M} \qquad \frac{I\ M\ O}{L\ L\ L}$$

When the right thumb is a loop and the left thumb a whorl, the sequence is

$$\frac{S\ M\ L}{I\ I\ I} \qquad \frac{S\ M\ L}{M\ M\ M} \qquad \frac{S\ M\ L}{O\ O\ O}$$

I-M-O FILING SEQUENCE

MMM/III	OOO/III	MMM/IIM	OOO/IIM	MMM/IIO	OOO/IIO	MMM/IMI	OOO/IMI
MMI/III	OOM/III	MMI/IIM	OOM/IIM	MMI/IIO	OOM/IIO	MMI/IMI	OOM/IMI
MIO/III	OOI/III	MIO/IIM	OOI/IIM	MIO/IIO	OOI/IIO	MIO/IMI	OOI/IMI
MIM/III	OMO/III	MIM/IIM	OMO/IIM	MIM/IIO	OMO/IIO	MIM/IMI	OMO/IMI
MII/III	OMM/III	MII/IIM	OMM/IIM	MII/IIO	OMM/IIO	MII/IMI	OMM/IMI
IOO/III	OMI/III	IOO/IIM	OMI/IIM	IOO/IIO	OMI/IIO	IOO/IMI	OMI/IMI
IOM/III	OIO/III	IOM/IIM	OIO/IIM	IOM/IIO	OIO/IIO	IOM/IMI	OIO/IMI
IOI/III	OIM/III	IOI/IIM	OIM/IIM	IOI/IIO	OIM/IIO	IOI/IMI	OIM/IMI
IMO/III	OII/III	IMO/IIM	OII/IIM	IMO/IIO	OII/IIO	IMO/IMI	OII/IMI
IMM/III	MOO/III	IMM/IIM	MOO/IIM	IMM/IIO	MOO/IIO	IMM/IMI	MOO/IMI
IMI/III	MOM/III	IMI/IIM	MOM/IIM	IMI/IIO	MOM/IIO	IMI/IMI	MOM/IMI
IIO/III	MOI/III	IIO/IIM	MOI/IIM	IIO/IIO	MOI/IIO	IIO/IMI	MOI/IMI
IIM/III	MMO/III	IIM/IIM	MMO/IIM	IIM/IIO	MMO/IIO	IIM/IMI	MMO/IMI
III/III		III/IIM		III/IIO		III/IMI	

Figure 165—Part 1

Figure 165 (continued) — a combinatorial grid of fractions. Each cell is of the form (numerator)/(denominator) with three-letter strings over the symbols M, I, O.

$\frac{MMM}{IMM}$	$\frac{OOO}{IMM}$	$\frac{MMM}{IMO}$	$\frac{OOO}{IMO}$	$\frac{MMM}{IOI}$	$\frac{OOO}{IOI}$	$\frac{MMM}{IOM}$	$\frac{OOO}{IOM}$
$\frac{MMI}{IMM}$	$\frac{OOM}{IMM}$	$\frac{MMI}{IMO}$	$\frac{OOM}{IMO}$	$\frac{MMI}{IOI}$	$\frac{OOM}{IOI}$	$\frac{MMI}{IOM}$	$\frac{OOM}{IOM}$
$\frac{MIO}{IMM}$	$\frac{OOI}{IMM}$	$\frac{MIO}{IMO}$	$\frac{OOI}{IMO}$	$\frac{MIO}{IOI}$	$\frac{OOI}{IOI}$	$\frac{MIO}{IOM}$	$\frac{OOI}{IOM}$
$\frac{MIM}{IMM}$	$\frac{OMO}{IMM}$	$\frac{MIM}{IMO}$	$\frac{OMO}{IMO}$	$\frac{MIM}{IOI}$	$\frac{OMO}{IOI}$	$\frac{MIM}{IOM}$	$\frac{OMO}{IOM}$
$\frac{MII}{IMM}$	$\frac{OMM}{IMM}$	$\frac{MII}{IMO}$	$\frac{OMM}{IMO}$	$\frac{MII}{IOI}$	$\frac{OMM}{IOI}$	$\frac{MII}{IOM}$	$\frac{OMM}{IOM}$
$\frac{IOO}{IMM}$	$\frac{OMI}{IMM}$	$\frac{IOO}{IMO}$	$\frac{OMI}{IMO}$	$\frac{IOO}{IOI}$	$\frac{OMI}{IOI}$	$\frac{IOO}{IOM}$	$\frac{OMI}{IOM}$
$\frac{IOM}{IMM}$	$\frac{OIO}{IMM}$	$\frac{IOM}{IMO}$	$\frac{OIO}{IMO}$	$\frac{IOM}{IOI}$	$\frac{OIO}{IOI}$	$\frac{IOM}{IOM}$	$\frac{OIO}{IOM}$
$\frac{IOI}{IMM}$	$\frac{OIM}{IMM}$	$\frac{IOI}{IMO}$	$\frac{OIM}{IMO}$	$\frac{IOI}{IOI}$	$\frac{OIM}{IOI}$	$\frac{IOI}{IOM}$	$\frac{OIM}{IOM}$
$\frac{IMO}{IMM}$	$\frac{OII}{IMM}$	$\frac{IMO}{IMO}$	$\frac{OII}{IMO}$	$\frac{IMO}{IOI}$	$\frac{OII}{IOI}$	$\frac{IMO}{IOM}$	$\frac{OII}{IOM}$
$\frac{IMM}{IMM}$	$\frac{MOO}{IMM}$	$\frac{IMM}{IMO}$	$\frac{MOO}{IMO}$	$\frac{IMM}{IOI}$	$\frac{MOO}{IOI}$	$\frac{IMM}{IOM}$	$\frac{MOO}{IOM}$
$\frac{IMI}{IMM}$	$\frac{MOM}{IMM}$	$\frac{IMI}{IMO}$	$\frac{MOM}{IMO}$	$\frac{IMI}{IOI}$	$\frac{MOM}{IOI}$	$\frac{IMI}{IOM}$	$\frac{MOM}{IOM}$
$\frac{IIO}{IMM}$	$\frac{MOI}{IMM}$	$\frac{IIO}{IMO}$	$\frac{MOI}{IMO}$	$\frac{IIO}{IOI}$	$\frac{MOI}{IOI}$	$\frac{IIO}{IOM}$	$\frac{MOI}{IOM}$
$\frac{IIM}{IMM}$	$\frac{MMO}{IMM}$	$\frac{IIM}{IMO}$	$\frac{MMO}{IMO}$	$\frac{IIM}{IOI}$	$\frac{MMO}{IOI}$	$\frac{IIM}{IOM}$	$\frac{MMO}{IOM}$
$\frac{III}{IMM}$		$\frac{III}{IMO}$		$\frac{III}{IOI}$		$\frac{III}{IOM}$	

Figure 165—continued

$\frac{MMM}{100}$ $\frac{MMI}{100}$ $\frac{MIO}{100}$ $\frac{MIM}{100}$ $\frac{MII}{100}$ $\frac{IOO}{100}$ $\frac{IOM}{100}$ $\frac{IOI}{100}$ $\frac{IMO}{100}$ $\frac{IMM}{100}$ $\frac{IMI}{100}$ $\frac{IIO}{100}$ $\frac{IIM}{100}$ $\frac{III}{100}$

$\frac{OOO}{100}$ $\frac{OOM}{100}$ $\frac{IOI}{100}$ $\frac{OMO}{100}$ $\frac{OMM}{100}$ $\frac{OMI}{100}$ $\frac{OIO}{100}$ $\frac{OIM}{100}$ $\frac{OII}{100}$ $\frac{MOO}{100}$ $\frac{MOM}{100}$ $\frac{MOI}{100}$ $\frac{MMO}{100}$

$\frac{MMM}{MII}$ $\frac{MMI}{MII}$ $\frac{MIO}{MII}$ $\frac{MIM}{MII}$ $\frac{MII}{MII}$ $\frac{IOO}{MII}$ $\frac{IOM}{MII}$ $\frac{IOI}{MII}$ $\frac{IMO}{MII}$ $\frac{IMM}{MII}$ $\frac{IMI}{MII}$ $\frac{IIO}{MII}$ $\frac{IIM}{MII}$ $\frac{III}{MII}$

$\frac{OOO}{MII}$ $\frac{OOM}{MII}$ $\frac{OOI}{MII}$ $\frac{OMO}{MII}$ $\frac{OMM}{MII}$ $\frac{OMI}{MII}$ $\frac{OIO}{MII}$ $\frac{OIM}{MII}$ $\frac{OII}{MII}$ $\frac{MOO}{MII}$ $\frac{MOM}{MII}$ $\frac{MOI}{MII}$ $\frac{MMO}{MII}$

Figure 165—continued

MMM/MIM	OOO/MIM	MMM/MIO	OOO/MIO	MMM/IMM	OOO/IMM	MMM/MMM	OOO/MMM
MMI/MIM	OOM/MIM	MMI/MIO	OOM/MIO	MMI/IMM	OOM/IMM	MMI/MMM	OOM/MMM
MIO/MIM	OOI/MIM	MIO/MIO	OOI/MIO	MIO/IMM	OOI/IMM	MIO/MMM	OOI/MMM
MIM/MIM	OMO/MIM	MIM/MIO	OMO/MIO	MIM/IMM	OMO/IMM	MIM/MMM	OMO/MMM
MII/MIM	OMM/MIM	MII/MIO	OMM/MIO	MII/IMM	OMM/IMM	MII/MMM	OMM/MMM
IOO/MIM	OMI/MIM	IOO/MIO	OMI/MIO	IOO/IMM	OMI/IMM	IOO/MMM	OMI/MMM
IOM/MIM	OIO/MIM	IOM/MIO	OIO/MIO	IOM/IMM	OIO/IMM	IOM/MMM	OIO/MMM
IOI/MIM	OIM/MIM	IOI/MIO	OIM/MIO	IOI/IMM	OIM/IMM	IOI/MMM	OIM/MMM
IMO/MIM	OII/MIM	IMO/MIO	OII/MIO	IMO/IMM	OII/IMM	IMO/MMM	OII/MMM
IMM/MIM	MOO/MIM	IMM/MIO	MOO/MIO	IMM/IMM	MOO/IMM	IMM/MMM	MOO/MMM
IMI/MIM	MOM/MIM	IMI/MIO	MOM/MIO	IMI/IMM	MOM/IMM	IMI/MMM	MOM/MMM
IIO/MIM	MOI/MIM	IIO/MIO	MOI/MIO	IIO/IMM	MOI/IMM	IIO/MMM	MOI/MMM
IIM/MIM	MMO/MIM	IIM/MIO	MMO/MIO	IIM/IMM	MMO/IMM	IIM/MMM	MMO/MMM
III/MIM		III/MIO		III/IMM		III/MMM	

MMM/MMO	OOO/MMO	MMM/MON	OOO/MON	MMM/MOM	OOO/MOM	MMM/MOO	OOO/MOO
MMI/MMO	OOM/MMO	MMI/MON	OOM/MON	MMI/MOM	OOM/MOM	MMI/MOO	OOM/MOO
MIO/MMO	OOI/MMO	MIO/MON	OOI/MON	MIO/MOM	OOI/MOM	MIO/MOO	OOI/MOO
MIM/MMO	OMO/MMO	MIM/MON	OMO/MON	MIM/MOM	OMO/MOM	MIM/MOO	OMO/MOO
MII/MMO	OMM/MMO	MII/MON	OMM/MON	MII/MOM	OMM/MOM	MII/MOO	OMM/MOO
IOO/MMO	OMI/MMO	IOO/MON	OMI/MON	IOO/MOM	OMI/MOM	IOO/MOO	OMI/MOO
IOM/MMO	OIO/MMO	IOM/MON	OIO/MON	IOM/MOM	OIO/MOM	IOM/MOO	OIO/MOO
IOI/MMO	OIM/MMO	IOI/MON	OIM/MON	IOI/MOM	OIM/MOM	IOI/MOO	OIM/MOO
IMO/MMO	OII/MMO	IMO/MON	OII/MON	IMO/MOM	OII/MOM	IMO/MOO	OII/MOO
IMM/MMO	MOO/MMO	IMM/MON	MOO/MON	IMM/MOM	MOO/MOM	IMM/MOO	MOO/MOO
IMI/MMO	MOM/MMO	IMI/MON	MOM/MON	IMI/MOM	MOM/MOM	IMI/MOO	MOM/MOO
IIO/MMO	MOI/MMO	IIO/MON	MOI/MON	IIO/MOM	MOI/MOM	IIO/MOO	MOI/MOO
IIM/MMO	MMO/MMO	IIM/MON	MMO/MON	IIM/MOM	MMO/MOM	IIM/MOO	MMO/MOO
III/MMO		III/MON		III/MOM		III/MOO	

Figure 165—Part 2

MMM/IIO	OOO/IIO	MMM/MIO	OOO/MIO	MMM/OIO	OOO/OIO	MMM/IMO	OOO/IMO	MMM/MMO	OOO/OMM
MMI/IIO	OOM/IIO	MMI/MIO	OOM/OIO	MMI/OIO	OOM/OIO	MMI/IMO	OOM/IMO	MMI/OMM	OOM/OMM
MIO/IIO	IOO/IIO	MIO/MIO	IOO/OIO	MIO/OIO	IOO/OIO	MIO/IMO	IOO/IMO	MIO/MMO	IOO/OMM
MIM/IIO	OMO/IIO	MIM/MIO	OMO/OIO	MIM/OIO	OMO/OIO	MIM/IMO	OMO/IMO	MIM/MMO	OMO/OMM
MII/IIO	OMM/IIO	MII/MIO	OMM/OIO	MII/OIO	OMM/OIO	MII/IMO	OMM/IMO	MII/OMM	OMM/OMM
IOO/IIO	OMI/IIO	IOO/OIM	OMI/OIM	IOO/OIO	OMI/OIO	IOO/IMO	OMI/IMO	IOO/OMM	OMI/OMM
IOM/IIO	OIO/IIO	IOM/OIM	OIO/OIM	IOM/OIO	OIO/OIO	IOM/OIO	OIO/IMO	IOM/OMM	OIO/OMM
IOI/IIO	OIM/IIO	IOI/OIM	OIM/OIM	IOI/OIO	OIM/OIO	IOI/IMO	OIM/IMO	IOI/OMM	OIM/OMM
IMO/IIO	IIO/IIO	IMO/OIM	IIO/IIM	IMO/OIO	IIO/OIO	IMO/IMO	IIO/IIO	IMO/OMM	IIO/IIO
IMM/IIO	MOO/IIO	IMM/OIM	MOO/OIM	IMM/OIO	MOO/OIO	IMM/IMO	MOO/MOM	IMM/OMM	MOO/OMM
IMI/IIO	MOM/IIO	IMI/OIM	MOM/OIM	IMI/OIO	MOM/OIO	IMI/IMO	MOM/IMO	IMI/OMM	MOM/OMM
IIO/IIO	IOM/IIO	IIO/OIM	IOM/OIM	IIO/OIO	IOM/OIO	IIO/IMO	IOM/IIO	IIO/OMM	IOM/OMM
IIM/IIO	OMW/IIO	IIM/OIM	OMW/OIM	IIM/OIO	MMO/OIO	IIM/IMO	OMW/IMO	IIM/OMM	MMO/OMM
III/IIO		III/OIM		III/OIO		III/IMO		III/OMW	

$\frac{MMM}{OMO}$	$\frac{OOO}{OMO}$	$\frac{MMM}{IOO}$	$\frac{OOO}{IOO}$	$\frac{MMM}{OOM}$	$\frac{OOO}{OOM}$	$\frac{MMM}{OOO}$	$\frac{OOO}{OOO}$
$\frac{MMI}{OMO}$	$\frac{OOM}{OMO}$	$\frac{MMI}{IOO}$	$\frac{OOM}{IOO}$	$\frac{MMI}{OOM}$	$\frac{OOM}{OOM}$	$\frac{MMI}{OOO}$	$\frac{OOM}{OOO}$
$\frac{MIO}{OMO}$	$\frac{OOI}{OMO}$	$\frac{MIO}{IOO}$	$\frac{OOI}{IOO}$	$\frac{MIO}{OOM}$	$\frac{OOI}{OOM}$	$\frac{MIO}{OOO}$	$\frac{OOI}{OOO}$
$\frac{MIM}{OMO}$	$\frac{OMO}{OMO}$	$\frac{MIM}{IOO}$	$\frac{OMO}{IOO}$	$\frac{MIM}{OOM}$	$\frac{OMO}{OOM}$	$\frac{MIM}{OOO}$	$\frac{OMO}{OOO}$
$\frac{MII}{OMO}$	$\frac{OMM}{OMO}$	$\frac{MII}{IOO}$	$\frac{OMM}{IOO}$	$\frac{MII}{OOM}$	$\frac{OMM}{OOM}$	$\frac{MII}{OOO}$	$\frac{OMM}{OOO}$
$\frac{IOO}{OMO}$	$\frac{OMI}{OMO}$	$\frac{IOO}{IOO}$	$\frac{OMI}{IOO}$	$\frac{IOO}{OOM}$	$\frac{OMI}{OOM}$	$\frac{IOO}{OOO}$	$\frac{OMI}{OOO}$
$\frac{IOM}{OMO}$	$\frac{OIO}{OMO}$	$\frac{IOM}{IOO}$	$\frac{OIO}{IOO}$	$\frac{IOM}{OOM}$	$\frac{OIO}{OOM}$	$\frac{IOM}{OOO}$	$\frac{OIO}{OOO}$
$\frac{IOI}{OMO}$	$\frac{OIM}{OMO}$	$\frac{IOI}{IOO}$	$\frac{OIM}{IOO}$	$\frac{IOI}{OOM}$	$\frac{OIM}{OOM}$	$\frac{IOI}{OOO}$	$\frac{OIM}{OOO}$
$\frac{IMO}{OMO}$	$\frac{OII}{OMO}$	$\frac{IMO}{IOO}$	$\frac{OII}{IOO}$	$\frac{IMO}{OOM}$	$\frac{OII}{OOM}$	$\frac{IMO}{OOO}$	$\frac{OII}{OOO}$
$\frac{IMM}{OMO}$	$\frac{MOO}{OMO}$	$\frac{IMM}{IOO}$	$\frac{MOO}{IOO}$	$\frac{IMM}{OOM}$	$\frac{MOO}{OOM}$	$\frac{IMM}{OOO}$	$\frac{MOO}{OOO}$
$\frac{IMI}{OMO}$	$\frac{MOM}{OMO}$	$\frac{IMI}{IOO}$	$\frac{MOM}{IOO}$	$\frac{IMI}{OOM}$	$\frac{MOM}{OOM}$	$\frac{IMI}{OOO}$	$\frac{MOM}{OOO}$
$\frac{IIO}{OMO}$	$\frac{MOI}{OMO}$	$\frac{IIO}{IOO}$	$\frac{MOI}{IOO}$	$\frac{IIO}{OOM}$	$\frac{MOI}{OOM}$	$\frac{IIO}{OOO}$	$\frac{MOI}{OOO}$
$\frac{IIM}{OMO}$	$\frac{MMO}{OMO}$	$\frac{IIM}{IOO}$	$\frac{MMO}{IOO}$	$\frac{IIM}{OOM}$	$\frac{MMO}{OOM}$	$\frac{IIM}{OOO}$	$\frac{MMO}{OOO}$
$\frac{III}{OMO}$		$\frac{III}{IOO}$		$\frac{III}{OOM}$		$\frac{III}{OOO}$	

Figure 165—Part 3

Final and Key Sequences

Since both final and key subdivisions of the classification consist of numerals representing ridge counts, their filing sequence is numerical, beginning with 1.

SML Subsecondary Extension Sequence

SML subsecondary extension allows for 729 combinations, from $\frac{SSS}{SSS}$ to $\frac{LLL}{LLL}$. The following sequence can appear in both the denominator and the numerator: SSS, SSM, SSL, SMS, SMM, SML, SLS, SLM, SLL, MSS, MSM, MSL, MMS, MMM, MML, MLS, MLM, MLL, LSS, LSM, LSL, LMS, LMM, LML, LLS, LLM, LLL. The numerator follows the sequence from SSS to LLL over the denominator SSS, before repeating the same numerator sequence over denominator SSM, much in the same fashion as was done for the subsecondary IMO filing sequence illustrated in Figure 165.

Numerical Loop Extension Sequence

The numerical extension used by the FBI in its all-loop sections and in a few other primaries gives a total of 117,649 combinations, going from 111 through 117, 121 through 127, 131 through 137, and so on through 777 in denominator and numerator. A partial sequence is illustrated in Figure 166.

WCDX Extension Sequence

Used mainly in the all-whorl group (primary 32-over-32), the WCDX extension filing sequence goes from $\frac{W}{W}$ to $\frac{xX3x}{xX3x}$ following the sequence W, cW, dW, xW, Wc, Wd, Wx, cWc, cWd, cWx, dWc, dWd, dWx, xWc, xWd, xWx, W2c, Wcd, Wcx, Wdc and so on to xX3x. This sequence, it should be observed, follows the same pattern as that established for the small-letter secondary illustrated in Figure 164.

Essentially, the process of filing fingerprints is the same as that used in searching. By working one's way through the files while being guided by the classification formula, the exact location where a particular set of prints must be placed will be found. At that point, there may be other sets of prints that have exactly the same classifi-

$\underline{111}$	$\underline{112}$	$\underline{113}$	$\underline{114}$	$\underline{115}$	$\underline{116}$	$\underline{117}$
111	111	111	111	111	111	111

$\underline{121}$	$\underline{122}$	$\underline{123}$	$\underline{124}$	$\underline{125}$	$\underline{126}$	$\underline{127}$
111	111	111	111	111	111	111

$\underline{131}$	$\underline{132}$	$\underline{133}$	$\underline{134}$	$\underline{135}$	$\underline{136}$	$\underline{137}$
111	111	111	111	111	111	111

$\underline{141}$	$\underline{142}$	$\underline{143}$	$\underline{144}$	$\underline{145}$	$\underline{146}$	$\underline{147}$
111	111	111	111	111	111	111

$\underline{151}$	$\underline{152}$	$\underline{153}$	$\underline{154}$	$\underline{155}$	$\underline{156}$	$\underline{157}$
111	111	111	111	111	111	111

$\underline{161}$	$\underline{162}$	$\underline{163}$	$\underline{164}$	etc., to		$\underline{777}$
111	111	111	111			777

Figure 166.

cation through all subdivisions and extensions because classification is based on a formula derived from studying the ten patterns on the fingers of one individual rather than from comparing friction ridge detail. When the spot is located where the prints should be filed, a check is first made among the prints in that location to determine whether or not a set of prints for the same individual is already on file. The check is made by visually studying the friction ridge characteristics on one of the fingers of the new card and comparing them with the ridge detail on the same finger in the other sets having the same classification. To allow for possible variations in ridge counting among different experts, a search of two ridges over and under the one counted is conducted in the key and final classifications.

REFERENCING

Questionable patterns were studied in Chapter 3. When it comes to filing and searching for sets of prints containing patterns the interpretation of which is uncertain, reference classifications are made on the basis of all possibilities. Approximating patterns may well be

interpreted differently by two fingerprint classifiers. What one calls
a tented arch might be called a loop by another equally qualified
technician. During the blocking-out process, a technician may en-
counter a set of prints with a pattern on the left index that leaves
him in doubt whether it is an ulnar loop or a tented arch. After
studying the pattern, he may decide that the pattern looks more
like a loop; but since it is so difficult to decide, he thinks another
technician might well call it a tented arch. He can therefore interpret the pattern as a loop and reference it as a tented arch. In
blocking out, he will mark the pattern /?T. The slanting line is his
first interpretation of the pattern as an ulnar loop on a left-hand
finger, while the T, separated from the slanting line by a question
mark, represents his second choice. The set is filed according to the
first interpretation. In searching, however, the technician would
make another classification based on the possible interpretation of
the pattern as a tented arch and search in that location of the files,
too.

Similar instances of doubt may occur in ridge counting or ridge
tracing. When there is doubt whether a ridge count is 9 or 10,
blocking out on the fingerprint card reveals that doubt in the form
of a 9?10 designation for the pattern. The same is true for ridge
traces in whorls, marked I?M or even I?M?O if it is impossible to
determine the ridge trace of a whorl with any degree of accuracy.

Reference searches are also conducted whenever an amputation
exists in a set of prints. It was explained in Chapter 3 how such sets
are classified. In searching through the file, however, one must keep
in mind that the subject's fingerprints might have been recorded
before the amputation occurred. For that reason, the file should be
searched under all combinations of classifications that could have
existed for a full set. The following example illustrates the practice:

I	M		9	
W	W	AMP	U	A
A	T	U	T	U
		7		5

In order to obtain the first classification for this set of prints, the
right middle amputation would be given the same interpretation as
that of the corresponding finger on the left hand, namely an ulnar
loop with a ridge count of 7. The classification would therefore be

7	17	W– –a	
17	aT–t		5

In searching, however, all other possible combinations would be substituted for the AMP on the right middle finger.

I	M		9					
W	W	A	U	A	9	17	Wa–a	
A	T	U	T	U		17	aT–t	5
		7		5				

I	M		9					
W	W	T	U	A	9	17	Wt–a	
A	T	U	T	U		17	aT–t	5
		7		5				

I	M	1?19	9					
W	W	R	U	A	1?19	17	Wr–a	
A	T	U	T	U		17	aT–t	5
		7		5				

I	M		9					
W	W	W	U	A	9	17	W– –a	
A	T	U	T	U		25	aT–t	5
		7		5				

When searching for the original classification, the key would have to be searched for from 1 through 19 (19 being the highest likely ridge count) because the key of 7 was arrived at by taking the ridge count of the left middle finger and because we have no way of knowing what the ridge count of the right middle finger would have been had it been an ulnar loop. The same is true for the third reference classification, where we substituted for the amputated pattern a radial loop interpretation of unknown ridge count. Because we are dealing with a small-letter secondary classification, there is no need to envision I, M or O combinations for the whorl in the fourth reference classification: they would not affect the formula.

DETERMINING HANDS AND FINGERS

It is not unusual at crime scenes to discover one or more series of latent prints which, from their relative positions, can be attributed to a right or a left hand, and even to specific fingers on the hand. Some ingenuity on the investigator's part is required, but the general shape and height of the prints provide some clues. Most latent prints are plain prints. And it is known that, in a set of inked plain prints, the middle fingerprint is highest in relative position to the

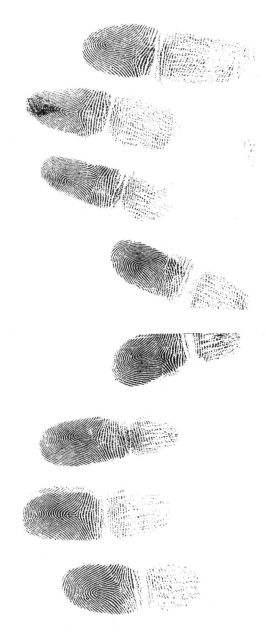

Figure 168. Left-hand plain prints.

Figure 167. Right-hand plain prints.

others, with the ring and index fingers successively lower. So it is possible to determine from fragments which fingers made the latent prints. Figure 167, for example, shows the plain prints of a right hand, and similar prints made by a left hand are shown in Figure 168. Even if some of the latent prints are blurred and are therefore useless for identification purposes, they can still sometimes aid the investigator in naming the fingers of the identifiable latent prints.

Most series of latent prints found at crime scenes are from index, middle and ring fingers. Thumb prints are usually found alone. On double-faced surfaces, fingerprints are usually found on one side and thumb prints on the other side because that is the natural way of grasping objects. While it is not always possible to determine from which hand a thumb print came, some indication can often be found in the shape and in the location of the prints, as well as in the size (thumb prints are usually larger than other fingerprints). A series of left- and right-hand thumb prints is shown in Figure 169. A careful study of them will reveal definite clues and correlations in size among the various left and right prints.

Experience has also taught us that most loops are ulnar loops and that most radial loops occur on index fingers. Radial loops seldom occur on thumbs; if they do, they are usually nutant loops. Central pocket loops and almond-shaped whorls usually have an ulnar trend (see Figure 170). Left-hand spiral whorls usually show clockwise spiraling, while right-hand whorls are most frequently counterclockwise spirals. Central pocket loops occur most frequently on ring fingers; double loops appear more often on thumbs than on other fingers.

SANDBERG KEY SEARCHING

Earlier in this chapter we indicated that it is practically impossible to search a few isolated latent prints found at a crime scene through the main ten-finger collection, unless to compare them with the fingerprints of known suspects. While it is possible to search the main files even if only one latent print is available, provided enough reference searches are made to allow for all possibilities, the task is almost hopeless. But it is not so seemingly futile when a number of latent prints from the same individual are found, and the probability for success is further improved when the search is conducted in small or medium-sized files.

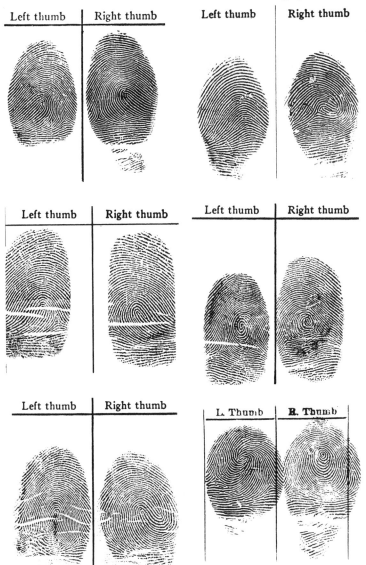

Figure 169. Left- and right-hand thumb prints.

In order to limit the primary classification to be searched when a partial set of prints is found, the late Lieutenant Fred Sandberg of the Metropolitan Police Department of Washington, D. C., devised a special "key" that, when used properly, eliminates irrelevant primary classifications in the ten-finger file (see Figure 171). In it, the

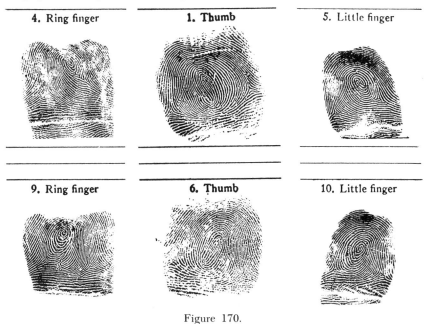

Figure 170.

capital letter W indicates a numerical pattern and blank squares represent nonnumerical patterns (loops and arches).

Suppose that five latent fingerprints are discovered at a crime scene and that from the positions of the latent prints it has been determined that four of the prints are from right-hand fingers (index, middle, ring and little fingers) while the fifth is assumed to be a left thumb print. The following patterns appear in the latent prints: right index, whorl; middle, ring and little, loops; left thumb, loop. Placing these known patterns in their natural sequence (as they would appear on a fingerprint card) and inserting question marks

NUMERATORS	1	2	3	4	5	6	7	8	9	10	11	12	13	14	15	16	17	18	19	20	21	22	23	24	25	26	27	28	29	30	31	32
R. Index Finger																	W	W	W	W	W	W	W	W	W	W	W	W	W	W	W	W
R. Ring Finger									W	W	W	W	W	W	W	W									W	W	W	W	W	W	W	W
L. Thumb					W	W	W	W					W	W	W	W					W	W	W	W					W	W	W	W
L. Middle Finger			W	W			W	W			W	W			W	W			W	W			W	W			W	W			W	W
L. Little Finger		W		W		W		W		W		W		W		W		W		W		W		W		W		W		W		W
DENOMINATORS	1	2	3	4	5	6	7	8	9	10	11	12	13	14	15	16	17	18	19	20	21	22	23	24	25	26	27	28	29	30	31	32
R. Thumb																	W	W	W	W	W	W	W	W	W	W	W	W	W	W	W	W
R. Middle Finger									W	W	W	W	W	W	W	W									W	W	W	W	W	W	W	W
R. Little Finger					W	W	W	W					W	W	W	W					W	W	W	W					W	W	W	W
L. Index Finger			W	W			W	W			W	W			W	W			W	W			W	W			W	W			W	W
L. Ring Finger		W		W		W		W		W		W		W		W		W		W		W		W		W		W		W		W

Figure 171. Sandberg Key.

for fingers with unknown pattern types, we arrive at the following ten-finger sequence:

?	W	U	U	U
U	?	?	?	?

By using the Sandberg Key it now becomes possible to determine which sections of the primary files might contain this set of prints. Because we know that the right index is a whorl pattern, the Key tells us that whorl patterns on right index fingers appear in primary numerators 17 through 32 (see Figure 172A, top row under Numerators). We also know that the right ring finger, which is a numerator finger in primary classification, has a loop on it. According to the Key, loops on right ring fingers, when there is also a whorl in the right index, can occur only in primaries 17 through 24 of the numerator (see Figure 172B, first two rows under Numerators). But we can narrow the search to even fewer primary numerators because we also know that the pattern type of the left thumb (also a numerator finger) is a loop. When we know that the right index is a whorl, that the right ring is a loop and that the left thumb is also a loop, the Key tells us that a set of prints with these three known patterns can be found only in primaries 17 through 20 (see Figure 172C, first three rows under Numerators). We know now that the primary numerator for the set of prints must be 17, 18, 19 or 20. If that were all the information we had, we would have to search all the cards on file with numerators 17 through 20 among all the denominators 1 through 32. That is, the search would have to include all of these primary classifications:

17	18	19	20	17	18	19	20	17	18	19	20	17	18	19	20
1	1	1	1	2	2	2	2	3	3	3	3	4	4	4	4

and so on up to $\frac{17}{32}$ $\frac{18}{32}$ $\frac{19}{32}$ and $\frac{20}{32}$.

However, our hypothetical criminal also left two latent prints from fingers that are represented in the denominator of the primary —the loops on the right middle and right little fingers. In consulting the Key under Right Middle Finger we note that a nonnumerical pattern such as a loop can appear in primary denominators 1 through 8 and 17 through 24 (see Figure 172A, wavy line under Denominators). We have therefore eliminated half of the primary

A

NUMERATORS	1	2	3	4	5	6	7	8	9	10	11	12	13	14	15	16	17	18	19	20	21	22	23	24	25	26	27	28	29	30	31	32
R. Index Finger																	w	w	w	w	w	w	w	w	w	w	w	w	w	w	w	w
R. Ring Finger									w	w	w	w	w	w	w	w									w	w	w	w	w	w	w	w
L. Thumb					w	w	w	w					w	w	w	w					w	w	w	w					w	w	w	w
L. Middle Finger			w	w			w	w			w	w			w	w			w	w			w	w			w	w			w	w
L. Little Finger		w		w		w		w		w		w		w		w		w		w		w		w		w		w		w		w
DENOMINATORS	1	2	3	4	5	6	7	8	9	10	11	12	13	14	15	16	17	18	19	20	21	22	23	24	25	26	27	28	29	30	31	32
R. Thumb																	w	w	w	w	w	w	w	w	w	w	w	w	w	w	w	w
R. Middle Finger									w	w	w	w	w	w	w	w									w	w	w	w	w	w	w	w
R. Little Finger					w	w	w	w					w	w	w	w					w	w	w	w					w	w	w	w
L. Index Finger			w	w			w	w			w	w			w	w			w	w			w	w			w	w			w	w
L. Ring Finger		w		w		w		w		w		w		w		w		w		w		w		w		w		w		w		w

B

NUMERATORS	1	2	3	4	5	6	7	8	9	10	11	12	13	14	15	16	17	18	19	20	21	22	23	24	25	26	27	28	29	30	31	32
R. Index Finger																	w	w	w	w	w	w	w	w	w	w	w	w	w	w	w	w
R. Ring Finger									w	w	w	w	w	w	w	w									w	w	w	w	w	w	w	w
L. Thumb					w	w	w	w					w	w	w	w					w	w	w	w					w	w	w	w
L. Middle Finger			w	w			w	w			w	w			w	w			w	w			w	w			w	w			w	w
L. Little Finger		w		w		w		w		w		w		w		w		w		w		w		w		w		w		w		w
DENOMINATORS	1	2	3	4	5	6	7	8	9	10	11	12	13	14	15	16	17	18	19	20	21	22	23	24	25	26	27	28	29	30	31	32
R. Thumb																	w	w	w	w	w	w	w	w	w	w	w	w	w	w	w	w
R. Middle Finger									w	w	w	w	w	w	w	w									w	w	w	w	w	w	w	w
R. Little Finger					w	w	w	w					w	w	w	w					w	w	w	w					w	w	w	w
L. Index Finger			w	w			w	w			w	w			w	w			w	w			w	w			w	w			w	w
L. Ring Finger		w		w		w		w		w		w		w		w		w		w		w		w		w		w		w		w

C

NUMERATORS	1	2	3	4	5	6	7	8	9	10	11	12	13	14	15	16	17	18	19	20	21	22	23	24	25	26	27	28	29	30	31	32
R. Index Finger																	w	w	w	w	w	w	w	w	w	w	w	w	w	w	w	w
R. Ring Finger									w	w	w	w	w	w	w	w									w	w	w	w	w	w	w	w
L. Thumb					w	w	w	w					w	w	w	w					w	w	w	w					w	w	w	w
L. Middle Finger			w	w			w	w			w	w			w	w			w	w			w	w			w	w			w	w
L. Little Finger		w		w		w		w		w		w		w		w		w		w		w		w		w		w		w		w
DENOMINATORS	1	2	3	4	5	6	7	8	9	10	11	12	13	14	15	16	17	18	19	20	21	22	23	24	25	26	27	28	29	30	31	32
R. Thumb																	w	w	w	w	w	w	w	w	w	w	w	w	w	w	w	w
R. Middle Finger									w	w	w	w	w	w	w	w									w	w	w	w	w	w	w	w
R. Little Finger					w	w	w	w					w	w	w	w					w	w	w	w					w	w	w	w
L. Index Finger			w	w			w	w			w	w			w	w			w	w			w	w			w	w			w	w
L. Ring Finger		w		w		w		w		w		w		w		w		w		w		w		w		w		w		w		w

Figure 172. Sandberg Key. (Courtesy: Institute of Applied Science.)

denominators. We know that the right little finger is also a nonnumerical pattern (a loop), or the combination of two loops in the denominator on the right middle and right little fingers can only occur in primary denominators 1 through 4 and 17 through 20 (see Figure 172B, wavy line under Denominators). Thus we can locate the criminal's prints by searching all primary numerators 17 through 20 over all denominators 1 through 4 and 17 through 20. We therefore have only thirty-two possible primary combinations to search through (instead of 1,024 possible primary divisions), in one of which the criminal's complete set of prints will be found if they are on file. These are the only possible primary combinations in our hypothetical case:

| $\frac{17}{1}$ | $\frac{18}{1}$ | $\frac{19}{1}$ | $\frac{20}{1}$ | $\frac{17}{2}$ | $\frac{18}{2}$ | $\frac{19}{2}$ | $\frac{20}{2}$ | $\frac{17}{3}$ | $\frac{18}{3}$ | $\frac{19}{3}$ | $\frac{20}{3}$ | $\frac{17}{4}$ | $\frac{18}{4}$ | $\frac{19}{4}$ | $\frac{20}{4}$ |

| $\frac{17}{17}$ | $\frac{18}{17}$ | $\frac{19}{17}$ | $\frac{20}{17}$ | $\frac{17}{18}$ | $\frac{18}{18}$ | $\frac{19}{18}$ | $\frac{20}{18}$ | $\frac{17}{19}$ | $\frac{18}{19}$ | $\frac{19}{19}$ | $\frac{20}{19}$ | $\frac{17}{20}$ | $\frac{18}{20}$ | $\frac{19}{20}$ | $\frac{20}{20}$ |

MECHANICAL SEARCHING

Although the largest identification bureaus maintain that it is possible to search for a specific card in their gigantic collections and retrieve it within fifteen minutes, in practice many factors hinder searches for hours or even days. It is not surprising, then, that many attempts have been made to speed searches of identification records. Among the means suggested and used have been mechanical searches using IBM punch cards and sorters, microfilm, and electronic optical scanners and retrievers. In early 1969, the Atlanta, Georgia, police identification bureau became the first department to begin storing its identification records on a microfilm information-retrieval system, which reduced the standard fingerprint records to quarter-inch images on a 100-foot-long roll of microfilm. The system's capability is said to reduce a search to 18 seconds. Other research is now developing even more sophisticated optical scanners for ten-finger files.

Searching fingerprint files by means of IBM sorters dates back to the 1930s and the New York State Division of Criminal Identification, now part of the New York State Identification and Intelligence System (NYSIIS). As early as 1937, the New York state bureau searched loop patterns in the 1-over-1 primary by mechanical means. (Even earlier, though, the National Bureau in Washington employed a similar method, but little is known about it.) In April, 1953, the New York bureau extended its search to all primary groups as a result of converting its fingerprint files to a serial number searching system. Instead of filing by classification, the agency started keying its cards mechanically. The system is still used. Upon receipt of a fingerprint card, a technician counts the ridges of every loop and whorl in the set, then records the counts in the upper right-hand corner of each block in the space normally reserved for the ridge count during the blocking-out process under conventional filing methods. The card passes next to a classifier who writes in the special New York classification in the customary place. From that station, the card moves to one of two electronic sorting machines and IBM punch cards (see Figure 173) are made from the data. They can be sorted at the rate of 450 cards per minute by a machine that automatically separates the punch cards having the same ridge counts as the set of prints being searched. When a small number of cards with "possible idents" is turned up, a further search of the cards is made using primary classification and any other available identification data. The final check is a visual comparison of the selected punch cards and the fingerprints they represent. If the search fails to turn up a matching set, an IBM punch card for that set is prepared and placed in the proper section of the file. Fingerprint records are filed chronologically according to date of receipt, rather than by fingerprint classification, and the file number is noted on the punch card for easy cross-reference.

William E. Cashin, director of the New York bureau in 1953, explained the twelve advantages of this method to a meeting of identification officers held in New York when the method was introduced. He observed that:

1. While all ten fingers are considered in the search, each finger is considered separately as well.

2. Tolerances for human error in ridge counting are provided for

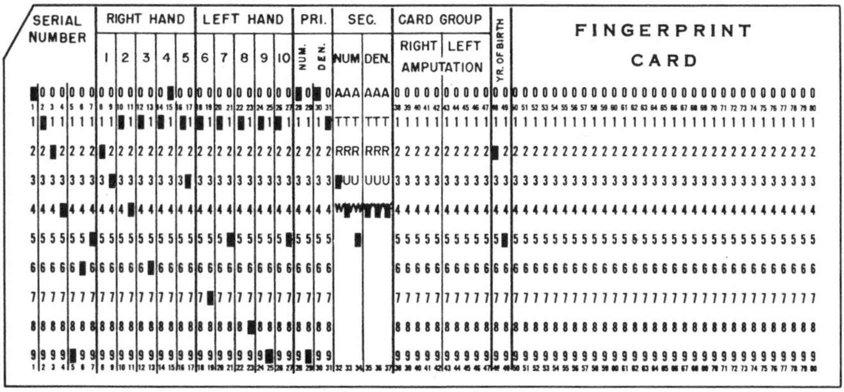

Figure 173. An IBM punch card used in 1953 by the New York State identification bureau for searching fingerprints at the rate of 450 cards per minute. (Courtesy: New York Department of Corrections.)

by searching two counts higher and lower if the ridge count is 15 or less, or three counts higher and lower if the count is above 15.

3. By searching each finger at the same time, any type of pattern that can appear in the particular set of prints is searched. If, for example, the set of prints contains loops, whorls, an arch and a small-letter radial loop, all of these combinations are searched at the same time.

4. Reference searches according to primary, secondary and final classifications are made simultaneously with the original search.

5. If the reference search involves a primary classification, the searching machine prints the primaries searched as well as the total number of cards handled, and includes the date of birth and serial number for each possible identification.

6. When the ridge count for a finger is unknown because the finger was bandaged and no print was obtained, or because the finger was amputated or its skin scarred or blurred, a provision can be made to select all possibilities for the particular finger or fingers.

7. The process of electronic searching reduces the classification to a series of numbers; the technical sequence is no longer a consideration. For that reason, fingerprints are filed in chronological order, which of course means that a 32-over-32 primary might well be filed before a 1-over-1 primary.

8. The speed of the search, 450 cards per minute, is faster and affords more accuracy than any other known method.

9. Latent impressions and personal descriptions can also be searched more rapidly and easily because of the great tolerance that can be built into the search. This advantage avoids considerable eye strain because the machine does all preliminary elimination work and reduces visual scanning to only those cards that fall within the tolerances.

10. Filing fingerprints is easier and less subject to error. Since they are filed by serial number, they are more easily located in a numerical file than by looking through fingerprint classifications.

11. The print out of the primary classification shows that reference searches have been made. The print out of other data, such as serial numbers and dates of birth, permits quicker comparison of prints.

12. The carbon copy of all machine printing provides a daily report that is valuable for statistical and budgetary purposes.

AUTOMATIC CLASSIFICATION

The New York system of mechanical searching instituted in 1953 still requires the intervention of fingerprint experts to interpret fingerprint patterns, to count ridges and to assign classifications to sets of prints. For many decades, it was felt that the expertise of the technician or classifier could not be done away with, that a machine could never replace the human element. One of the primary reasons for that belief was that the prints of one finger do not show up as identical on subsequent recording attempts. The thickness of the lines vary depending on the amount of ink used and on the amount of pressure applied while printing. The physical measurements of distances between certain ridge characteristics within two subsequent prints of the same finger may contain extremely minute variances depending on the amount of pressure applied by the finger, a factor known to technicians as pressure distortion. It does not present a great deal of trouble to an experienced technician, but it could disrupt machine processing.

Independent of the continuing research of the New York bureau and the FBI, John A. Fitzmaurice, a scientist working for Baird-Atomics, Inc., of Cambridge, Mass., devoted considerable research to the problem of optical scanning in the early 1960s.

Fitzmaurice arrived at the conclusion that no headway toward computerization could be made so long as the traditional method of classification and interpretation of patterns remained the cornerstone of fingerprinting. Machines could not be effectively programed to make distinctions among questionable pattern types based on arbitrary rules of interpretation on which technicians often disagree. Proceeding from the premise that as far as establishing identity was concerned interpretation and classification are irrelevant because identity is established by comparing individual ridge characteristics rather than pattern types, Fitzmaurice and others concluded that interpretation could profitably be bypassed if a machine could be devised to catalog, file and compare fingerprints by individual characteristics alone.

Approaching the problem from that standpoint, Fitzmaurice studied ridge minutiae and decided that, since a computer would have difficulty distinguishing between ridge endings and bifurcations, he would make no distinction between the two and consider them as one characteristic only. In attempting to mark all such ridge characteristics and assign a value of one to each of them (see Figure 174C), he also assigned an arbitrary value of zero to all areas of the pattern not exhibiting characteristics. This process would have rather limited use unless a scheme could be provided by which these locations could be correlated. Fitzmaurice suggested placing a grid of 2,500 squares over the fingerprint so that the locations of the characteristics could be designated by counting the number of squares horizontally and vertically from the lower left-hand corner of the grid (see Figure 174D and E). The most critical test of any automatic classification system is the capability of the apparatus to allow for pressure distortion, and Fitzmaurice indicated that he solved this problem by providing "cells" of nine squares for each ridge characteristic, with the ridge detail theoretically placed in the center square (as illustrated in Figure 174D),

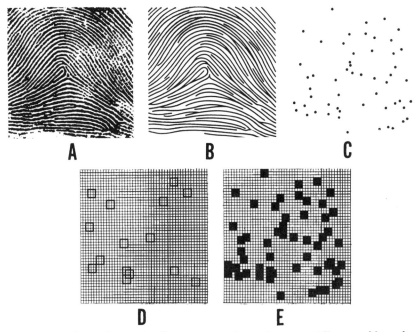

Figure 174. After reducing the fingerprint in A to what essentially resembles a line drawing (see B), Fitzmaurice pointed out all of the ridge characteristics in a pattern, as shown in C. By superimposing a grid upon the patterns and allowing for reference indications in eight surrounding squares of the grid, as shown in D, enough flexibility was provided to take pressure distortion into account. The location coordinates of the characteristics in pattern A are illustrated in E. (Courtesy: Baird-Atomics, Inc.)

which would provide for location coordinates that afford a degree of flexibility.

For the system to be workable and practical, the fingerprint file has to be converted to a new type of classification system that is based on the location of the individual characteristics within a print. The new classifications are stored in the memory core of a computer. Fitzmaurice advocates scanning the prints by a spot of light moving horizontally across the print while oscillating vertically at high speed, one row of cells on the grid at a time. The output signal of the scanner transforms the ordinary fingerprint image into a sharp line image (compare Figure 174A and B), after which recognition of individual characteristics becomes relatively easy. The final output of this detector stage is stored on magnetic tape. The scanner can operate in such a manner that approximately thirty-six sets of ten fingers are handled by each machine, which can classify about six thousand sets of prints per week of continuous operation.

That is a relatively slow speed compared to the high speed at which magnetic tape is usually operated in normal computer operations. For control purposes, therefore, the scanning output tape is first stored in a small computer. It can be transferred later to magnetic tape for high-speed use in the core memory banks of a larger computer. The fingerprints themselves are stored numerically according to a system similar to that used for years by the New York bureau.

In searching through the core memory, the technician orders the grid coordinates of individual characteristics of a latent print to be compared with the playback of the memory tape through a two-dimensional "shift register." Whenever a close match is found, a print out of the file number of the fingerprint is made. The cards with matching coordinates can then be manually pulled from the numerical file and visually compared.

Fitzmaurice's system incorporates some excellent concepts of the machine searching and scanning of fingerprints, but it also suffers from considerable defects. There is the seemingly insoluble problem of fitting the grid over a fingerprint in such a way that different technicians can properly locate it time after time, although Fitzmaurice suggested that the grid could be multiply tested and placed in varying positions. The problem of natural finger growth —youth versus adult—is also vexing, and to solve it Fitzmaurice suggested that grids of various sizes be made in a manner directly proportional to the average spacing of the ridges. But that seems highly impractical. Nevertheless, Fitzmaurice's contributions to computerized retrieval systems in fingerprinting are valuable, especially his conception of the need to abandon traditional classification procedures in favor of a totally new approach. That concept has been responsible for the advances made in recent years by a number of other scientists.

THE NYSIIS EXPERIENCE

A tremendous breakthrough in fingerprint information retrieval and information sharing has been noted in New York State in the last decade. While research has by no means been limited to that state, New York deserves the credit for approaching information sharing and fingerprint automation as part of an overall revision of traditional methods of communication in law enforcement. The impetus for this research effort was provided, ironically, by a frustrating incident in which fingerprints did not play a major role.

In November, 1957, more than one hundred of the nation's top mobsters gathered at a lonely resort in New York State for a high-level conference on ways to improve the gains of organized crime. After the event, soon dubbed the notorious "Appalachian Meeting," a special commission was created in the state to determine the purpose of the meeting and the identity of all who attended.

Since not much cooperation was forthcoming from the participants in the main event, the task of gathering information on these men proved to be formidable. After two years of work the task was still far from done. One participant was the subject of more than two hundred separate police files in New York alone. It was the frustration generated by their old-fashioned system of record keeping that prompted the New York state authorities to do something about bringing information sharing and retrieval up to date. Governor Nelson Rockefeller started the New York State Identification and Intelligence System (NYSIIS) in May 1963 and assigned it the task of studying the feasibility of applying electronic data-processing techniques to criminal justice.

A team of top experts and renowned scientists in both computation and identification published a feasibility report in November, 1963, envisioning a complete overhaul of record keeping and information sharing in law enforcement. Almost immediately thereafter, the old state identification bureau was transferred from the Department of Correction to NYSIIS under the general directorship of Robert R. L. Gallati. The noted fingerprint expert Paul D. McCann, formerly head of the state identification bureau, became a deputy director in NYSIIS in charge of identification.

Affecting the whole system of criminal justice, NYSIIS started working immediately to streamline fingerprint work by instituting intensive field testing of the transmission of fingerprints over telephone lines. By the beginning of 1968, the network of direct communication links of this nature to the central bureau in Albany reached some 3,600 law enforcement agencies in the state. Any local station can now transmit fingerprints to Albany within fourteen minutes, and the results of the search through the main file reach the initiating department within a matter of hours. Before the network became operative, arrest fingerprint cards required about a week for processing. But local departments that send fingerprint cards for routine checks against the main FBI file in Washington, D. C., sometimes still wait ten to fourteen days for a reply because of the volume of cards handled by the FBI.

Along with its new services in information sharing, the NYSIIS team has also studied electronic classifying and searching of fingerprints and has achieved remarkable results. By July, 1968, the system's computerized procedure made it possible to compare arrest fingerprint cards with over 1,600,000 sets of prints on file within twenty-five seconds. Within a matter of minutes, the department contributing the arrest cards over the facsimile network is notified whether or not a prior record exists. Before the computer's installation, mechanical searches often took as long as an hour.

Research is continuing into how latent prints discovered at crime scenes can be electronically searched against the entire ten-finger file rather than against the latent print base file, which contains the records of some twenty thousand habitual criminals. No such system exists at present, but the research of NYSIIS indicates that the technical requirements can be met by a system that is expected to become operational within a few years.

Several approaches are being considered. The favored one involves optical enlargement on the screen of a special console. The person assigned the responsibility of classifying the print would point to each ridge detail with a special electronic pencil in order to establish its numerical classification, which would be automatically recorded in a computer. Searching the file would be a computer function. By using fingerprint identifiers such as hand, finger and pattern type, as well as the distance between the core and the delta, the computer would eliminate large portions of the file from scanning. The remaining fingerprint records stored in the memory of the computer would then be searched by being compared with the coordinates of the ridge characteristics computed by the technician during classification. All file prints whose characteristics match a prescribed number of locations in the questioned print would be printed out for visual comparison. If no identification of the latent print were made, the computer would of course add the print to the unidentified latent print file. Because all incoming arrest cards would thereby be compared with the unidentified latent print, unsolved problems might well be cleared up automatically. Even though it is still only on the drawing board, the NYSIIS team feels that such a system of computer searches will be sufficiently accurate, when introduced, to limit tentative matches to several possibilities.

OTHER RESEARCH

The NYSIIS project is by no means the only one that is being effectively pursued. In the early part of 1969, the Cornell Aeronautical Laboratory at Buffalo, New York, demonstrated an engineering model of a fingerprint reader designed for an evaluation of the feasibility of developing a computerized fingerprint classification and searching system. According to the scientists working on the system being developed for the FBI, the engineering model is able to process one fingerprint every twelve seconds, and it is expected that much higher speeds can be obtained. Not designed to match fingerprints, the reader is able only to find and code ridge minutiae. The system will make it possible for a computer to examine a fingerprint and to identify and locate ridge endings and bifurcations. It employs a combination of electro-optical, analog computer and digital computer techniques.

At the First and Second Symposia on Law Enforcement, Science and Technology, sponsored by the Illinois Institute of Technology Research Institute (IITRI) and held in 1968 and 1969, several papers were presented that dealt with the application of computer technology to fingerprint searching. In reviewing the available data, C. B. Shelman of the Argonne National Laboratory, a researcher in the field, determined that automatic fingerprint-processing systems should be built according to these standards:

1. The scanners should accept the standard 8 x 8 inch filing cards, so as not to render obsolete the present filing system.

2. The prints must be reduced by the machine to a numerical code-type classification for bulk storage purposes.

3. The code should be processed in such a manner that prints can be categorized into at least two levels of classification, to make it unnecessary to search the entire file to identify an unknown print.

4. Partial latent impressions should be processed so that a high degree of probability exists that the print can be matched with the one on file, if one exists in the collection.

5. It must also be possible for the automated system to accept human intervention if a latent print is beyond machine interpretation.

Shelman also felt that the following capabilities should be included in any special-purpose scanning equipment:

1. Complete automation by translating and rotating a print to establish a reference system, which could be accomplished by the development of a translational- and rotational-invariant descriptor.

2. An ability to scan small areas of a fingerprint, both in the horizontal and vertical directions. [The data-reduction schemes that Shelman's study developed required the availability of ridge coordinates of a given area in both the horizontal and vertical directions.]

3. Considerable computing capacity, because each print produces about 50,000 points of raw data to be translated and assimilated in the computation system. To prevent the need for prohibitively large and expensive storage, each area of the print must be processed before proceeding to the next area.

4. An ability to accept a given area for processing, or to reject the area if it is beyond machine interpretation. The condition of an impression requires the equipment to process prints where a portion is beyond machine interpretation, in some cases beyond human interpretation. The system should be capable of processing the data that are available.

5. An ability to categorize and store all prints.

Shelman's research at Argonne was conducted with a flying spot scanner, which was under the control of a small general-purpose

Figure 175. A fingerprint with a grid overlay and symbol designators, as used by Shelman in Argonne National Laboratory experiments with the CHLOE flying spot scanner and the ASI 210 computer. (Courtesy: Argonne National Laboratory.)

computer. Input/output was by magnetic tape, paper type or typewriter. He also utilized a grid overlay (see Figure 175) and, following Fitzmaurice's lead, considered only ridge endings and bifurcations. The machine extracted two types of information from the fingerprints: ridge slopes (to be used as a type of primary classification) and ridge minutiae (endings and bifurcations, to serve as a secondary classification as well as for positive identification).

While totally automated filing and searching systems are not yet a reality, they should certainly become operational within a decade. Does that mean the next generation will have no need for fingerprint experts? Not at all. Every automated system requires human operators with specialized knowledge in fingerprint identification. The final determination of the identity, or lack of it, of any two prints will still have to be made by a trained and experienced fingerprint expert. A shift in job emphasis will undoubtedly occur, since classifiers, filers and searchers will probably see their jobs become obsolete, but the same technicians will find new responsibilities in the jobs created to operate automated systems. So automation will not reduce manpower needs but rather will dramatically increase the fingerprint-processing capabilities of present staffs. Instead of being able to search for a few latent prints a day in a limited five-finger or single-print file containing only thousands of cards, fingerprint technicians will direct and work with machines that will be able to search for latent prints discovered at crime scenes among the millions of cards filed in regional and national identification bureaus.

Chapter 10

Comparison of Fingerprints

FUNCTIONS IN THE IDENTIFICATION BUREAU

A number of functions are associated with working in an identification division. Some of them require a great deal of training and experience; others demand very little. The lowest ranking function would be that of recording fingerprints of arrestees. In most police departments this job is handled by a patrolman, a police cadet, or a civilian employe whose duties include a wide variety of work unconnected with the fingerprint technique itself. He probably does not receive more than an hour or so of training before assuming the duties of *fingerprint recorder*. The man who fulfills that function, then, is *not* a fingerprint technician and need not have any knowledge of the principles of fingerprint identification.

A second function in fingerprinting is the searching of crime scenes to discover latent impressions. This requires more training. The *latent print technician* must know the basic nature of latent prints, as well as the various techniques involved in making hidden impressions visible on a variety of surfaces, using a diversity of developing media (powders, vapors, chemicals). He must also be able to lift and photograph crime scene prints, and know how to deal with evidential materials. The latent print technician, in other words, requires training as well as experience. Yet, his training and experience may be in the limited field in which he is asked to function. He need not necessarily be skilled in the interpretation of various finger patterns, nor does he have to know the techniques of
252

comparing latent and inked impressions. In some departments, members of the detective division are trained in searching crime scenes for chance impressions.

A third function in fingerprinting is that of interpreting and classifying the recorded impressions received in the identification division. This is truly a function of the *fingerprint technician,* for he must be thoroughly schooled in all of the phases of the science of fingerprints. The responsibility rests upon him of classifying and filing fingerprints according to proper procedures so that the files may serve the purpose for which they were intended. He must, by similar procedures, search the files to determine if arrestees have been previously fingerprinted. He must, then, also know how to establish identity by fingerprints. Yet, if his function were limited to the work just described, he would not need to have practical experience in comparing latent prints with inked impressions. In fact, in many large departments fingerprint technicians may do nothing but interpret fingerprint cards, while others may do nothing but search the files, or work out classifications on cards.

The ultimate function in fingerprinting involves the comparison of latent and inked impressions to determine whether the latent image was made by the same finger that printed the inked impression. This responsibility is the most difficult in the broad field of fingerprinting, yet it is also designated by the term fingerprint technician, permitting possible confusion with respect to the exact work a "fingerprint technician" is called upon to do. It would probably be better for the profession to reserve the designation of fingerprint technician for the specialists who compare inked and latent impressions, and call those who are primarily engaged in interpreting and filing fingerprint cards "fingerprint classifiers."

The fingerprint technician, using the term in its ultimate function of a person comparing latent and inked prints, requires a thorough knowledge of all of the phases of fingerprinting. He must have, therefore, adequate training as well as long practice and experience.

Interpreting and classifying fingerprint patterns is generally referred to as a "science," but the comparison of latent and inked impressions is more properly classifiable as an art. Despite adequate guidelines and rules to aid the technician, the actual comparison requires skill acquired through long experience in working with latent and inked impressions. Moreover, good fingerprint classifiers may never acquire the necessary skill and practice to become good identification technicians.

There are a number of subsidiary functions in the fingerprint field and in the work of identification bureaus, especially in the larger ones which tend to have specialized and departmentalized functions, but of all concerned with fingerprints the "fingerprint technician" deserves undoubtedly to rank highest. In some departments, especially the smaller ones, an individual may be fully qualified in all or several of the functions associated with fingerprint work. This is generally also true of the supervisory personnel in bureaus of all sizes.

No reference has been made to the designation of fingerprint "expert," since that title is not a function associated with identification work. A person is an expert when a court of law decides that, on the basis of his special skills and training in a given field, he is allowed to render opinion evidence on the witness stand. An ordinary witness may generally testify only as to facts within his own knowledge. A person who has qualified as an expert in the eyes of the court, however, may not only testify as to facts within his knowledge but also express opinions with respect to the conclusions to be drawn from his specialist's findings. A fingerprint "expert," then, is simply a fingerprint technician who has demonstrated to the satisfaction of a court that he has such knowledge and experience in his field as will qualify him to express opinions about identity or nonidentity of fingerprints.*

Since there are a number of different fingerprint tasks, the training required to become proficient at one's tasks will be more or less depending on the stature of the function. We need concern ourselves only with the requirements of proficiency which lead to the highest function, that of the technician who is asked to testify in court concerning the identity or nonidentity of fingerprints connected with a legal controversy, civil or criminal.

In law, an expert is a person who is permitted by the court to give opinion evidence in a field which requires special skills that a jury might not be expected to possess. Before the court will determine that a witness is an expert, the witness must be shown to have special competence or proficiency which has been acquired *through*

---

* The legal aspects of fingerprint work, as well as examples of direct and cross-examination of fingerprint witnesses, are explored in another book by the same author, titled *Fingerprints And The Law*, published by Chilton in 1969.

study or experience or both. While this purports to be a fairly accurate statement of the law with respect to expert testimony in general, the fingerprint profession could not agree with these requirements in its own field. An individual could not possibly become a fingerprint technician with the skills necessary to render testimony in court solely on the basis of study. In fingerprinting, *both are required:* experience is the indispensable element.

There are various ways in which the requirement of "study" can be met. One can satisfactorily complete special training courses; one could receive training from a qualified fingerprint technician who himself has the knowledge and experience required to qualify as an expert in court; or one could make a thorough study of the available literature in the field. Any of these three might result in acquiring the necessary training or study. Experience, however, can only be achieved by actually working with latent and inked impressions. There would be no hard and fast rule to determine the length of time that should be devoted to actual work with latent and inked impressions, inside or outside a law enforcement agency, because it would depend obviously on individual ability. It would seem, however, that *a minimum* of two years of full-time work with fingerprints would be required, *after* one had already acquired a thorough understanding of all of the various aspects of fingerprinting through study or training.

Reference was made to acquiring the basic knowledge in the field by taking fingerprint courses. There are no college or university-level degree programs in fingerprint identification. Undergraduate or graduate degrees, therefore, have no relevance to determining the proficiency of an individual *in fingerprint identification.* Training courses are available from private sources (such as the Institute of Applied Science in Chicago), law enforcement agencies on the federal, state, and local level, and a few isolated colleges, universities or schools. No course of study, however, qualifies an individual to be a fingerprint "expert" and none purports to do so. At the most, the training thus provided gives one a sufficient and necessary background to start actual work in the field. Study can never be a substitute for experience in fingerprint identification, although it is an essential adjunct.

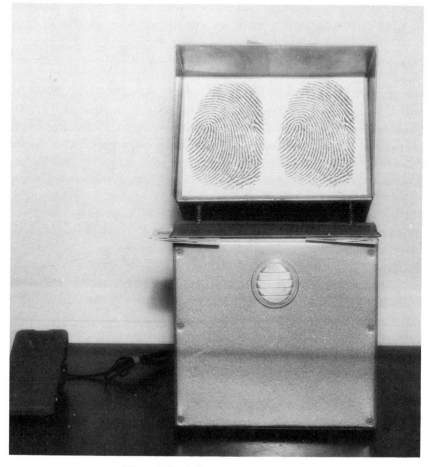

Figure 176. A fingerprint comparator.

ESTABLISHING IDENTITY BY FINGERPRINTS

The equipment necessary for studying and evaluating fingerprints is simple and inexpensive. It consists basically of at least one
good fingerprint magnifier and a ridge counter. A fingerprint magnifier is a magnifying lens (magnification of 3x to 6x) mounted in a
special stand with a horseshoe base. The base of the magnifier is
grooved to accommodate special fingerprint reticles which are useful
in interpreting and classifying. For the purpose of studying the individual ridge characteristics, however, such reticles are not necessary. A ridge counter is essentially a pointed instrument about 5–7

inches long, looking much like a crochet needle with a point rather than a hook at the end.

Comparison of latent and inked prints is usually done without enlargement other than that provided by the magnifier. There are certain instruments on the market, called "comparators," which consist essentially of a light box with a mirror arrangement, enlarging lenses and a viewing screen approximately 10 to 12 inches high and 20 to 25 inches wide. One such comparator is illustrated in Fig. 176. Two natural-size fingerprints can be positioned under the two lenses of the instrument. When the light is activated, an enlargement of about 5 x 7 inches of each fingerprint appears side by side on the viewing screen for easy comparison. Many departments use such comparators, but most skilled technicians prefer to use fingerprint magnifiers.

Apart from the traditional horseshoe fingerprint magnifiers, a number of other optical enlarging systems and instruments have been manufactured and enjoy limited use. They are worthwhile accessories for the technician who prefers working with them. The one thing all of these instruments must have in common to make them suitable for fingerprint comparison work is that they enlarge a whole fingerprint, not just a small portion of it, which is why microscopes are not suitable for ordinary fingerprint comparison work.

In discussions about microscopes in fingerprint identification, the instrument that is usually referred to provides great enlargement (from 25 to 1000 times) of a small area. The higher the power of magnification of the optical instrument, the smaller the area that is seen through the lens. Depending on the degree of magnification, one might not see any ridges at all but simply fragments of a ridge or particles of fingerprint powder in latent prints, or wood or paper fibers if the prints are on wood or paper.

In comparing fingerprints, it is necessary to study the various ridge characteristics and their interrelationships. Compound microscopes do not permit such examination.

Magnification provided by optical viewing instruments must be distinguished from photographic enlargement, which enlarges the whole area of a print rather than progressively smaller portions of it. Photographic enlargements are not necessary for the technician's study of fingerprints. They are made only after he has decided that the prints are identical and when he wishes to prepare exhibits to aid him in explaining his conclusions to a court or jury.

To determine whether or not two prints are identical, a technician must evaluate four variable factors.

General Pattern Agreement

The known and unknown prints must be of the same pattern
type. Obviously, prints from different classes of patterns, such as an
arch and a loop, could not possibly be made by the same finger. But
similarity of pattern is only a class characteristic, since all fingerprint patterns fall within three main classes and eight secondary
groups in the Henry system (loops, whorls, arches; radial and ulnar
loops, plain whorls, central pocket loops, double loops, accidentals,
plain arches and tented arches). While agreement in pattern type is
required, it does not by itself establish identity unless the other
three variable factors also agree.

Essential though pattern concordance is for proving identity,
such agreement can be proven circumstantially in some instances.
It is not necessary that the unknown print show to what pattern
type it belongs because it is not required that a complete pattern be
shown to establish identity. As long as the friction skin area of the
latent has sufficient ridge detail to satisfy the third variable factor
in identification (the quantitative factor), it is possible to identify
the print positively. Most latent prints do not show all of the ridge
detail on a finger. Parts are often blurred. Yet only a minor portion
of the print is necessary to provide positive identification. Eighteen
identical points have been charted in Figure 177, proving that the
latent print on the left was made by the same finger that recorded
the inked impression on the right. It is impossible, from that illustration, to determine pattern type. However, from the identical flow
of the ridges, and from the similarity in general shape and form of
the visible ridges, it may be deduced that both are of the same pattern type.

Qualitative Concordance

A comparison of both prints must reveal that the ridge characteristics of both are of the same type and shape. Ridge endings, bifurcations, enclosures, and so forth must be the same in both prints.
They must also be of the same shape and face the same direction. It
is not sufficient to establish the presence of a bifurcation at a given

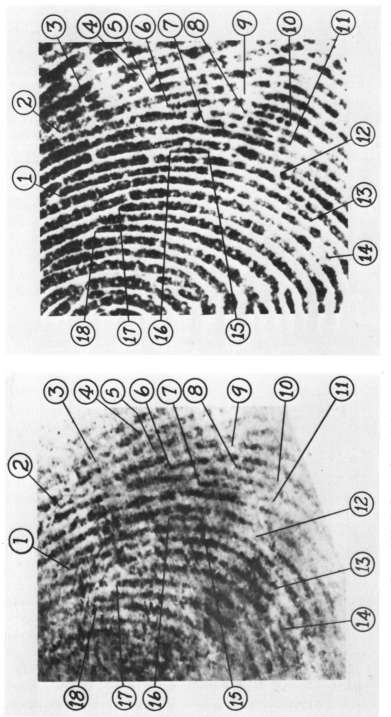

Figure 177. Eighteen identical characteristics in a latent print and an inked impression.

place in both prints, for example, because the bifurcation must fork in the same direction in both prints.

Quantitative Factor

The quantitative factor involves determining how many ridge characteristics are needed to prove identity. It is generally agreed in this country that ten to twelve matching points are needed to prove identity, but those figures are only a rough guide that provides a safety factor. It is impossible to say definitely how many characteristics are needed to prove identity because it is essentially a determination that must be made by the technician on the basis of his experience. Fewer than ten characteristics can be sufficient to prove identity. In fact, it is possible for a technician to prove identity on the basis of only seven or eight characteristics, if some of them are very unusual types or combinations.

Some characteristics occur more often than others. Ridge endings and bifurcations are among the most frequent. Islands (ridge dots), enclosures and trifurcations occur far less frequently. Finding several of the latter characteristics closely interrelated would have much more value as proof of identity than finding the same number of ridge endings in the same relationship.

Relationship of Ridge Characteristics

The final variable factor in the examination of known and unknown prints is determining that the same ridge characteristics found in both prints are similarly interrelated, or intervene in the same way, in both. This means that the number of ridges that intervene between two given characteristics in the latent print must be the same as the number of ridges intervening between the same two characteristics of the inked print.

COMPARING FINGERPRINTS

A basic premise in identification is that a given number of identical ridge characteristics must occur in two prints, as determined by an evaluation of the four variable factors, without unexplained dissimilarities. Many dissimilarities between latent and inked prints can be explained, so they are insignificant. A latent print is never a mirror image, never an exact reproduction, of an inked impression. The study of dissimilarities, then, tests the knowledge and experience of the technician.

An inked print is purposely rolled from nail to nail. It will therefore give a complete image of all of the ridge detail present on the friction skin of the finger, provided, of course, that the print was properly rolled and recorded.

A latent print, on the other hand, is left by accidental touching. Clearly, a much smaller area of the finger will be impressed, in fact only that portion of the finger which actually touched the surface, such as the ball of the finger, or the tip or one of the sides. A portion of that latent impression would most likely be blurred or smudged, and therefore unusable for the purpose of comparison.

In addition to these factors which make a latent print look different from an inked impression of the same finger, are other factors that cause apparent dissimilarities. The surface may have been dirty, causing certain areas to show up less clearly than others; the skin may not have secreted as much perspiration in some areas as in others, accounting for stronger and weaker ridge detail; the skin may have been dirty and foreign objects (dust particles) between the friction ridges would give an odd though characteristic image to certain areas of the ridge detail. Excessive use of powder, when used to develop a latent print, might cause some of the furrows to be clogged. It is clear that many factors contribute to the appearance of dissimilarities between latent and inked impressions which are known to have been left by the same finger. It is here that the practical experience and training of the technician are needed. Examining latent prints and comparing them with known inked impressions cannot be learned from a book, which can provide only guidelines. Skill is acquired through actual work and practical experience.

The basic guideline is that the fingerprint technician, when making a comparison, must first look at the latent impression to determine whether sufficient ridge characteristics are present in the latent image to satisfy the quantitative factor, the minimum number of ridge characteristics needed to establish identity. If enough characteristics are present, the technician must then find the same characteristics in the known inked impression in the same interrelationship.

It is an error of the inexperienced to start with the inked print and then to try to discover the characteristics of the inked print in the latent impression. One might be influenced by the much clearer inked image toward discovering the same ridge characteristics in the latent impression even though they are not distinct. If one were bent on discovering dissimilarities, it would be easy to point out a great number of ridge characteristics in the inked impression that are not visible in the latent print. These dissimilarities are not true dissimilarities but only apparent ones; they do not impair or prevent identification.

At the outset of this section, it was stated that a given number of identical characteristics must be found in both prints being compared, without any unexplained dissimilarities. Theoretically, if one unexplained dissimilarity were found in areas where the ridge detail was clear and distinct in both the latent and inked print, identity could not be established.

This raises the question of how many ridge characteristics might be found to be identical in quality and quantity in two prints known to be made by different fingers. Much research has been done by this author as well as by a great number of technicians and researchers who have shared their findings in the scientific literature. This research involved isolating small areas of friction skin which showed only three to five ridge characteristics, and comparing that small area with thousands of other limited portions of different fingerprints. It is possible, in some instances, to isolate three ridge characteristics in a given interrelationship and find a friction skin area in a different print which shows the same three ridge characteristics in a similar interrelationship, but this author has never been able to find, in different impressions, four similar ridge characteristics in identical interrelationships. Despite intense research, only one case has ever been publicized, to this author's knowledge, where four characteristics which appeared identical were found in dissimilar prints. Even in that case, however, a very close study of the characteristics revealed differences of a less obvious nature than usually encountered. In any event, it may be concluded that when technicians adhere to the rule of no less than 10 identical characteristics, they are playing it safe, as of course they must do to avoid error. This does not preclude, however, the possibility of establishing identity on fewer than ten identical characteristics in the appropriate case.

When a competent technician uses the required margin of safety in establishing identity (presence of a sufficient number of identical characteristics in both prints), it is virtually impossible for another equally competent technician to disagree. In fingerprinting, then, there is no such thing as a "probable" identification; there is no such thing as experts arriving at conflicting conclusions on identity. The only possible difference of opinion might occur among qualified experts in a marginal case when one man feels that identity is established (on, say, fewer than eight characteristics) and the other man feels that this is insufficient ridge detail to arrive at a definite conclusion.

COMPARING PALMPRINTS AND SOLEPRINTS

The comparison of latent palm and soleprints with inked impressions of palms and soles proceeds on exactly the same basis as that used for comparing fingerprints. It has been clearly shown that there is no biological, physiological, or physical difference between the type of friction skin on the end joints of fingers and that on the palmar and plantar surfaces.

An example of an identification of a latent palmprint fragment is shown in Figure 178. Only 20 identical points are charted, but it is obvious that at least twice as many can be pointed out. There is no general rule for how many points of comparison in palm and soleprints are needed in order to prove identity. Presumably, the accepted guideline of ten to twelve points of identity could be defended as valid for palm and soleprints, but technicians usually chart no fewer than fifteen characteristics because palm and soleprint skin areas are generally more extensive.

A good example of the value of searching crime scenes for palmprints is from a Norwegian case in which a safecracker wore gloves but unwittingly left partial palmprints of both hands on a glass-topped desk. The burglar forgot to fasten the snaps that close the slits of the gloves near the wrists, thus leaving a roughly triangular area of the palmar skin exposed.

The latent images were developed with lead white powder which produced impressions in which the ridges showed white. A photographic tone reversal was made to show the powdered ridges in black (see left impression of Figure 179 which represents a partial right palmprint).

The Oslo Police Headquarters possessed a palmprint file, but a search of the records failed to reveal a prior recorded palmprint of the burglar. Copies of the prints were sent to the national identification bureaus of surrounding countries that maintained palmprint files, but there too the search was fruitless. Nearly three years later,

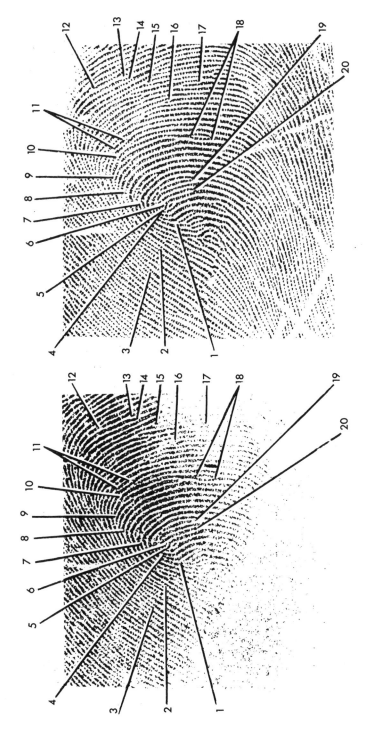

Figure 178. Twenty identical characteristics in a latent palmprint fragment and an inked impression.

however, incoming prints taken from three suspects arrested for a safeblowing job in another Norwegian city provided the final solution when one of them proved to be identical to the latent print in the Oslo file. The portion of the right inked palmprint in the carpal delta zone which matches one of the latents is shown at the right in Figure 179. This identification helped to solve thirty-four burglaries.

Since the friction skin on the palms and soles may have loops, whorls, and areas where the friction skin ridges run roughly parallel without forming patterns, care must be taken to label such latent fragments correctly. Whenever small latent images are found that present whorls or loops without clear finger-shaped outlines, the possibility must not be overlooked that they are partial palmprints, instead of fingerprints. Failing to consider that possibility may lead to searching the wrong files.

For easy identification of palm areas, names are assigned to the various portions of the palm. Generally, the finger end of the palm is called the distal end, the wrist end is called the proximal end, the radial side is the side toward the thumb, and the ulnar side is toward the little finger of each hand. The large cushion-type pad at the base of the thumb is called the thenar zone. It frequently shows loops, whorls, or combinations of both of these patterns, though in a significant number of palmprints no definite pattern is noticed. The

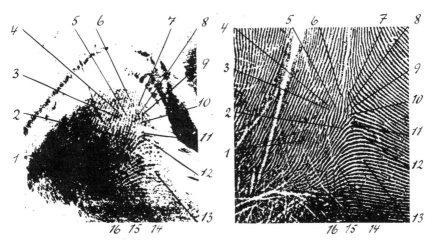

Figure 179. Identical characteristics in latent palmprints. (Courtesy: Identification Bureau, Oslo Police Headquarters, Oslo, Norway.)

large cushion below the little finger is called the hypothenar zone and may or may not be covered with definite friction ridge patterns. The palmar zone is the area which lies immediately below the fingers across the width of the palm. It is divided into interdigital areas because of the appearance of a delta-like ridge formation between or at the base of the fingers. Loop or whorl-type patterns may also occur in the palmar zone between the interdigital deltas. The carpal delta zone lies at about the center of the palm near the wrist where a delta called the carpal delta is frequently present.

Palmprint classification systems are largely based upon these various palmar areas. (See Figure 154.)

Footprints can also be identified by friction ridge characteristics according to the same procedures followed in identifying fingerprints. Foot traces are uncommon in this country, but a number of cases are on record in which identification was based on soleprint evidence. Toeprint evidence has rarely been used as the only basis for identification. However there is at least one case on record in which this occurred.

The distal end of the foot is the toe end; the proximal end is the heel end. The ball zone is the large cushion at the base of the big toe; the cushion below the small toes next to the ball zone is called the plantar zone. It is not unusual to find loops and whorls on the ball and plantar zones. The heel is also called the calcar area. Most frequently, this area does not contain any definite ridge patterns; in fact, the skin formations often look more like latitudinal striations than ridges.

The fibular side of the foot is the little toe side; the tibial side is the big toe side. On the tread area or center of the sole, a pattern may occasionally be found in the small fibular area, which is located immediately under the plantar zone on the little toe side of the foot, as well as in the small tibial area, which is located midway between the ball and calcar zones on the big toe side of the foot.

As with fragmentary palmprints, care must be taken to properly characterize latent soleprints. When a dancing school in Durham County, England, was burglarized and the latent fragment illustrated in Figure 180A was discovered on a glass-topped table, local police officers developed the print but erroneously labeled it a palmprint. The scientific aids officer of the county police, to whom the evidence was turned over, realized that it was a latent soleprint. The identification bureau kept no soleprint records, but the print of

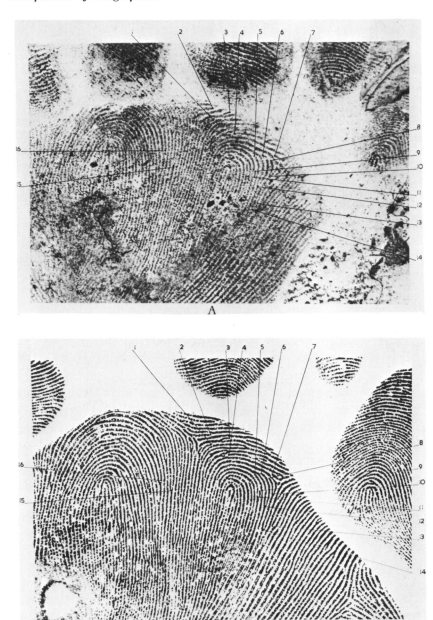

Figure 180. Identical characteristics in a latent soleprint and an inked impression. (Courtesy: Divisional Scientific Aids Officer, Durham County Police, England.)

a known suspect was found to match the latent soleprint (see Figure 180B).

Identification of infant footprints is made by following the same guidelines as those which apply to the identification of other friction skin areas. Theoretically, at least, such identification should be much easier, since we are dealing here with the comparison of two sets of inked impressions taken at different times, rather than comparing a latent print with an inked print. Yet, successful identification of infant footprints (taken at the time of delivery in the hospital) often fails simply because the footprints are improperly recorded. The friction ridge structure on the feet of the newly born is extremely delicate and minute. Only if the hospital record is carefully made will subsequent identification be possible. In many cases, the hospital prints made by the nurse are hastily made. Too much pressure and ink are applied with the result that the print is a big, black ink blob, showing no ridge detail. Because of the minute ridge detail, if it is visible at all, technicians will ordinarily enlarge the impressions photographically to arrive at a final conclusion of identity or nonidentity, rather than reach a conclusion solely on the basis of an examination with the fingerprint magnifier.

PRESSURE DISTORTION

The illustrations of friction ridge comparisons used in this book are considered to be excellent. This fact makes it necessary to caution the defense attorney in a criminal case who might have a copy of this book in hand and be confronted with fingerprint evidence that appears far less clearcut. He might be tempted to conclude that the evidence with which he is faced should not be used because of the lack of clarity in the latent impression. Yet, as any competent fingerprint technician knows, most identifiable latent prints are not of as good quality as those used in this book. But the bulk of these cases would not even necessarily be termed "difficult comparisons." The results of the comparison are simply less obvious to the non-expert.

Comparisons may become quite difficult when comparing prints from the same digit if they have a superficial appearance of dissimilarity caused by extreme pressure distortion in recording one of the prints. The danger is not so much that an erroneous identification will be made, but that the apparent dissimilarity may cause the technician to reject the prints as not from the same finger. The two finger impressions illustrated in Figure 181, for example, are apparently dissimilar in general pattern configuration. Yet, a close study of the ridge detail and individual characteristics reveals conclusively that they were made by the same finger. When the print on the right was recorded, excessive pressure caused the pattern outline to become distorted.

Distortion may come about because of the resiliency and elasticity of the finger and because of the angle at which the latent or inked print touches the surface upon which it is recorded.

The distortion referred to is of the extreme type, which actually causes a changed appearance between two impressions of the same digit. To a much slighter extent, some distortion is always present when, for example, a rolled impression is compared with a plain impression of the same digit. The difference would become highly noticeable if the prints were greatly enlarged. This is one of the reasons why no system of distance measurements between characteristic points, or geometric projections, can be used to determine identity. Differences would be found quite logically under those circumstances in prints known to be from the same person. The same invalid and erroneous conclusions would be reached by the "system of triangulation that involves drawing an imaginary axis between similar points on each print," devised by a now thor-

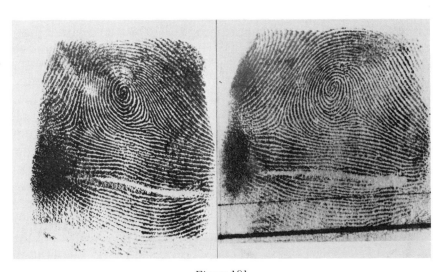

Figure 181.

oughly discredited pseudo-expert whose only claim to expertise in fingerprinting was training as a microscopist.

Cases of accidental or intentional mutilation of the friction skin may present special difficulties in comparison. Due allowance must be made for pattern contractions in and around the area of scarring which may make the pattern look quite different from pre-scarification impressions. In some such cases the pattern appears to have changed completely, but the change is localized in the area of scarification. By ignoring the mutilated area along with the ridge detail immediately adjoining it, just as would be done with the blurred or unidentifiable portion of a latent print, identity can be established from the remaining unaltered ridge detail if sufficient characteristics are present in that unchanged area.

THE FINGERPRINT WITNESS IN COURT *

We have said that there are three kinds of fingerprint technicians: those who search for and develop latent fingerprints; those who interpret, classify, and file inked fingerprints; and those who compare latent and inked prints to establish identity. We also recognized that two, or indeed all three, of these functions might be performed by one individual. In the latter case, the technician must be prepared to explain each step of the work involved in every area of fingerprint identification. This also means that, throughout the investigation of a case, the technician must conduct himself so that every step of his work can be related to the court and jury.

Case Preparation

It is important to preserve an unbroken chain of evidence. In order to do so, fingerprint evidence discovered at a crime scene must be carefully preserved from the time of discovery until the time of trial, and possession of the evidence must be accounted for. Whenever the evidence is handed over to another individual, it is important to note carefully when and to whom it was given. Preferably, as few people as possible should handle the evidence during

---

* In the book *Fingerprints and the Law* (Chilton Book Co., 1969), three chapters are devoted to courtroom testimony on fingerprints. Since a number of prosecutors and defense attorneys consult that book, it would obviously be useful to the fingerprint witness to be familiar with the approaches specifically suggested there. A few portions of the material covered in this section are also discussed in Chapter 11 of *Fingerprints and the Law*, though with a different emphasis.

that period. While not actually being used for examination purposes, the evidence should be locked in the evidence room or in a vault with restricted access.

If latent prints are to be lifted from a surface, a photograph of the latent print on the object itself must be made before lifting, so that it can be established that the lifted print actually came from that surface. Of course, if the object bearing the print is small or moveable, it should be preserved as well, so that it can be introduced into evidence at trial.

In a certain burglary case, a latent fingerprint was discovered on a pane of broken glass under the window through which access was gained. After development of the latent print with powder, the print was lifted and transferred to a latent print card. The glass itself was thrown away. No photograph had been taken while the latent print still was on the glass. At the trial, the defendant contended that the latent print which he admitted was his did not come from the broken glass at the crime scene but was a plant by the police and had been taken from a smooth object that he had held while incarcerated after arrest. Without the original glass, or a photograph showing the latent print on the glass before lifting, some courts might have excluded the evidence. In this case, the court admitted the evidence, but a vigorous defense attorney, on cross-examination, had very little difficulty in seriously undermining the value of the fingerprint evidence when the technician who developed the latent prints was on the witness stand. This line of questioning followed:

Q. You stated that after you had dusted a piece of glass you discovered a fingerprint. Is that right?
A. Yes.
Q. And after you found this print, you then lifted it off that piece of glass. Correct?
A. Yes.
Q. Would you tell us again how this was done?
A. (The witness explains the lifting process).
Q. In essence, then, you just put the cellophane tape which has the latent fingerprint image sticking to it on a card, so that the fingerprint shows through the tape?
A. Yes, sir.
Q. And that can be done with any kind of powdered fingerprint from any kind of hard surface?

A. Yes.

Q. So, when you have that piece of paper with the latent finger-print sticking to it only, and nothing else, you can't tell, from that piece of paper and the fingerprint alone, from what surface it was lifted, can you?

A. No, you cannot tell.

Q. Once that print has been lifted with the cellophane tape and placed on a latent print transfer card, it can be kept indefinitely, can it not?

A. Yes.

Q. So, on the basis of this latent transfer card with the powdered print sticking to it, there is no way to tell where it came from without referring to what you have written on it. Isn't that right?

A. Yes.

Q. If you developed my client's latent print from any other piece of glass, like from the glass top on this table here in the courtroom, and then lifted it, that latent print wouldn't look any different from the one you have shown us here, would it?

A. True, it would not look any different.

Q. And from the latent transfer card with the print on it alone, you could not tell whether this print was developed three days ago or three years ago. Isn't that right?

A. Yes.

Q. Isn't it true that a latent print which has been developed with powder and then lifted to a transfer card from a glass pane, cannot be distinguished from one lifted from any other glass surface, or indeed from any other smooth, hard surface?

A. That is true.

Q. What this amounts to, then, and correct me if I am wrong, is that a well qualified fingerprint expert who has only this transfer card, and not the piece of glass from which the print was allegedly lifted, cannot state that this print in fact came from a piece of glass?

A. No, you can't tell.

Q. Once a latent print has been developed on glass or any other hard, smooth surface, and lifted from it, there still remains some residue of the perspiration print on the surface. Isn't that true?

A. Yes, in most cases.

Q. In other words, fingerprint technicians agree that in some instances you can redevelop the same latent on the same surface after one, two, or three successive lifts. Isn't that correct?

A. Yes, at times.

Q. So, if we had that so-called piece of glass, our own experts would be able to determine whether this latent print on the card actually came from the glass, couldn't they?

A. Well, if the print was left too long ago, it might not be possible to redevelop it anymore.

Q. But, after dusting a pane of glass, some powder adheres to the whole surface and not only to the latent print. Isn't that true?

A. A small amount of it, true.

Q. So when that latent print was lifted, the cellophane or scotch tape used would also lift the dust particles around the print so that where the cellophane had touched the glass there would actually be a clean area of exactly the size of the cellophane lifter. Is that not true?

A. Yes.

Q. So either way, whether by redevelopment, or by observing and measuring the dimensions and nature of the cellophane lift, our experts would be able to tell whether this lift on the transfer card came from that piece of glass. Right?

A. Yes, they could.

Q. But you conveniently lost the glass?

Not preserving the piece of window pane, then, not only deprived the defendant of the opportunity to verify the validity of the evidence against him, but also brought added problems for the prosecution, problems which might have raised a sufficient doubt about the worth of the evidence in the minds of the jurors. Now observe how the defense attorney hammered his points home when another expert testified for the state and identified the latent print on the transfer card as one of the defendant's fingerprints. Without disputing the truth of the identification, the lawyer continued to demolish the validity of the evidence by suggesting that the prints could have been lifted from some other object.

Q. The transfer card with the latent print on it is permanent, is it not?

A. Yes.

Q. From the print on that card alone, you cannot tell whether it was developed this morning or years ago. True?

A. Yes.

Q. Once a latent print has been developed with powder and then lifted, the print can be redeveloped again in most cases, can it not?

A. Yes, it can.

Q. If you had the object here from which this latent print had been lifted, it would still be possible to establish beyond a doubt that the lifted print actually came from that object, could you not?

A. Yes, you could.

Q. But from this latent print card alone, you have no way of knowing from what kind of hard surface it came. Isn't that true?

A. True.

Q. In fact, from this latent print card you cannot tell that it was lifted from glass, right?

A. True, you can't tell for sure.

Q. As far as you are concerned, then, since you did not actually develop and lift this print, it could have come from any smooth, hard object in the defendant's house, or something he touched after the police had thrown him in jail. You can't tell, right?

A. True.

Preparing Court Exhibits

In order to help the jury to understand why he has reached a conclusion of identity, the fingerprint technician will, in most cases, prepare enlarged photographs of both the latent print and the inked impressions on which the location of individual ridge characteristics that appear in both prints are indicated and consecutively numbered. Such exhibits are not indispensable, since they are not evidence by themselves.

The actual object on which the latent prints are found is evidence, as are the inked comparison prints of the defendant. When the latent print has been identified as belonging to the defendant, it is the testimony of the fingerprint technician who qualified as an expert that serves as evidence. The jury, composed of persons having no special knowledge of fingerprints, might understand the expert witness's conclusions better if it could visually observe how the expert reached his conclusions. For that purpose, the witness may use charted exhibits as "demonstrative" evidence.

Among forensic scientists there has been disagreement with respect to the wisdom of using exhibits. Some prominent experts prefer not to use any exhibits at all, relying instead upon the persuasiveness of their findings as presented in oral form. Those who believe in this theory suggest that the jury should believe them because on their qualifications they have been shown to have special knowledge in this field. If the jury doubts their testimony, so they argue, they might also doubt the propriety of the photographic exhibits. Other experts hold to the belief that in all cases fingerprint experts should prepare charted exhibits for use in court.

The better practice might be to adopt some elements of both positions. Keeping in mind that the purpose of demonstrative evidence is to help the jury to understand the expert witness's conclusions, it would certainly be advantageous to demonstrate identity by enlarged charted exhibits in those cases where the latent print is fairly clear and where identity can be easily explained by referring to individual characteristics on the enlargements. But if the latent print is a partial one, not showing core or delta areas, and somewhat smudged in certain areas, it might be better not to make enlarged photographic exhibits at all, where the use of such exhibits before a jury might tend to confuse.

When exhibits are used, the following suggestions should be followed in order to insure that the demonstrative evidence will serve its purpose properly:

1. Both the latent and inked impressions should be enlarged with the same degree of magnification. While there is no set rule as to size, exhibits of 5 x 7 or 8 x 10 inches would show the ridge detail clearly.

2. After the prints have been enlarged, they should be dry-mounted on illustration board of not less than 14 x 20 inches, with the latent print on the left, and at least a one-inch margin around each print.

3. In marking the exhibits, projection lines should be drawn from the identifying characteristics that appear in both prints, always starting with those appearing in the latent print. If the latent is unusually clear, it is not necessary to draw projection lines to all of the characteristics; point out about 16 to 18 in a fingerprint and no less than 20 in a palmprint or soleprint. (It must be observed again that identity can be positively established by fewer characteristics,

but if more are shown the exhibit is likely to be more persuasive to the jury.)

In drawing projection lines, it is important for clarity's sake not to have them cross each other. They should project evenly around the whole pattern. The projection lines should be drawn with a fine pen so that the lines do not obscure ridge detail.

4. The ridge characteristics should be numbered consecutively in both the latent and inked prints. The same number assigned to a characteristic in the latent print must be assigned to the corresponding characteristic in the inked print. It is customary to number the characteristics in a clockwise fashion.

5. A ridge break should not be considered to be a ridge characteristic unless the break qualifies as a ridge ending. Enclosures should be assigned one number. The same is true for short ridges, though some experts prefer to consider them as two ridge endings, one at each end of the short ridge. If identification were established by, say, eight points only, and the eight points were reached by counting two short ridges and an enclosure for a total of six points, the validity of that identification could be questioned by an argument that in truth only five characteristics exist: two short ridges, one enclosure, and two other ridge characteristics. For that reason, it appears to be better practice to assign only one number to an enclosure, and one number to a short ridge. Those points where the ridges stop at the edges of prints should not be considered to be ridge characteristics because they are not true ridge endings but merely the places where the friction ridges ceased to touch the surface of the objects on which they were found.

6. It is a good idea to make additional copies of all photographed exhibits before the trial so that extra copies, correctly marked, will be available if first copies are lost or in some way made unusable or if several lawyers might wish to examine the photographs of the evidence at the same time.

The defense attorney may ask for photographic copies of the fingerprint evidence, or an opportunity to inspect the evidence itself. In the past, a number of law enforcement identification men have been reluctant to cooperate with experts for the defense, even after they have been ordered to do so by the prosecutor or by the court. Yet, if the police expert's work has been done properly, he stands to benefit from the independent corroboration which must clearly result from such an inquiry. As a result of this examination, defense counsel is generally assured that the fingerprint identification was properly done. He may, in that case, subject the witness to a more limited cross-examination than otherwise as he attempts to grope his way through evidence of which he has little understanding and where, because of his suspicious nature with respect to police practices, he suspects foul play. Competent fingerprint technicians should not fear defense inquiry into their work prior to trial; they should welcome it, provided they know the defense expert to be a competent person. But even if he is not, as has proved to be the case in a few instances, the police officer is obligated to cooperate with the defense if a statute, court rule, or court order gives discovery rights that encompass fingerprint evidence.

On the Witness Stand

The testimony given by the fingerprint technician is in the form of questions and answers. The questions are asked by the attorneys for both sides, the answers are provided by the witness. The side which calls the witness to court is first to ask questions of the witness; this is called direct examination. The attorney for the opposite side may next ask questions of the same witness; this is cross-examination. After the cross-examination, the first attorney may ask additional questions during re-direct examination, just as thereafter the cross-examiner may have re-cross-examination. On rare occasions, the judge also asks a few questions of the witness.

The direct examination of the fingerprint expert usually comprises three parts. The first part involves eliciting, from the witness, his background and experience in order to show that he is truly competent and qualified to give testimony as an expert; the second part lays the foundation for the evidence through a series of questions concerned with the general principles upon which fingerprint identification is based, the techniques that are used, and how identity can be established by fingerprints. The final part deals with the actual examination of the evidence.

Cross-examination is a basic right guaranteed to any litigant; it also serves to expose ineptitude or deception. Customarily, the cross-examiner confines himself to matters discussed within the scope of direct examination, but since great latitude is given on cross-examination, he may go considerably beyond the immediate bounds of cross-examination if "the door was opened" to a particular line of questions. The trial judge, in his discretion, may restrict questioning on collateral matters which unduly disgrace, degrade, or embarrass the witness, as well as on matters which are clearly outside the scope of cross-examination.

The effectiveness of an expert's testimony depends in large measure on the total impression created by his appearance, demeanor, and facility of expression. While he should know all of the details of the case and be adequately prepared to answer all relevant questions, the jury will weigh his testimony not only by his answers, but also by all the factors that influence human beings observing a man on the witness stand. For that reason, the following suggestions may aid in presenting the expert's testimony in the most favorable light:

1. Dress should be conservative and neat. A well-pressed business suit is preferable over a uniform, since it projects a more objective attitude.

2. Answers to questions should be given frankly, honestly, and truthfully, without evasion. If the witness does not know the answer to a question, he should not hesitate to say so. He should never guess or estimate, unless an estimate is asked for.

3. If an objection is raised to a question, the witness should refrain from answering the question and wait until the judge has overruled it to answer. If the objection is sustained, no answer may be given to that question.

4. Answers given should be responsive to the questions. Information beyond what is called for by the question should not be volunteered.

5. A witness should never allow himself to become angry because of cross-examination which seems to impugn his honesty or competency. When the person testifying loses his temper in the courtroom, the jury may interpret his behavior as indicating bias, unfairness, and instability on his part.

6. If a cross-examiner insists on a "yes" or "no" answer only, and the witness honestly feels that the question cannot be answered that way, it is proper for the witness to turn to the judge and advise him that the question cannot be answered with a "yes" or "no" because either answer would be misleading and that an explanation is needed.

7. The witness should use plain language, avoid professional jargon as much as possible and explain technical terms with which the

jury might not be familiar. He should also avoid using language which, because of the peculiar connotations attached to legal terminology, always seems more monumental than the facts warrant. For example, the typical statement, "Upon entering the premises I observed the subject discarding an object in the lavatory," sounds unduly sinister; the facts could be just as effectively communicated by saying "When I entered the house I saw Mr. Jones throw an envelope into the toilet stool."

8. If one of the questions asked on cross-examination calls for a response which the police witness feels may appear to damage the prosecution's case in the eyes of the jury, he should nevertheless answer the question truthfully and in a responsive manner without attempting to avoid the issue. If the prosecutor was properly briefed during a pre-trial conference, he will pick up the point on re-direct and ask him to explain or elaborate.

9. Above all, the witness should remember that his duty is not to determine the guilt or the innocence of a defendant. He should not take a partisan attitude in the matter being tried. His only purpose is to testify to the results of his expert examination of items of scientific evidence, and to render an opinion based upon his study of the friction skin details in the latent and inked impressions.

While on the stand, it may happen that the witness cannot recall specific details from memory, but has a record of what is asked for. In such case, the court will permit him to consult his notes before answering the question. The notes themselves, however, are not evidence, and the witness may not read the answer to the question from his notes. He may use them only to refresh his recollection and jog his memory. After he has done so, he must then again testify from his memory rather than from the notes. It must be remembered, however, that the opposing counsel is entitled to inspect the notes to which the witness has referred and frame questions on cross-examination around data found in the instrument itself.

Where simply refreshing one's recollection by quickly referring to notes is insufficient to jog the memory of the witness, but where he has a precise record of the facts that was made at the time of their occurrence, the instrument that embodies this record may in some instances be introduced as evidence itself on the legal theory of "past recollection recorded." Before such documents are admissible in evidence, however, certain legal requirements must be met.

When it is contemplated that such a record may be necessary, it would be advisable to discuss this matter also with the prosecutor prior to trial.

Establishing Identity by Microscopic Ridge Detail

Poroscopy

As stated earlier, it is the perspiration on the fingers and hands that is partly responsible for leaving latent images of the friction skin upon touched objects. This perspiration flows to the surface of the friction ridges through the pore openings. From the enlargement of friction skin in Figure 182 it can be clearly observed that the shape of the pores varies, as does their location in relation to the edges of the friction ridges. Pores are rectangular, triangular,

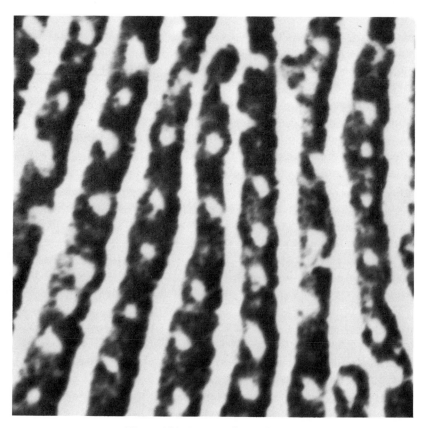

Figure 182. Variety of pore shapes.

circular, or oval; some are placed in the middle of the friction ridge, others are at the edge. It can also be observed that the distance between the pores is not constant. In some instances two pores are side by side.

Such observations led the French criminologist Edmond Locard to conclude, in the first decade of this century, that identity could be established by a comparison of the pore structure in an unknown latent print with that of the inked impression. He discovered that there is an almost limitless variety in shapes and locations of pores. They may cover nearly the whole width of a ridge or they may appear in the center or on either side. They may be evenly or unevenly distributed. Between 9 and 18 pores per centimeter may be found on a single ridge. In continued studies Locard established, that while the size of pores may vary between childhood and old age, their general form and relative position remain constant throughout life.

The method of establishing identity by a comparison of the pores was called poroscopy. Locard's unit of measurement in comparing pores is the "micron," which is 1/1000th of a millimeter, or approximately 1/25000th of an inch, a unit of measurement employed by microscopists. Size of the pores varies from 88 to 220 micra. Locard stated that the largest pores had three times the diameter and nine times the area of the smallest. He contended that poroscopy was an ideal method for identifying individuals where only an infinitesimal portion of friction skin was available. He claimed it was possible to find up to 1,500 pores in a single fingerprint, as opposed to the maximum of 100–150 ridge characteristics. Locard never seems to have postulated a mathematical calculation for the chances of duplication in pore characteristics.

In 1912, Dr. Locard proved the value of poroscopy in the now famous case of Boudet and Simonin, where he showed the concurrence of 901 separate sweat pores in Boudet's latent fingerprint on a piece of furniture at the burglarized premises, and more than 2,000 in a latent impression left by Simonin's palm. He charted out the pores in inked and latent prints in the same manner as ridge characteristics in fingerprints are matched.

One of the disadvantages of poroscopy is that many latent fingerprints do not show pore structure, especially after powder development. The relatively coarse powder granules tend to fill up the pore openings in the sweat deposits. Pore structure is generally visible only when latent prints are developed by chemical means, or are impressed in a liquid, such as blood. Even then, however, the ridges may not reveal visible pore structure. This may be because the pore openings are too small or inactive. The appearance of pores may also vary from one print to another because the small openings are easily plugged up partially or totally. This calls for extensive experience in evaluating and analysing pore data. It is doubted whether any experts in fingerprints in this country ever seriously studied and used poroscopy to an extent that might qualify them as experts in identifying individuals by pore structure only.

It is true, of course, that poroscopy might be used as an adjunct to fingerprint identification made on a low number of matching characteristics. If the technician discovered, say, five matching characteristics and concluded that identity was established, he might still want to reinforce his findings by doing a pore comparison in order to be more convincing in court. However, to this author's knowledge this has never been done in any important criminal cases in the United States. This is probably so because, on the whole, fingerprint technicians experienced in comparing latent and inked impressions are conservative and tend to discard, as unidentifiable, latent prints that do not show sufficient ridge characteristic detail.

Another difficulty is in obtaining suitable comparison records. In general, the great bulk of fingerprint cards in identification files throughout the country do not show pore detail, whether because the recorders used too much ink to show the structure or whether the pores are too small. This means that careful recording of fingerprints may still not make it possible to obtain adequate pore images. In experiments conducted by the author with forty individuals of both sexes and random age, it was discovered that the inking process, cautiously employed in recording four sets of prints of each individual, permitted reproduction of useable pore detail in the prints of eight subjects only—a bare 20%. Even by placing latent impressions of these subjects on paper and developing the impressions with silver nitrate, it was possible to record adequate pore detail in the prints of only eighteen—still less than 50%. While the sampling is too low to permit use of the results as a reliable statistical guide, it nevertheless shows the difficulties that may be encountered in poroscopy.

The principles of poroscopy, as established by Dr. Locard, appear to be valid. No one doubts the correctness of the premise that identity can be established by pore structure comparison. The difficulties in its practical application, however, will probably prevent poroscopy from ever gaining use on a wide scale.

Edgeoscopy

The fingerprint scientist Salil K. Chatterjee devised a totally new concept of personal identification which uses papillary ridges but abandons traditional fingerprint concepts. Chatterjee found in his study of papillary ridges that the characteristics of the edges were widely divergent and as persistent as the ridges and pores themselves. Around these facts he designed an auxiliary system of personal identification based upon comparison of the edges of papillary ridges, and termed this method *Edgeoscopy* (a choice of term resoundingly criticized by scientists for its combination of an English with a Greek word).

Chatterjee found that there are basically seven types of edge formations (see Figure 183), and that their characteristics may occur on both sides of a ridge. They are: (1) straight edges; (2) convex edges; (3) peaked edges, protruding with a broad base and pointed top; (4) table edges, protruding with a narrow base and broad flat top; (5) pocket edges, formed by a sweat pore with one side open; (6) concave edges; and (7) angular edges. He added an eighth group to include edges that did not fall within one of these divisions.

Chatterjee determined that the edge characteristics are permanent and do not change during the life of an individual. Impressions of the same patterns taken many years apart show the same characteristics. (See Figure 184.) The size of the characteristics may vary between childhood and maturity, but their shape, relative position and distance, persist throughout life. While no attempt was made

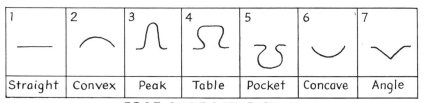

EDGE CHARACTERISTICS

Figure 183.

to provide a classification system based on ridge edges, Chatterjee offered his method as an adjunct to fingerprint identification, much along the same theories that motivated Locard's development of poroscopy.

As such, edgeoscopy suffers from the same defects as Locard's method. While no one has disputed the inherent correctness of Chatterjee's theories, edgeoscopy appears to be of little practical value. The minuteness of the edge detail causes variations in printing due to pressure distortion. There seems to be little practical value in edgeoscopy.

FORGERY OF FINGERPRINTS

The question of whether or not fingerprints can be forged is a serious one, though it has been easily dismissed or avoided by many identification men who regard the possibility as preposterous. The question deserves a serious answer.

Courts have held that fingerprints lack probative value if they are found in a location where they could have been impressed innocently. If the imprints are found where the defendant did not have

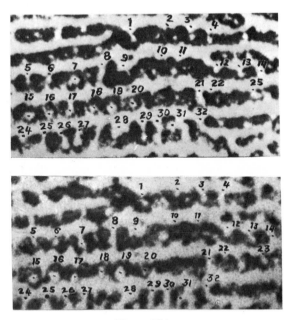

Figure 184.

legitimate access, and he contends that he was never there, then the presence of his fingerprints is a circumstance from which an inference of guilt can be drawn. If it were seriously contended, however, that the fingerprints could have been forged, another problem might arise. Just as it would be inconceivable to assert that a man did *not* commit a crime merely because his fingerprints were *not* found at the scene, so it would have to be said that the mere presence of the defendant's prints where he could not have had innocent access does not necessarily raise the inference that the defendant actually deposited the prints. If forgery is claimed the prosecution would have to prove that the latent crime scene prints were genuine, and not forgeries.

It would be utterly foolish to summarily dismiss the notion that fingerprints cannot be forged. In the present state of the graphic arts, almost anything can be faithfully reproduced. The intricate designs on paper currency have often been counterfeit and have fooled many "experts." Those details are more complex than fingerprint ridge structure. It is equally foolish to insist, as many identification technicians do, that forgeries are easy to detect, especially when most technicians have never seen (or are at least not aware that they have ever seen) a forged fingerprint. It does not inspire confidence in the competency of a man to see him confidently answer "yes" to the question whether he would be able to detect a forged fingerprint, and immediately thereafter hear him admit that he has never seen one!

Dispassionate scientists like Dr. Harold Cummins and others have stated unequivocally that fingerprints can be forged, and that such forgeries can be done so skilfully that experienced fingerprint technicians cannot detect the fraud. Cummins proved it in 1934 by carrying out a very simple experiment. He placed two genuine and two forged prints, all of the same finger, on one card and submitted the card to eight persons whom he knew to be qualified fingerprint experts. He told them that there were both genuine and forged prints on the card without indicating how many of each, and asked them to identify the forgeries. Only two experts correctly identified them; a third was correct but questioned one of his (correct) findings; two experts were entirely incorrect; and three experts arrived at one erroneous finding.

When the results of this experiment were published in the *Journal of Criminal Law and Criminology*, the editor of the publication,

Professor Fred E. Inbau, himself a former director of a crime laboratory, reported in a footnote that he had submitted the same prints to six heads of police identification bureaus whom he considered qualified, and that the percentage of accuracy in their responses approximated that obtained by Dr. Cummins.

The claims that fingerprints can be forged must be taken seriously, and a careful study of the factors going into the possible existence of forged fingerprints and of ways to detect forgeries must be made.

The subject is not a recent one. In 1907, Dr. Edmond Locard, who was then working as an assistant in the laboratory at Lacassagne, discovered a procedure for making counterfeit prints by the use of a mold of gutta-percha which permitted placing latent perspiration prints on bloody impressions. A Los Angeles handwriting expert is said to have been the first person in the United States to forge a fingerprint, in 1919. In 1924, Wehde and Beffer published a book titled *Finger Prints Can Be Forged*. Wehde, a former convict and expert jewelry engraver, claimed to be able to counterfeit a fingerprint that would baffle science. He was given the privilege to demonstrate his technique in Chicago in 1923, before a special meeting of officers of the International Association for Identification, but his counterfeit was so crude that it could be termed a forgery even without the use of magnifier or microscope. When he published his book, however, he gave a quite different account of the meeting with IAI officers than that recorded in the association's minutes. Beginning in 1926, a British medium claimed to be in touch with a deceased individual and as proof that he still existed offered a thumbprint of the deceased which she had asked him to deposit during a seance. Upon investigation, the impression turned out to belong to the medium's dentist who had furnished the impression in wax, not knowing that the impression was going to be used to make a stamp with which to fool participants in the seance.

Many more examples are on record. All but a few, however, deal largely with claims that fingerprints can be forged, rather than with actual forgery cases in criminal prosecutions. Fingerprint technicians readily say that they have never encountered a case where fingerprints had been forged. This really does not answer the question of whether or not fingerprints *can* be forged. When questioned most of them will admit that they had never considered the possibility of a forgery in their latent print work, and had never examined crime scene prints to determine genuineness. Inquiry into the subject is not stimulated among fingerprint technicians. Earlier textbooks do not warn or advise the latent print searcher to check for possible forgeries. When discussing the subject at all, such texts give the impression that there is no need to consider the possibility that a forgery will slip by them. In other words, if it is a forgery, it will be so obvious that the technician will recognize it without special inquiry. Yet, as was seen before, scientists and researchers, who cannot be classed as other than dispassionate, unequivocally state that fingerprints can be forged and that the forgery may easily be overlooked unless a deliberate attempt is made to investigate the print for genuineness. Luckily, an ever greater number of enlightened fingerprint technicians are willing to face reality and are now examining fingerprints in the effort to detect possible attempts at forgery.

Types of Forgeries

Original fingerprints are those discovered at a crime scene and those recorded by the inking process on a fingerprint card. Reproductions of such fingerprints, then, are not forgeries unless the reproduction is done with the intent to deceive. Furthermore, the copying of the ridge pattern must be done by a method designed to produce accurate one-to-one reproductions. This excludes free-hand drawings or paintings of friction ridge patterns, which of course could not fool even the uninitiated. Among the types of forged fingerprints which may be encountered, we must consider three types: the *stamped print* which is a replication of a fingerprint by a rubber stamp, cast, molding, plate, or die; the *transferred print* which is a true perspiration latent lifted from one place and transferred to another where it is left to be discovered as if the latter surface had been touched by the finger leaving the impression; and the *transferred powdered lift* which is a latent developed with powder on one surface, then lifted with Scotch tape and the tape placed onto another incriminating surface.

Of these three types of so-called forgeries, the first is relatively easy to dismiss, since attempts to counterfeit fingerprints by this method are not too hard to spot. The second type may present real problems to the technician. Nevertheless, a series of tests makes it possible for the technician who has made a study of and experimented with intentionally forged prints of that type to discover the spurious origin of the impression. The third type, which really requires participation by the identification officer and must assume his dishonesty, cannot be detected from the prints themselves. Claims that such fraud was perpetrated, however, can be effectively rebutted by the careful technician who does his job in a thorough and professional manner and who can prove and demonstrate every step of his work.

THE STAMPED PRINTS. Stamped prints require the replication of the ridge structure in a soft surface such as wax, moulage, or other substance suitable for making casts. The indentations of the ridges in the substance then provide a negative form from which a positive casting can be made. This casting can be used much like a rubber stamp, which it could actually be, to impress a so-called latent impression by covering the ridged surface of the stamp with perspiration, blood, or other substances.

This method suffers from all of the defects that ordinary rubber stamps suffer from. The edges of the forged impression are not always even and show ragged detail which distinguishes the "latent" from the genuine latent, even though the stamp is made from a genuine latent. The loss of detail in the print itself does not necessarily point to forgery by stamped impression (most latents are of uneven quality and partially blurred). However, ragged edging is highly characteristic in stamps. Also, telltale ghost edges of the casting medium frequently occur with this method.

Most important, of course, is that repeated use of the stamp will result in "latent" impressions which are absolutely identical in detail, something which defies the law of probabilities. It is impossible to place two latent fingerprints in succession that show exactly the same amount of ridge detail and identical ridge cut-off. Yet, if a forger were to go to the trouble of "planting" a spurious latent impression, he would certainly leave more than one because to do so would increase the chance that at least one would be discovered. The obvious, and quite visible, spurious "latent" fingerprint placed in a most prominent position would by its very nature call special attention to it, since in the experience of latent print technicians "those things just don't happen!" Also, the stamped latent is usually going to be clearer than a true latent, since details of common blurring are hard to reproduce.

THE TRANSFERRED PRINTS. A transferring medium, which may be one of a wide group of materials understandably unnecessary to name, is brought into close contact with an undeveloped perspiration print so that part of the sweat deposits are transferred to the medium. The transferring medium is then placed in contact with the object or surface upon which it is intended that the latent print appear. From the description of the process alone, it can at once be noted that there must be a considerable loss of perspiration secretion.

William W. Harper, then a consulting physicist with the Pasadena Police Department, published the results of his experiments with transferred prints of this kind in 1937. He made several hundred transfers from and to microscope slides under carefully controlled, ideal conditions. He examined the genuine and transferred latents under the microscope at 10 and 50 magnifications. He also made approximately one hundred photomicrographs of genuine and transferred prints. Various fingerprint experts in the Los Angeles area, to whom the prints were submitted for examination, were unable to identify the forged prints. Harper found that no significant criteria could be established whereby microscopic examination of the deposited secretion would unerringly lead to the detection of forgeries.

However, a number of other factors may be used to determine whether a latent impression is forged or genuine. These factors do not rely primarily on microscopic examination of the deposited sweat secretions and give reliable indications of genuineness or forgery. Some of these factors are:

1. Forged transferred prints will appear to be weak, even when one begins with a latent image placed with a copious amount of perspiration. This is largely in line with Harper's own findings but derives from a study of the overall quality of the print as well as of ridge fragments.

2. A study of the position of the latent may reveal whether the print could have been left there during normal handling. Considering that a fingerprint is an impression made by the end phalange of a digit, just the fact that the pattern producing skin surface dangles at the end of a finger, which is attached to a hand, which in turn is attached to an arm, makes it impossible for fingerprints to be found in some given positions on certain surfaces, unlikely in others, and

likely and probable in the remainder. A forger, unless he is also an accomplished fingerprint technician, might very easily overlook the importance of the relative position of a fingerprint upon a certain surface. Therefore, much can be learned from an examination of the position or slant of the latent.

3. Depending on the forgery technique used, the examiner should be alert to the possibility of a tone and/or a position reversal. This, too, is easily overlooked even by the skillful forger, and yet just as easily spotted by the alert and experienced fingerprint technician.

4. An examination must be made of the surface upon which the latent print is found, and especially the area immediately surrounding the latent itself. Depending upon the type of transferring medium used, foreign particles may be transferred from the old to the new surface. By impressing the transferring medium to the new surface and then removing it so that the perspiration print will remain on it, particles of the new surface are likely to be removed from the area around the impression, often leaving an area of increased cleanliness around the latent print of the same size and shape of the transferring medium.

5. If more than one latent print of the same finger is discovered with identical shape and pattern characteristics, a forgery is clearly apparent, since no two genuine impressions of the same finger, placed at different times, will be exactly identical in the ridge area shown.

6. If the transferring medium contained adhesives, as most do, traces of the adhesive will also be discovered on the surface on which the perspiration print was planted. Microscopic analysis of the area would reveal the presence of the most minute adhesive particles, but such examination might not be necessary since in all but a few cases an examination with the fingerprint magnifier would give the same result.

7. In most *undeveloped* perspiration prints some pore structure is visible, though the pore openings readily clog up during powder development. Since the pore structure is small and delicate, it is difficult to preserve that delicate pore structure in the transfer process. The minute pore designs would tend to flatten when pressure is applied to the perspiration print with the transferring medium, and again when additional pressure is applied in placing the transferring medium on the second surface. While the absence of pore openings in a latent perspiration print is not, by itself, indicative of

a forgery, such absence would become highly revealing if it is shown that the person whose print is left normally does show clearly identifiable pore detail in inked or other perspiration prints.

8. If the transferring medium is extensively coated with adhesives, as many are, the traces of adhesive left on the surface after "depositing" the transferred perspiration print may make it impossible to dust that latent impression, since the fingerprint powder would indiscriminately stick to the whole surface coated with adhesive, not just to the perspiration outline of the ridge detail.

None of these factors, taken singly, can establish genuineness beyond a reasonable doubt, though some of them may clearly establish the existence of a forgery by themselves. Taken in combination, however, they provide a solid basis for a determination that the latent fingerprint is authentic and not transferred.

These examination techniques for the detection of forgery require an investigation of the latent print details prior to development. This is quite easy, of course, when we are dealing with visible latent prints, such as those made in blood, paint, or other substance which does not require development. When dealing with perspiration prints however, an effort must be made to determine their presence on a given surface before the application of powders to the surface. As described in an earlier chapter dealing with latent print techniques, this can be done by shining light at a low angle over the surface, holding the object up to the light and inspecting it from several angles, or by breathing on the surface. The possibility should also be considered of developing the latent impressions with other developing media, especially iodine fumes. Iodine fumes do not alter the perspiration in any fashion, and after the image has faded away the latent print can still be redeveloped with powder, iodine, or other chemical methods.

Apart from all the considerations discussed earlier, forging of fingerprints by the methods described lacks practical value for the criminal. It also requires the combination of a number of other factors which makes practical use of forgeries unlikely. The forger must have more than a rudimentary knowledge of fingerprint identification as well as of latent print techniques. He must also know something of photography and engraving, and therefore requires access to considerable equipment if the stamp method is used. In addition, he must procure a usable latent impression of an innocent person. This may not be too hard, but still requires certain determination. He then ends up with an inferior end product that he must use repeatedly which, in itself, gives his efforts away, or go to the even greater trouble of obtaining different latents of the same innocent individual in order to make several stamps. He still runs the risk that the planted latent will not be discovered; that if discovered, it will be exposed as a fraud which may tend to prove to be worse for him in the long run; and that even if discovered and not exposed as a fraud, the print may never be identified because nothing ties the innocent person to the crime. Also, no name index search will reveal the fingerprint classification for comparison purposes. The innocent person's prints may not even be on file. If the forger intends to cast suspicion upon an individual whom he knows will be considered a likely suspect, he may be even more limited in getting a latent fingerprint from that person, and furthermore, that individual's prints might be discarded as lacking probative value if he has had legitimate access to the crime scene.

With all these factors militating against successful use of a "forged" fingerprint, the true criminal might still become implicated because he forgot to remove his own fingerprints from the crime scene. The use of forged fingerprints, then, is really not a practical or useful proposition and does not constitute a great threat to the detection of crime or the conviction of an innocent person.

THE TRANSFERRED POWDERED LIFT. More serious than the two previously discussed means of "forging" latent fingerprints is the allegation that the police themselves have "planted" the fingerprints at a crime scene of an individual whom they desired to "frame." It is a claim easily made, a suspicion easily cast, and frequently it is impossible to disprove by scientific evidence. But such things have happened.

When a federal grand jury reports that crime laboratory technicians went to a crime scene with the specific intention of "discovering" evidence to corroborate the findings of the detectives, and when proof is introduced to show that one technician in fact did back up, falsely, the untrue statements of the detectives, suspicion is cast, in the public's eyes, on all police evidence specialists, including fingerprint technicians.

It is conceded that a fingerprint expert could easily manipulate fingerprint evidence in such a way as to "frame" an individual for a crime. As a man trained in the field, he could without great difficulty obtain a latent impression from a suspect who has been questioned or arrested, since the very presence of the suspect on police premises would assure that he leaves latent impressions in areas or on objects which the technician could have seen him handle. The technician could then just as easily develop the latent print and lift it, then claim to have found and lifted the latent print at a crime scene. He could back up his claim by leaving the cellophane lift on the surface where he alleges he found it or by placing it on a latent print transfer card with appropriate annotations on the card as to the origin of the latent.

The fingerprint technician, accordingly, must be alert to the possibility that such an accusation may be made and make sure that he can prove every step of his actions. After all, his honesty, integrity, and credibility are always at issue when he takes the witness stand, just as is the case with any witness. He should, therefore, resort to making sure there were witnesses to his work at the crime scene, to his development of latent impressions, and to his lifting (if necessary) and photographing of such prints. His attitude as a witness, his dignity, appearance, demeanor, and professional care in his work, must convince the judge and jury that he is a believable witness. By observing all of the proper procedures which are standard in his work, he will avoid the pitfall of appearing to be an incompetent or dishonest police officer. Juries are quite ready to believe the fingerprint technician who displays an attitude of professionalism, discreet confidence, unassuming firmness, clear impartiality, and an unbiased devotion to scientific truth.

Chapter 11

Medical and Related Research in Fingerprint Applications

The public has come to associate fingerprinting almost exclusively with criminal identification and police work, although the use of fingerprints for civilian identification purposes is firmly established and may offer an even greater potential for the future. Apart from identification of individuals in criminal and civil fields, another area of research deals with medical applications. This should not come as a surprise when we realize that the first individuals to draw attention to friction skin patterns were anatomists and other scientists. Among the early researchers, beginning with Dr. Nehemiah Grew in 1671 through Dr. Henry Faulds in 1880, was not a single law enforcement officer. When law enforcement officials saw the potential value of using fingerprints for identification, they seized the initiative and more or less monopolized the field.

Medical research in fingerprinting then went somewhat into eclipse, although it never ended totally. Dedicated researchers in several countries continued their work, but it is largely due to the persistence and genius of an American scientist, Dr. Harold Cummins, Professor Emeritus of Anatomy and former dean of the medical school at Tulane University, that medical research in fingerprint applications has again become a reality. Dr. Cummins became interested in fingerprints in 1921 and since then has become probably the world's most outstanding authority on *dermatoglyphics*, a term he coined in 1926 when he discovered that anatomists and others in related sciences did not have a technical name for fingerprint research.

Dermatoglyphics, a term derived from the Greek and meaning

294

skin designs, is now in general use in the scientific writings of anatomists, physical anthropologists, zoologists, geneticists, and medical doctors. Much of the knowledge of the nature of fingerprints, including their embryology and their physical and physiological characteristics, derives from the efforts of Dr. Cummins, his associates and colleagues. But these men have contributed greatly to other uses of fingerprinting. Among them are the study of correlations between ridge abnormalities and congenital defects, thereby leading to the use of fingerprints as a possible diagnostic aid; the study of inherited pattern types and racial distributions of patterns, suggesting that it might be possible to develop techniques to determine paternity by fingerprints, and other such endeavors.

INHERITANCE OF FINGER PATTERNS

When we speak of inherited fingerprints, it must be made clear at once that the premise that no two fingerprints are identical is not being eroded or disproved. Medical research has established that certain pattern traits, even certain groupings of characteristics, may be transmitted genetically. It has been clearly established that there is a greater average likeness in the finger markings of two brothers than in those of two persons taken at random. Heredity, therefore, does have some influence on the finger patterns. There are numerous instances where children bear the same pattern types found in at least one parent, though not invariably. Research along these lines was conducted in 1908 by Cevidalli, and later by Elderton, Bonnevie, Poll, and Cummins, who all concluded that there was a tendency to inherit certain patterns. They disagreed with earlier reports of Sir Francis Galton and Rene Forgeot who, in the late 1800s, had stated that fingerprint patterns were not inherited. The more recent studies show undeniable correlations which prove that fingerprints are indeed inherited.

The bulk of the investigative material was obtained through studies of twins, triplets, and quadruplets, although thousands of other families and family relationships were also studied. Some close family traits and resemblances have been discovered in fingerprints, although the prints were *never* identical in the minute ridge characteristics. In other cases, no resemblance whatever could be noted. In a study of 436 children, Cummins found a frequency of whorls on the children's fingers which closely matched the percentage of whorls on the parents' fingers. These indications provided only a mass comparison to which some individuals did not conform. He also suggested that the characteristics which are known to be inherited are the type of pattern, including a tendency to double-core structures (as in double loops), breadth-height proportions of patterns (such as broad, medium, or narrow), and pattern size determined by ridge count.

Similarly, it was discovered that the congenital absence of clearly defined ridge patterns could be inherited. Persons with dissociated ridge patterns most frequently had ancestors with similar freak ridge characteristics. It was announced in 1969 that six members of one family had no classifiable finger or palmprints. However, the palmar surfaces were not actually printless, but rather patternless, since friction ridge pebbles in the form of dissociated ridges were present.

Turning from the smallest unit of human groups, the family, to the largest, we find that studies involving human races show that there is also a correlation between frequency of incidence of certain pattern types and race or ethnic groups. A study of 500 sets of prints of white Europeans, conducted by the author in 1952, revealed the following frequency of pattern appearance on the fingers:

	RIGHT HAND			LEFT HAND		
	Arches	*Loops*	*Whorls*	*Arches*	*Loops*	*Whorls*
Thumb	3	52	45	5	64	31
Index	16	54	30	16	56	28
Middle	8	77	15	8	76	16
Ring	2	52	46	3	67	30
Little	1	86	13	2	90	8
Total %	6	64.2	29.8	68	70.6	22.6

This yields overall percentages of 6.4 percent arches, 67.4 percent loops, and 26.2 percent whorls. A similar study conducted ten years later on 500 sets of prints of American prisoners, about one third of whom were not Caucasian, yielded overall percentages of 6.2 percent arches, 63.9 percent loops, and 29.9 percent whorls. The German researcher G. G. Wendt found the following percentage frequencies of the three basic patterns in populations of different genetic background:

GROUP	Percentage Frequencies of		
	Arches	*Loops*	*Whorls*
Bushmen	13.4	68.2	18.4
Europides	6.4	64.8	28.8
Negroes	6.0	62.8	31.2
Hindus	3.0	59.4	37.6
American Indians	5.4	56.0	38.6
Mongolians	2.4	51.8	45.8

On the basis of these and many other studies, other interesting results have been obtained. Another German scientist, Dr. G. Geipel, proved that the Ayom pygmies in New Zealand have a different genetic background from that of the pygmies of central Africa. African pygmies were found to have 12.8 percent arches and 17.7 percent whorls, while the Ayom pygmies have only 0.4 percent arches against 57.8 percent whorls. In reporting on Geipel's study, Professor Walter Hirsch also indicated that in Africa, Asia, and the Americas, whorl frequency decreases from North to South, whereas in Europe the frequency of whorls decreases from South to North: from Mediterraneans (about 30 percent) to Nordics (about 25 percent). He also reports that Arabs and Jews have more whorls (about 35 percent) than European Mediterraneans (29–30 percent). Whorl distribution in black races (average 30 percent), despite extensive variations, is said to be similar to that of Europeans. Mongolians (yellow race) on the other hand are reported to have a high percentage (about 45 percent) of whorls.

The Japanese scientist Dr. Tanemoto Furuhata, assisted by many other researchers of the Institute of Legal Medicine at the University of Tokyo, did a study of the Ainos, an "isolated island race," about whose racial origin the scholars are not yet agreed. Since the Ainos are remarkably different from their surrounding races, Dr. Furuhata and his staff conducted a fingerprint study and correlated pattern frequency in an attempt to determine genetic origin. They concluded that, on the basis of the arch-loop-whorl pattern frequencies, the Ainos do not belong to the Asiatic types and are more closely related to the Polish and Americans of European descent, and that the Ainos are therefore of Caucasian origin. Findings such as these show that studies of human ethnic group fingerprint pattern frequencies are important to our knowledge of the development of mankind.

FINGERPRINTS AS PROOF OF PATERNITY

Having seen that there is a correlation in pattern distribution among races as well as among families, the logical question is whether fingerprints can be used to establish paternity? Not long ago, fingerprint experts would have answered that question in the negative. But then, they would also have said that fingerprint patterns are never inherited. In a report on a survey taken by the New York City Civil Service Commission in 1936 it was stated that practically all fingerprint experts believe that patterns are never inherited.

Today, different answers would obtain. The beliefs of the earlier fingerprint men are not surprising, for the research done in dermatoglyphics by geneticists and other scientists over the past fifty years was seldom if ever brought to the attention of police identification men. It was not until Dr. Harold Cummins started his long-lasting collaboration with the editors of *Finger Print and Identification Magazine* that the fingerprint profession became familiar with his research. Contributing to the negative attitude of fingerprint experts toward inheritance of patterns was misunderstanding of the scientific conclusions. Since one of the basic tenets of the fingerprint technician is that no two fingerprints are ever alike in their minute ridge details, the concept that patterns might be inherited appeared as a threat. Yet, when persons in the medical and related professions talk about inheritance of patterns, they do not suggest that inherited patterns are exactly like those of an ancestor, but rather that they conform to a general configuration including, at times, a close resemblance in repeated groupings of ridge characteristics. At no time have they suggested that in inherited patterns the minute ridge detail is duplicated.

It seems that paternity could, in some instances, be established by fingerprints, but as yet insufficient data have been accumulated to make the results accurate enough to translate into formulas or procedures. A Hungarian scientist, Dr. Sandor Okros, published a book on *The Heredity of Papillary Patterns* in 1965, in which he agrees with this evaluation. He reports investigating the fingerprints of 1,500 families for the specific purpose of tracing the genetic sequences of fingerprint patterns. He also discussed several hundred cases where paternity or nonpaternity was a legal issue, and related cases in which he testified in court on the subject. Of 534 cases the possibility of paternity was not excluded by blood in 463 cases. (Blood analysis, according to experts in this field, can never positively establish paternity, though it can be used to exclude the possibility of paternity.) In the 463 cases, he established paternity in 327 and excluded it in 136 by an examination of the fingerprints. As a control, he investigated the 71 cases in which blood tests had excluded the possibility of paternity, and his fingerprint analysis agreed in 59 instances but showed paternity in 12 cases. A reexamination of the fingerprints in the 12 discrepancies showed that errors had been committed in seven of the original cases, dramatically illustrating the present lack of certainty and the absence of easily formulated standards of procedure.

Expert testimony on determinations of paternity or nonpaternity by fingerprint studies has been used by courts in Hungary, Germany, and Austria, but never as the sole basis for a decision. Fingerprint experts obviously could not qualify as experts in paternity suits unless they could show significant and authoritative independent research in that specific area. This author does not know of any such research having been conducted by American experts whose main job is criminal identification.

FINGERPRINTS AS A DIAGNOSTIC AID

Largely as a result of Dr. Cummins' early publications on dermatoglyphics, many people in the medical profession have given intense scrutiny in the past twenty years to papillary ridge designs on the fingers and hands. The main thrust of the research has been toward discovering whether any correlations existed between fingerprint patterns or fingerprint abnormalities and congenital diseases or defects. Significant results have been reached, particularly with respect to congenital heart disease diagnoses, mongolism, schizophrenia, and phenylketonuria. The medical literature abounds with reports on such research. Discussion on the findings must of necessity be selective. A general conclusion, however, is that dermatoglyphics is emerging as a worthwhile clinical instrument and tool.

One study was concerned with discovering whether certain noncardiac congenital differences are associated with congenital cardiovascular defects. In order to investigate this possibility, the palmprints (a noncardiac congenital difference) of 157 patients with congenital heart disease and of 143 patients with acquired heart disease were examined. The result showed a significant increase in frequency of certain hypothenar ridge formations and other ridge characteristics in patients with congenital heart disease as opposed to those patients who had acquired the heart disease. In a similar study in Japan, which involved a comparison of palmprints of 44 patients with congenital heart disease and those of 362 patients with acquired heart disease, it was found that the distal displacement of a ridge characteristic (palmar axial triradii) occurred in 64 percent of the palmprints of patients suffering from congenital heart disease and in only 17 percent of those with acquired heart disease.

A Spanish study conducted at the Department of Cardiology and Genetics of the Institute for Medical Research in Madrid in 1963 attempted to obtain similar correlations in a study of fingerprints. For purposes of comparison, the fingerprints of 150 patients afflicted with congenital heart disease were compared with those of 50 control subjects. The association between different fingerprint patterns, and their frequency of appearance led to the conclusion that cardiovascular anomalies are genetically determined in a large proportion of cases.

Along similar lines, a study was made at Ypsilanti State Hospital in Michigan to determine whether fingerprint patterns are found to have special characteristics in persons with schizophrenia. By carefully selecting a group of one hundred male schizophrenics so as to exclude any patients who might have suffered from possible complicating features such as mental deficiencies, mongolism, convulsiveness, infantile paralysis, and even left handedness, it was discovered that there was a marked increase in the incidence of whorls, arches, and particularly tented arches, along with a marked decrease in ulnar loops in these patients as compared with the averages for unafflicted persons. In addition to these findings, it was found that the schizophrenics had a very marked tendency toward dissociation of ridges. The anomaly was found to exist on one or more of the fingers of 18 percent of the schizophrenics, as opposed to a percentage of 0.5 percent in a study of the prints of 4,000 convicts.

Cummins also reports that fingerprint areas of ridge dysplasia are very common and often extensive in persons suffering from mongolism, a congenital anomaly occurring about once in 700 births, and resulting in many physical peculiarities, widely dispersed in the body, and a mental state usually at the level of idiocy. He also found unlike frequency of normal features, such as pattern distribution, and a much higher frequency of all-ulnar-loop sets with a corresponding decrease in frequency of whorls, arches, tented arches, and radial loops. Ridge counting to determine the size of the patterns showed that the loops had smaller than average ridge counts. Palmar and plantar abnormalities from the norm were also very pronounced and in unusually high frequency. He states that the difference between mongols and normal people in the location of the distally located palmar axial delta is so great that this single feature would allow a correct distinction in 88 percent of the persons examined. While some newborn mongols are easily recognized as such by other physical defects and features, a study of the palmprints (dermatoglyphic features) could aid greatly in an early diagnosis of doubtful cases.

These and many other similar studies which have been conducted all over the world show that there is much more to fingerprints than simply a means of personal identification. Great promise is held out for possible use of finger, palm and soleprints as a diagnostic aid, and extensive research continues to be carried out along those lines.

Bibliography

BOOKS

Abreu Gomez, *La identificacion criminal y la policia cientifica en Mexico*, Merida, 1951.

Anon., *The Science of Fingerprints*, Washington, D. C., 1963.

Bakhsh, *Identification by Finger-Prints, Palms, Soles and Toes*, Dacca, 1966.

Baptista, *Sistema Portugues de identificacao dactiloscopica*, Lisbon, 1958.

Battley, *Single Finger Prints*, New Haven, 1931.

Block, *Fingerprinting: Magic Weapon Against Crime*, New York, 1969.

Bose, *Finger Print Companion*, Calcutta, 1926.

Brayley, *Arrangement of Finger Prints*, Boston, 1910.

Bridges, *Practical Fingerprinting* (rev. ed.), New York, 1964.

Browne and Brock, *Fingerprints: Fifty Years of Scientific Crime Detection*, New York, 1954.

Calaber, *La Dactyloscopie en Belgique*, Brussels, 1951.

Castellanos, *Identification Problems—Civil and Criminal*, New York, 1939.

Castellanos, *Dermopapiloscopia clinica*, Havana, 1953.

Chapel, *Fingerprinting—A Manual of Identification*, New York, 1941.

Chatterjee, *Finger, Palm and Sole Prints*, Calcutta, 1953.

Cherill, *The Fingerprint System at Scotland Yard*, London, 1953.

Cherill, *Fingerprints Never Lie*, New York, 1954.

Costello and Gibbs, *The Palms and Soles in Medicine*, Springfield, 1967.

Cummins and Midlo, *Finger Prints, Palms and Soles*, Philadelphia, 1943.

Daae, *Identifizierung von Personen speziell durch Fingerabdrucke*, Mannheim, 1905.

de Pina, *Dactiloscopia*, Lisbon, 1938.

Dubois, *Classificacion de las impressiones palmares*, Buenos Aires, 1908.

Duncan, *An Introduction to Fingerprints*, London, 1942.

Faulds, *Guide to Finger Print Identification*, Hanley, 1905.

Faulds, *Manual of Practical Dactylography*, London, 1923.

Ferrer, *Manual de identificacion judicial*, Madrid, 1921.

Field, *Fingerprint Handbook*, Springfield, 1959.

Galton, *Finger Prints*, London, 1892 (Da Capo ed., New York, 1965).

Galton, *Finger-Print Directories*, London, 1895.

Gauthier, *Tratado de papiloscopia*, Santiago, 1953.

Gettings, *The Book of the Hand*, London, 1965.
Heindl, *System und Praxis der Daktyloskopie* (3rd ed.), Berlin, 1927.
Henry, *Classification and Uses of Finger Prints* (8th ed.), London, 1937.
Herschel, *The Origin of Finger Printing*, London, 1916.
Holt, *Finger Prints Simplified*, Chicago, 1920.
Holt, *The Genetics of Dermal Ridges*, Springfield, 1968.
Kuhne, *The Finger Print Instructor*, New York, 1916.
Larson, *Single Fingerprint System*, New York, 1924.
Ljebjedewjew, *Daktiloskopija*, St. Petersburg, 1909.
Locard, *L'Identification des Recidivistes*, Paris, 1909.
Locard, *La Preuve judiciaire par les empreintes digitales*, Lyons, 1914.
McGinnis, *American System of Fingerprint Classification*, Albany, 1963.
Midlo and Cummins, *Palmar and Plantar Dermatoglyphics in Primates*, Philadelphia, 1942.
Moenssens, *Fingerprints and the Law*, Philadelphia, 1969.
Okros, *The Heredity of Papillary Patterns*, Budapest, 1965.
Ortiz, *La identificacion dactiloscopia*, Havana, 1913.
Regenbook, *Dactyloscopie*, Purmerend, 1935.
Rhodes, *Alphonse Bertillon*, New York, 1956.
Ribeiro, *Dactilo-Diagnose*, Rio de Janeiro, 1940.
Roscher, *Handbuch der Daktyloskopie*, Leipzig, 1905.
Scott, *Fingerprint Mechanics*, Springfield, 1958.
Sharp, *Palm Prints: Their Classification and Identification*, Capetown, 1938.
Vucetich, *Dactiloscopia comparada*, La Plata, 1904.
Wehde and Beffel, *Finger Prints Can Be Forged*, Chicago, 1924.
Wilder and Wentworth, *Personal Identification* (2nd ed.), Chicago, 1932.
Wilton, *Fingerprints: History, Law and Romance*, London, 1938.
Wilton, *Fingerprints: Scotland Yard and Henry Faulds*, Edinburgh, 1951.
Windt and Kodicek, *Daktyloskopie*, Vienna, 1904.

ARTICLES

CHAPTER 1

Ahmad, "The Development of the Henry System," *Finger Print and Identification Magazine* [hereafter referred to as *Finger Print Mag.*], Apr. 1964, p. 3.
Anderson, "Prehistoric Finger Prints," *Finger Print Mag.*, Sep. 1958, p. 3.
Bridges, "Personal Identification Through the Ages," *Finger Print Mag.*, Nov. 1937, p. 16.
Bridges, "Paries Palmatus," *Finger Print Mag.*, Sep. 1946, p. 3.
Bridges, "Pueblo Pottery," *Finger Print Mag.*, Jul. 1948, p. 3.
Bridges, "Pioneers of Finger Print Science," *Finger Print Mag.*, (I) Feb. 1954; (II) Mar. 1954; (III) Apr. 1954.
Cooke, "Mayan Hand Prints," *Finger Print Mag.*, Aug. 1951, p. 15.
Cummins, "Ancient Finger Prints in Clay," 52 *Scientific Monthly* 389 (1941).
Cummins and Kennedy, "Purkinje's Observations on Finger Prints and Other Skin Features," 31 *J. Crim. L. & Criminology* 343 (1940).
de Forest, "The Evolution of Dactyloscopy in the United States" (privately reprinted from *Proc. 16th-17th Ann. Conv., Int'l Ass'n for Ident., 1930-1931*).
Faulds, "On the Skin-Furrows of the Hand," *Nature*, Oct. 28, 1880, p. 605.
Faulds, "On the Identification of Habitual Criminals by Finger Prints," *Nature*, Oct. 4, 1894, p. 548.
Faulds, "The Hidden Hand" (pamphlet), circa 1920.

Faulds, "The Dawn of Dactylography," *Dactylography,* Jul. 1921, p. 12; Sep. 1921, p. 27.

Felsher, "A Quick Look at Dermatoglyphics," *Identification News,* Jul. 1962, p. 6.

Ferrier, "The Henry or Finger-Print System of Identification," *Mayer's Monthly Magazine,* Dec. 1904, p. 3.

Ferrier, "How St. Louis Obtained Its First Criminal Finger Prints," *Finger Print Mag.,* Dec. 1938, p. 3.

Galton, "Finger Prints in the Determination of Identity," *Scientific American,* 1897 (Supp. 17, p. 859).

Herrero, "Fifty Years of Dactyloscopy in Argentina," *Finger Print Mag.* Oct. 1943, p. 3.

Herschel, "Answer to 'On the Skin-Furrows of the Hand,' " *Nature,* Nov. 22, 1880.

Herschel, "The Origin of Fingerprinting" (pamphlet), 1916.

Klen, "Purkinje—A Man of Science," *Finger Print Mag.,* Mar. 1950, p. 6.

Laufer, "History of the Finger Print System," *Ann. Rep., Smithsonian Inst. 1912,* p. 631.

McClaughry, "History of the Introduction of the Bertillon System into the United States," *Finger Print Mag.,* Apr. 1922, p. 3.

Mairs, "Identification of Individuals by Means of Fingerprints, Palmprints and Sole Prints," 7 *Scientific Monthly* 4 (Oct. 1918).

Myers II, "Ancient Chinese Finger Prints," *Finger Print Mag.,* Sep. 1936, p. 18.

Myers II, "History of Identification in the United States," *Finger Print Mag.,* Oct. 1938, p. 3.

Myers II, "Supplemental History of Identification in the United States," *Finger Print Mag.,* Dec. 1942, p. 3.

Myers II, "A Third History of Identification in the United States," *Finger Print Mag.,* Apr. 1948, p. 3.

Myers II, "The Henry System Semi-Centennial," *Finger Print Mag.,* Jun. 1950, p. 3.

Myers II, "A Note on Tabor," *Finger Print Mag.,* Apr. 1965, p. 14.

Polson, "Finger Prints and Finger Printing: A Historical Study," 41 *J. Crim. L., Criminology & Pol. Sci.* 560 (1950).

Sannié, "Alphonse Bertillon and Finger Print Identification," *Finger Print Mag.,* Feb. 1951, p. 3.

Shreenivas and Sinha, "Personal Identification by the Dermatoglyphics and the E—V Methods," 31 *Patna J. Med.* 103 (1957).

Thompson, "National Identification Bureau is IACP Pioneers' Legacy," *The Police Chief,* Jan. 1968, p. 10.

Yasoshima, "Note on Henry Faulds," *Jap. J. Leg. Med. & Criminology,* Jun. 1958, p. 69.

Yasoshima, "Henry Faulds—Pioneer in Dactyloscopy," *Finger Print Mag.,* May 1960, p. 3.

CHAPTER 2

Anderson, "Prehistoric Finger Prints," *Finger Print Mag.,* Sep. 1958, p. 3.

Anon., "Finger Prints Reappear Despite Tortuous Mutilation," *Finger Print Mag.,* May 1930, p. 7.

Anon., "Evidentiary Value of Finger-Prints," 80 *Pa. L. Rev.* 887 (1932).

Anon., "Scarred Finger Tips of 'Dead' Jack Klutas *fail* to foil Identification Experts," *Finger Print Mag.,* Mar. 1934, p. 16.

Anon., " 'Live' Palm Prints, 50 Years Apart, Revealed," *Finger Print Mag.,* Apr. 1939, p. 3.

Anon., "Skin Grafting Operation on Felon's Fingers Fails to Hide His Identity," *Finger Print Mag.*, Feb. 1942, p. 11.

Anon., "Fingerprint Alterations and Clinical Dactyloscopy," *J.A.M.A.* Vol. 124, Jan. 8, 1944, p. 118.

Anon., "Michigan Quadruplets Finger Printed to Celebrate 16th Birthday," *Finger Print Mag.*, Oct. 1946, p. 16.

Anon., "His Attempt to Change Prints Ends in Failure," *Finger Print Mag.*, Dec. 1953, p. 16.

Anon., "Fingerprint Mutilation," *FBI Law Enforcement Bull.*, Jun. 1957, p. 19.

Anon., "The Question of Print Removal by Surgical Planing," *FBI Law Enforcement Bull.*, Mar. 1958, p. 18.

Anon., "Harold Cummins Explains Some Mighty Curious Ridge Patterns," *Finger Print Mag.*, Oct. 1960, p. 14.

Anon., "Prisoner Attempts Finger Print Scarring," *Finger Print Mag.*, May 1965, p. 11.

Anon., "Prints of Quintuplets Again Prove Individuality of Patterns," *Finger Print Mag.*, Dec. 1965, p. 3.

Anon., "Admits He 'Goofed' When Scarification of Print Failed," *Finger Print Mag.*, Oct. 1969, p. 16.

Baird, "Kindred Showing Congenital Absence of the Dermal Ridges (Fingerprints) and Associated Anomalies," *J. Pediatrics*, Vol. 64, No. 5 (1964).

Bogren, "The Discovery—Infallibility—and Permanence of Finger Prints As Means of Personal Identification," *Finger Print Mag.*, Jul. 1927, p. 23.

Braash and Nickson, "A Study of the Hands of Radiologists," 5 *Radiology* 719 (1948).

Burks, "Alteration of Finger Prints by Dermabrasion," *Finger Print Mag.*, Feb. 1958, p. 3.

Burks, "The Effect of Dermabrasion on Fingerprints," 77 *AMA Arch. Derm.* 8 (1958).

Castellanos, "The Biological Examination of Fingerprints," *Finger Print Mag.*, Dec. 1929, p. 3.

Cooke, "Intentional and Accidental Scarification of Finger Prints—Prints of Atomic Bomb Victims," *Finger Print Mag.*, Jun. 1953, p. 3.

Cooke, "Intentional and Accidental Scarification of Finger Prints—Inadvertent Pattern Destruction," *Finger Print Mag.*, May 1957, p. 3.

Cooke, "Finger Printing is Unscathed," *Finger Print Mag.*, Mar. 1958, p. 2.

Cooke, "Intentional and Accidental Scarification of Finger Prints—Willful Pattern Destruction," *Finger Print Mag.*, Apr. 1958, p. 3.

Coulson, "Permanence of Finger Prints," *J. Franklin Institute*, Jun. 1939, p. 819.

Cummins, "Dermatoglyphics: Significant Patternings of the Body Surface," 18 *Yale J. Biol. & Med.* 551 (1946).

Cummins, "Why Takeshita Lacks Patterned Friction Skin," *Finger Print Mag.*, May 1950, p. 3.

Cummins, "Loss of Ridged Skin Before Birth," *Finger Print Mag.*, Feb. 1965, p. 3.

Cummins, "Finger Prints: Normal and Abnormal Patterns," *Finger Print Mag.*, Nov. 1967, p. 3.

Darwish, "Intentional Scarification of Finger Prints," *Finger Print Mag.*, Nov. 1958, p. 6.

de Andres, "Finger-Tip Surgery," *Intl. Crim. Pol. Rev.*, Mar. 1955, p. 66.

Enklaar, "Principles and Problems in the Process of Identification," *Identification News*, Aug. 1964, p. 4.

Felsher, "A Quick Look at Dermatoglyphics," *Identification News,* Jul. 1962, p. 6.

Furuhata, Furuya, Tanaka and Nakajima, "A Family With Unclassifiable Papillary Patterns," 33 *Proc. Japan Academy* 410 (1957).

Furuhata and Kuwashima, "A Mysterious Man, who Has No Classifiable Papillar Ridge Pattern on Fingers and Toes," 26 *Proc. Japan Academy* 41 (1950).

Galton, "Identification by Finger-Tips," *The Nineteenth Century,* Aug. 1891, p. 303.

Gibbs, "Finger and Palm Alterations Due to Keratosis," *Finger Print Mag.,* Jul. 1965, p. 3.

Johnson, "Pads on Palm and Sole of the Human Foetus," *American Naturalist,* 1899, p. 729.

Kingston and Kirk, "Historical Development and Evaluation of the '12 point Rule' in Fingerprint Identification," *Intl. Crim. Pol. Rev.,* No. 186, p. 62 (1965).

Lacy, "Proof That Ridges Reappear After Demolishing or Burning," *Finger Print Mag.,* Jul. 1920, p. 4.

Lewisch, "Finger Print Identification," *Finger Print Mag.,* Sep. 1956, p. 4.

Mairs, "Can Two Identical Ridge Patterns Actually Occur—Either on Different Persons or on the Same Person?" *Finger Print Mag.,* Jul. 1953, p. 7.

Montagna, "The Skin," *Scientific American,* Feb. 1965, p. 56.

Okamoto, "The Extraordinary Finger Prints of the Boy of Nagoya," *Finger Print Mag.,* Jun. 1958, p. 15.

Osterburg, "An Inquiry Into the Nature of Proof—The Identity of Fingerprints," 9 *J. Forensic Sci.* 413 (1964).

Plotnick and Clor, "Destruction of Finger Print Pattern by Late Syphilis of the Palm," *Finger Print Mag.,* Dec. 1958, p. 4.

Robbins, "The Arizona Capture and Identification of 'The Dillinger Gang,' " *Finger Print Mag.,* Jun. 1934, p. 16.

Sannié, "The Value of Proof of Identification by Finger Prints," *Finger Print Mag.,* Dec. 1948, p. 15.

Scott, "Plastic Reproduction of Finger Ridge Patterns," *Identification News,* Nov. 1954, p. 6.

Singh, "Can Eight Corresponding Ridge Details in Fingerprints Justify Positive Identity?" *Identification News,* Apr. 1964, p. 11.

Taylor, "Doubles Do Not Exist," *Finger Print Mag.,* Apr. 1921, p. 2.

Wentworth, "Impossibility of Identical Finger Prints!," *Finger Print Mag.,* Jun. 1927, p. 16.

CHAPTER 4

Agate and Buckwell, "Mercury Poisoning from Fingerprint Photography," *The Lancet,* Sep. 10 1949, p. 451.

Anon., "New Method Develops Years-Old Fingerprints," *FBI Law Enforcement Bull.,* Nov. 1954, p. 14.

Anon., "Lifting Latent Fingerprints," *FBI Law Enforcement Bull.,* Jun. 1965, p. 14.

Blum and Lougheed, "Results of Time, Temperature, and Humidity on Latent Fingerprints," Flint, Mich., Police Dept. Research Paper, 1959.

Braught, "Lifting Latents for Keeps and for Court," *Finger Print Mag.,* Oct. 1959, p. 6.

Campbell, "Latent Finger Print Developers," *Finger Print Mag.,* Feb. 1950, p. 16.

de Resillac-Rose, "Copying Fingerprints—I" and "Copying Fingerprints—II," *Scientific American* (Supp.) Sep. 13, 1919, and Oct. 11, 1919.

Edwards, Hockey and Hudson, "Some Observations on the Detection of Fingerprints Using Ninhydrin," *J. Forensic Sci. Soc.,* Vol. 6, p. 183 (1966).

Ferrero, "Fingerprint Detection by Chemical Means," *Scientific American,* Nov. 8, 1913.

Graham, "Some Technical Aspects of the Demonstration and Vizualization of Fingerprints on Human Skin," *J. Forensic Sci.,* Vol. 14, p. 1 (1969).

Graham and Gray, "The Use of X-Ray Electronography and Autoelectronography in Forensic Investigation," *J. Forensic Sci.,* Vol. 11, p. 124 (1966).

Grodsky, "Variations in Latent Print Techniques," *Finger Print Mag.,* Dec. 1957, p. 16.

Hanggi and Alfultis, "Improved Technique in the Development and Lifting of Latent Fingerprints," *Identification News,* Jun. 1969, p. 5.

Harper, "Latent Prints at High Temperatures," 29 *J. Crim. L. & Criminology* 580 (1937).

Janakiram, "Intensifying Latent Finger Impressions on Single Colored Surfaces," *Finger Print Mag.,* Nov. 1968, p. 11.

Jones, "Fused Finger Prints," *Finger Print Mag.,* May 1967, p. 11.

Kirby, "Use of Chemicals in Developing Latent Prints," *Identification News,* Nov. 1968, p. 3.

Larsen, "The Starch Powder-Steam Method of Fixing Iodine Fumed Latent Prints," *Finger Print Mag.,* Jul. 1962, p. 3.

MacDonell, "The Use of Hydrogen Fluoride in the Development of Latent Fingerprints Found on Glass Surfaces," 51 *J. Crim. L., Criminology & Pol. Sci.* 465 (1960).

MacDonell, "Bristleless Brush Development of Latent Fingerprints," *Identification News,* Mar. 1961, p. 7.

MacDonell, "Recent Developments in the Processing of Latent Fingerprints," *Identification News,* Sep. 1961, p. 6.

MacDonell, "Recent Advancements in the Processing of Latent Fingerprints," *Identification News,* Jan. 1968, p. 4.

McLaughlin, "Developing Latent Prints on Absorbent Surfaces," *Finger Print Mag.,* Feb. 1961, p. 3.

McLaughlin, "Chemicals and Their Application for Developing Latent Prints," *Finger Print Mag.,* Jul. 1961, p. 3.

Mairs, "Handling Latent Friction Ridge Prints," *Finger Print Mag.,* Apr. 1951, p. 3.

Medlin, "The Flame Process," *Identification News,* Dec. 1967, p. 4.

Moenssens, "Ninhydrin Development of Latent Finger Prints: A Careful Reappraisal," *Finger Print Mag.,* Mar. 1968, p. 11.

Myers II, "Silver Chloride Reaction on Chance Impressions on Cloth," *Finger Print Mag.,* Jul. 1936, p. 11.

O'Neill, "The Development of Latent Fingerprints on Paper," 28 *J. Crim. L. & Criminology* 432 (1937).

Palla and Wiebe, "Development of Latent Finger Prints on Greasy Surfaces," *Finger Print Mag.,* Jul. 1950, p. 16.

Sandberg, "Developing Latents by Silver Nitrate," *Finger Print Mag.,* Feb. 1946, p. 16.

Speaks, "The Use of Ninhydrin in the Development of Latent Finger Prints," *Finger Print Mag.,* Mar. 1964, p. 11.

Speaks, "Ninhydrin Prints From Rubber Gloves," *Finger Print Mag.,* Sep. 1966, p. 3.

Theys, Turgis, Lepareux, Chevet and Ceccaldi, "New Technique For Bringing Out Latent Fingerprints On Paper: Vacuum Metallization," *Intl. Crim. Pol. Rev.,* Apr. 1968, p. 106.

Watson, "Now You Can Lift Prints From Dusty Surfaces," *California Peace Officer,* Nov.–Dec. 1960, p. 10.

Wiebe and Miles, "A Development in Iodine Fuming of Latent Finger Prints," *Identification News,* Feb. 1957, p. 4.

CHAPTER 5

Allen, "Fingerprint Photography With a '35'," *The Police Journal,* Feb. 1964, p. 68.

Anderson, "Prehistoric Finger Prints," *Finger Print Mag.,* Sep. 1958, p. 3.

Anon., "Procedures of the California State Department of Justice for Fingerprinting the Dead" (mimeographed materials, undated).

Anon., "Invents Way to Take Finger Prints of Mummies," *Finger Print Mag.,* May 1929, p. 9.

Anon., "Footprinting of Infants," *FBI Law Enforcement Bull.,* Jan. 1945.

Anon., "Problems and Practices in Fingerprinting the Dead," *FBI Law Enforcement Bull.,* Apr. 1949.

Anon., "Californian Designs Compact Print Outfit," *Finger Print Mag.,* Feb. 1958, p. 16.

Anon., "New Pad Revolutionizes Recording of Prints," *Finger Print Mag.,* Aug. 1963, p. 11.

Anon., "Digital Amputation in Post Mortem," *Finger Print Mag.,* Apr. 1965, p. 3.

Billinhurst, "Some Elementary Aspects of Fingerprint Photography," *The Police Journal,* Feb. 1966, p. 89.

Bowen, "It's HOW Baby Foot Prints Are Made That Makes the BIG Difference," *Finger Print Mag.,* Sep. 1957, p. 3.

Castellanos, "An Unusual Post Mortem Identification," *Finger Print Mag.,* Jul. 1964, p. 3.

Castellanos, "New Techniques of Skin Impressions (Dermatoscopy)," *Identification News,* Jan. 1970, p. 13.

Cherill, "A New Method of Taking the Finger Prints of Cadavers," *Intl. Crim. Pol. Rev.,* Jun.–Jul. 1951, p. 205.

Cooke, "Unusual Techniques in Post Mortem Finger Printing," *Finger Print Mag.,* Aug. 1958, p. 3.

Corr, "Post Mortem Printing Under Difficult Conditions," *Finger Print Mag.,* Feb. 1960, p. 3.

Cowan, "Preparation of Fingers for Post Mortem Printing Following Extreme Deterioration," *Finger Print Mag.,* Jul. 1959, p. 3.

Fletcher, "Obtaining Finger Prints from Cadavers," *Finger Print Mag.,* Jan. 1939, p. 3.

Forndran, "New Method for Recording Friction Skin Patterns," *Finger Print Mag.,* Sep. 1964, p. 3.

Fowler, "Further Thoughts on Casting Finger Prints," *Finger Print Mag.,* Feb. 1958, p. 6.

Goodman, "Identification of the Newly Born" (pamphlet), N.Y., 1957.

Hammond, Thomas and Heerman, "Footprinting the Newborn," 31 *Hospitals* 54 (Aug. 16, 1957).

Harrick, "Fingerprinting Via Total Internal Reflection," *Philips Technical Rev.,* 1962–63, No. 9, p. 271.

Harrison, "Fingerprinting Floaters," *Identification News,* Jul. 1961, p. 7.

Heathcote, "If You Can See It, You Can Photograph It," *The Police Journal,* Apr. 1963, p. 171.

Hunt, "Fingerprinting of Decomposed Bodies," *The Police Journal,* Nov.–Dec. 1960, p. 360.

Jenkins, "Identification of Disaster Victims," *Identification News,* Apr.–May 1957, p. 7.

Kimura, "The Electronic Finger Printing Method," *Finger Print Mag.*, Jan. 1965, p. 3.

Lieber, "Fingerprinting Partly Decomposed Bodies," *Identification News*, Aug.–Sep. 1958, p. 6.

Lucas, "Making Finger Prints Visible By Ultra-Violet Light," *Finger Print Mag.*, Aug. 1937, p. 3.

Mercer, "Obtaining Finger Prints From Mummified Fingers," *Finger Print Mag.*, Feb. 1966, p. 3.

Monti, "An Interesting Post Mortem Technique," *Finger Print Mag.*, May 1961, p. 6.

Osburn, "Outline of a Method for the Restoration of Desiccated Fingers," *Finger Print Mag.*, Sep. 43, p. 15.

Padron, "Necrodactylography—Advanced Post Mortem Finger Print Techniques," *Finger Print Mag.*, Dec. 1963, p. 3.

Padron, "Difficulties in Recording Finger Prints," *Finger Print Mag.*, Jan. 1967, p. 3.

Picard, "The Foto Focuser," *Law and Order*, Apr. 1958, p. 12.

Reeves, "A Newly Developed Method for Obtaining Dermal Impressions," *Finger Print Mag.*, Feb. 1957, p. 17.

Richards, "A New X-Ray Method for Finger Printing Badly Burned Fingers," *Finger Print Mag.*, May 1956, p. 3.

Rispling, "Obtaining Finger Prints of a Corpse," *Finger Print Mag.*, Aug. 1957, p. 17.

Scott, "Criminal Records and Fingerprint Photography," 4 *J. Forensic Sci.* 60 (1963).

Shepard, Erickson and Fromm, "Limitations of Footprinting as a Means of Infant Identification," 37 *Pediatrics* 107 (Jan. 1966).

Trotter, "Footprinting of Infants," *Finger Print Mag.*, Mar. 1959, p. 3.

Witte, "Macerated Fingers Identify Drowned Man," *Finger Print Mag.*, May 1959, p. 16.

CHAPTER 7

Cooke, "The Russak System Is Rough On Miami Crooks," *Finger Print Mag.*, Mar. 1962, p. 3.

Gootee, "Indianapolis, Indiana Simultaneous Classification System and General Appearance File," *Identification News*, Oct. 1959, p. 4.

Hayes and Roberts, "The Hayes-Roberts System for Latent Finger Print Identification," *Finger Print Mag.*, May 1968, p. 3.

Sharp, "The Five-Finger System of Finger Print Classification," *Finger Print Mag.*, Nov. 1951, p. 3.

Sharp, "The Ten-One File," *Finger Print Mag.*, Aug. 1961, p. 3.

CHAPTER 8

Anderson, "The Extension Primary Classification," *Finger Print Mag.*, Feb. 1965, p. 12.

Anon., "Single Finger Prints in the Los Angeles Police Bureau" [Barlow System], *Finger Print Mag.*, Dec. 1937, p. 16.

Anon., "RCMP Identification Branch Provides Modern Techniques," *Identification News*, Apr. 1961, p. 11.

Anon., "The Identification Branch" (pamphlet) RCMP, 1962.

Boolsen and Bridges, "Fifty-One Fingerprint Systems" (mimeographed materials), Berkeley, 1935.

Borgerhoff, "Le Service Belge d'Identification Judiciaire" (pamphlet), Imprimerie du Moniteur belge, 1924.

Bower, "The Bower System of Classifying Plain Arch Finger Print Patterns," *Finger Print Mag.*, Apr. 1952, p. 3.

Brogger Moller, "Classification of Palm Prints in Denmark," *Intl. Crim. Pol. Rev.,* Feb. 1952, p. 43.

Brogger Moller, "Palm Print File in Denmark," *Finger Print Mag.,* Aug. 1952, p. 3.

Brogger Moller, "The Classification of Palm Prints in Denmark," *Finger Print Mag.,* May 1954, p. 3.

Brown, "Single Finger Prints," *Finger Print Mag.,* May 1953, p. 15.

Brown, "A New Subdivision for Single Finger Prints," *Finger Print Mag.,* Jun. 1953, p. 3.

Calaber, "Three-Finger Classification," *Finger Print Mag.,* Apr. 1953, p. 16. (Also in *Intl. Crim. Pol. Rev.,* May 1952.)

Cataldo, "The Revised Cataldo System," *Finger Print Mag.,* Feb. 1959, p. 15.

Chatterjee, "Classification of Middle Phalange Impressions," *Finger Print Mag.,* Sep. 1959, p. 3.

Cooke, "The Decimal System of Classifying Single Finger Prints," *Finger Print Mag.,* Oct. 1950, p. 15.

Cooke, "An Extension to the Decimal System of Classifying Single Finger Prints," *Finger Print Mag.,* Jun. 1951, p. 15.

Dalstrom, "The Finger Print Registry of the National Institute of Technical Police at Stockholm," *Finger Print Mag.,* Jan. 1951, p. 3.

Field, "Single Hand Classification," *Identification News,* Jan. 1956, p. 4.

Geysen, "A Method of Classification for Plain Finger Prints," *Finger Print Mag.,* Oct. 1952, p. 16.

Griffiths, "A Short History of Finger Prints in Malaya" [includes discussion on Conley System], *Finger Print Mag.,* Feb. 1952, p. 3.

Hayes and Roberts, "The Hayes-Roberts System for Latent Print Identification," *Finger Print Mag.,* May 1968, p. 3.

Janakiram, "Effect of the Chatterjee Middle Phalange System on the Ten Digit Method," *Finger Print Mag.,* May 1964, p. 11.

Kalyanasundaram, "A Defense of the Chatterjee Middle Phalange System," *Finger Print Mag.,* Oct. 1960, p. 6.

Kehdy, "The Vucetich System of Classification and Filing," *Finger Print Mag.,* Feb. 1947, p. 3.

Maclean, "Searching Single Finger Prints" [Glasgow System], *Finger Print Mag.,* Feb. 1953, p. 3.

McGinnis, "American System of Fingerprint Classification" (pamphlet), N.Y. State Dept. of Correction, 1963.

Nayar, "Subclassification of the Ten-Arch Group," *Finger Print Mag.,* Mar. 1967, p. 3.

Preller, "Identification Section of the Argentine Federal Police," *Finger Print Mag.,* Apr. 1949, p. 3.

Regenboog, "Papillary Ridge Comparison in Holland," *Finger Print Mag.,* Mar. 1956, p. 6.

Sharp, "The Five Finger System of Finger Print Classification," *Finger Print Mag.,* Nov. 1951, p. 3.

Simons, "The Pateer System of Finger Print Classification," *Finger Print Mag.,* Apr. 1955, p. 3.

Singh, "Discussion on the Subclassification of the Ten-Arch Group," *Finger Print Mag.,* Mar. 1960, p. 3.

Singh, "Further Discussion on the Middle Phalange System of Subclassification," *Finger Print Mag.,* Jun. 1962, p. 3.

Singh, "Extension of the Henry Classification for the Ten-Loop Group," *Finger Print Mag.,* Sep. 1967, p. 14.

Stephenson, "Earle Fingerprint File System," *Identification News,* Apr. 1954, p. 7.
Stephenson, "The W-A-I-T-E Code," *Identification News,* Mar. 1960, p. 12.
Taylor, "One Finger System" (pamphlet), U.S. Govt. Print. Off., 1921.
Vonk, "Wat gebeurt er met de Dactyloscopische speuren," *Algemeen Politieblad,* Jun. 1960, p. 243.
Wedderburn, "Division of the Ten Arch Group," *Finger Print Mag.,* Nov. 1952, p. 3.
Wybrands, "Identification Methods at Barcelona," *Finger Print Mag.,* Sep. 1939, p. 16.

CHAPTER 9

Angst and Frieden, "Auswertung von daktyloskopischen Spuren mit electronischer Datenverarbeitung," *Kriminalistik,* Jun. 1968, p. 286.
Anon., "NYSIIS Fingerprint Classification and Identification System—Status Report" (mimeographed materials, Albany, N.Y.) Oct. 1965.
Anon., "Computerized Crime Fighting," *Police,* Mar.–Apr. 1967, p. 90.
Anon., "NYSIIS Against Crime" (pamphlet) NYSIIS Bureau of Public Inform., Apr. 1967.
Anon., "Automation and Information Sharing in New York," *Finger Print Mag.,* Jul. 1968, p. 3.
Anon., "Searching by Computer; A NYSIIS Reality," *Finger Print Mag.,* Sep. 1968, p. 16.
Cashin, "Electronic Fingerprint and Personal Appearance Identification" (pamphlet), circa 1953.
Cooke, "Electronics Speed Identification Service in New York State," *Finger Print Mag.,* Sep. 1953, p. 3.
Cooke, "The Russak System Is Rough On Miami Crooks," *Finger Print Mag.,* Mar. 1962, p. 3.
Fitzmaurice, "Automatic Single Fingerprint Identification," *Ident. News,* Nov. 1963, p. 4.
Hayes and Roberts, "The Hayes-Roberts System for Latent Finger Print Identification," *Finger Print Mag.,* May 1968, p. 3.
Horvath, Holeman and Lemmons, "Fingerprint Recognition by Holographic Techniques," *Police,* Sep.–Oct. 1967, p. 45.
Kingston, "Progress and Research in the Automation of Fingerprint Files," *Ident. News,* Sep. 1968, p. 4
O'Neill, "Automation in the Field of Identification," *Identification News,* Jan. 1964, p. 4.
Shelman, "Machine Classification of Fingerprints," *Argonne Natl. Lab. Reviews,* Apr. 1969, p. 21.
Snyders, "Facsimile Delivers The Message," *Business Automation,* Apr. 1960, p. 52.
Thomas and Verruso, "Fingerprint Identification and Facsimile Communications," *Muirhead Technique,* Apr. 1967, p. 11.
Trauring, "Automatic Comparison of Finger-Ridge Patterns," *Nature,* Mar. 3, 1963, p. 939.
Trotter, "Automation and the Fingerprint Expert," *Ident. News,* Oct.–Nov. 1966, p. 10.
Verruso, "NYSIIS—A New Era in Law Enforcement," *Finger Print Mag.,* Apr. 1967, p. 3.
Wegstein, "A Computer Oriented Single-Fingerprint Identification System" (pamphlet), Washington, D.C., 1968.
Wegstein, "A Semi-Automated Single Fingerprint Identification System" (pamphlet), Washington, D.C., 1969.

CHAPTER 10

Anon., "Defense Counsel Tries To Discredit Finger-Print Evidence," *Finger Print Mag.*, Aug. 1925, p. 3.

Anon., "More Opinions on Forgeries by Experts," *Finger Print Mag.*, Sep. 1928, p. 15.

Anon., "Can Finger Prints Be Forged???" *Finger Print Mag.*, Jul. 1931, p. 3.

Anon., "N.Y. State Bureau Develops Useful Print Viewer," *Finger Print Mag.*, Jan. 1955, p. 6.

Anon., "Fingerprint Forgery," *Identification News*, Jul. 1957, p. 5.

Anon., "The Truth About Forged Fingerprint Article," *Identification News*, Sep.–Oct. 1957, p. 4.

Anon., "FBI Director J. Edgar Hoover Denies Print Forgery Story," *Finger Print Mag.*, Nov. 1957, p. 15.

Anon., "Made by Same Digit, Yet They Differ In Appearance," *Finger Print Mag.*, Feb. 1958, p. 32.

Anon., "Bare Foot Prints At Dancing School Send Burglar to Prison," *Finger Print Mag.*, Nov. 1965, p. 16.

Anon., "Fingerprints Do *Not* Lie," *FBI Law Enforcement Bull.*, Sep. 1969, p. 20.

Anon., "FBI Director J. Edgar Hoover Sets the Record Straight," *Finger Print Mag.*, Oct. 1969, p. 3.

Anon., "Six Cazenovia Family Members Have No Finger or Palm Prints," *NYSIIS Newsletter*, Dec. 1969, p. 1.

Anon., "These Palms Could Cause Confusion," *Finger Print Mag.*, Mar. 1970, p. 24.

Arcano and Hernandez, "Dactyloscopic, Chiroscopic and Podoscopic Identification Cases," *Finger Print Mag.*, Aug. 1953, p. 15.

Baird, "Kindred showing congenital absence of the dermal ridges (fingerprints) and associated anomalies," 64 *J. Pediatrics* 621 (1964).

Bleben, "A Study in the Hereditary Transmission of Finger Patterns," *Proc. Iowa Acad. Sci. for 1901*, Vol. IX, p. 44.

Carlson, "Finger-Prints Can Be Forged," 5 *Va. L. Reg.* (*N.S.*) 765 (1920).

Carlson, "Dangers of Finger-Print Identification," 9 *Va. L. Reg.* (*N.S.*) 163 (1923).

Castellanos, "Types of Papillary Ridges," *Finger Print Mag.*, Nov. 1955, p. 16.

Chamberlain, "New Style Comparator Now Available," *Finger Print Mag.*, Nov. 1958, p. 15.

Chatterjee, "Edgeoscopy," *Finger Print Mag.*, Sep. 62. p. 3.

Cummins, "Counterfeit Finger-Prints," 25 *J. Crim. L. & Criminology* 666 (1934).

Cummins, "Attempts to Alter and Obliterate Fingerprints," 25 *J. Crim. L. &. Criminology* 982 (1935).

Cummins, "Notes on 'Walter' Thumbprints of the 'Margery' Seances," *Proc. Soc. Psychical Research*, Apr. 1935, p. 15.

Cummins, "The Identity of the 'Walter' Right Thumb," *Psychic Science* Jan. 1936, p. 289.

Cummins, "Finger Print Forgery," *Finger Print Mag.*, Apr. 1944, p. 16.

Cummins, "Finger Prints Modified by Scarring," *Finger Print Mag.*, Feb. 1956, p. 16.

Cummins, "Finger Prints of Phantoms!," *Finger Print Mag.*, Dec. 1960, p. 3.

Davis, "Pressure Distortion in Latent Prints," *Finger Print Mag.*, Dec. 1946, p. 3.

Davis, "Further Thoughts on Finger Print Comparisons," *Finger Print Mag.*, Jul. 1955, p. 15.

Engeset, "He Wore Gloves Yet Left Prints of Both Hands," *Finger Print Mag.*, Dec. 1964, p. 3.

Faulds, "Poroscopy, the Scrutiny of Sweat-Pores for Identification," *Nature*, Vol. 90, p. 635 (1913).

Furuhata, Furuya, Tanaka, Nakajima, Hasebe, Yokoyama, Nozawa and Fukumoto, "Genetic Investigation of Five Generations of One Family (Second Case) II. Fingerprint Patterns," 33 *Proc. Jap. Acad.* 673 (1957).

Furuhata, Ishii, Hasebe, Yokoyama, Furuya and Tanaka, "Genetical Investigation of a Family for Five Generations. II. Fingerprint Patterns," and "III. Palm Patterns," 32 *Proc. Jap. Acad.* 143 and 147 (1956).

Goddefroy, "Peut-on produire de fausses empreintes digitales?" 28 *Arch. d'anth. crim.* 207 (1913).

Guirguis, "Determining Paternity through Finger Prints," *Finger Print Mag.*, Aug. 46, p. 16, and *Finger Print Mag.*, Dec. 1949, p. 3.

Hardless, "Method of Comparing Thumb Impressions," *Identification News*, Mar. 1968, p. 3; Apr. 1968, p. 11; May 1968, p. 11; Jun. 1968, p. 14.

Harper, "Fingerprint 'Forgery'—Transferred Latent Fingerprints," 28 *J. Crim. L. & Criminology* 573 (1938).

Hoover, "Hoover Responds to—'Some Fingerprints Lie,'" *The Legal Aid Briefcase*, Jun. 1969, p. 221. (Also in *Identification News*, Sep. 1969, p. 11.)

Johnson, "Fingerprints Can Be Forged," (pamphlet; Orange County Sheriff's Dept., Santa Ana, Calif., undated).

Kasai, "On the Inheritance of Palmar Patterns," 5 *Jap. J. Leg. Med.* 108 (1951).

Kehdy, "Charting Ridge Characteristics in Brazil," *Finger Print Mag.*, Sep. 1955, p. 3.

Keyes, "Forgery of Finger Prints," *Finger Print Mag.*, Feb. 1967, p. 3.

Lauritis," Some Fingerprints Lie," *The Legal Aid Briefcase*, Oct. 1968, p. 35. (Also in *Identification News*, Sep. 1969, p. 3.)

Lee, "Finger Print Forgeries," *Finger Print Mag.*, Jun. 1925, p. 16.

Lee, "Easy to Detect Finger Print Forgeries," *Finger Print Mag.*, Sep. 1928, p. 16.

Lee, "Further Discussion of the Evidentiary Value of Finger-Prints," 81 *Pa. L. Rev.* 320 (1933).

Lee, "Finger Prints Can Be Forged," 25 *J. Crim. l. & Criminology* 671 (1934).

Locard, "Les Pores et l'identification des criminels," *Biologica*, Vol. 2, p. 357 (1912).

Locard, "La poroscopie, procede nouveau d'identification des criminels par les traces des orifices sudoripares," *Arch. d'Anthrop. Crim.*, 1913.

Maclean, "The Case of the Great Toe Print," *Finger Print Mag.*, Mar. 1953, p. 3.

Maclean, "Identification by Sole Prints," *Finger Print Mag.*, Aug. 1953, p. 3.

Mairs, "Can Two Identical Ridge Patterns Actually Occur—Either on Different Persons or on the Same Person?" *Finger Print Mag.*, Jul. 1953, p. 7

Moenssens, "The Legal Status of Finger Printing" (pamphlet), Chicago, 1964.

Myers II, "Prints of Prosthetic Fingers," *Finger Print Mag.*, Sep. 1946, p. 7.

Okajima, "Studies on the heredity of the whorl finger patterns," 3 *Jap. J. Leg. Med.* 78 (1949).

Shahan, "Heredity in Fingerprints," *Identification News*, Apr. 1970, p. 1.

Sing, "Pressure Distortion in Fingerprinting," *Identification News*, Sep. 1962, p. 14.

Srp, "Finger Print Forgeries," *Finger Print Mag.*, Jul. 1949, p. 3.

Steinwender, "Dactyloscopic Identification," *Finger Print Mag.*, Apr. 1960, p. 3.

Tyler, "You Can't Turn Jury Into Panel of Experts in Fifteen Minutes," *Finger Print Mag.*, Mar. 1970, p. 3.

Updegraff, "Changing of Fingerprints," *Amer. J. Surgery*, Dec. 1934, p. 533.

CHAPTER 11

Alter & Schulenberg, "Dermatoglyphics in the Rubella Syndrome," 197 *J.A.M.A.* 93 (1963).

Anon., "Her Unique Color Sensitive Fingers Bear Normal Ridge Patterns," *Finger Print Mag.*, May 1964, p. 3.

Anon., "Six Cazenovia Family Members Have No Finger or Palm Prints," *NYSIIS Newsletter*, Dec. 1969, p. 1.

Baird, "Kindred Showing Congenital Absence of the Dermal Ridges (Fingerprints) and Associated Anomalies," 64 *Jl. Pediatrics* 621 (1964).

Bleben, "A Study in the Hereditary Transmission of Finger Patterns," *Proc. Iowa Acad. Sci. for 1901*, Vol. IX, p. 44.

Braunberg & Clark, "Leprosy and Fingerprints," 20 *Med. Bull. Vet. Admin.* 324 (1944).

Castellanos, "The Biological Examination of Finger Prints," *Finger Print Mag.*, Dec. 1929, p. 8.

Cherill, "Fingerprints and Disease," *Nature* (Vol. 166), 1950, p. 581.

Cummins, "Dermatoglyphics: Significant Patternings of the Body Surfaces," 18 *Yale Jl. Biol. & Med.* 551 (1946).

Cummins, "Finger Prints: Research Contrasted With Identification Routine," *Finger Print. Mag.*, Oct. 1963, p. 3.

Cummins & Midlo, "Revised Methode of Interpreting and Formulating Palmar Dermatoglyphics," 12 *Am. Jl. Phys. Anthrop.* 415 (1929).

Felsher, "A Quick Look At Dermatoglyphics," *Identification News*, Jul. 1962, p. 6.

Forbes, "Fingerprints and Palm Prints (Dermatoglyphics) and Palmar-Flexion Creases on Gonadal Dysgenesis, Pseudohypoparathyrodism and Klinefelter's Syndrome," 270 *New Engl. Jl. Med.* 1268 (1964).

Furuhata, "The Difference of the Index Finger Prints According To Race," *The Japan Medical World*, June 1927, p. 161.

Furuhata, Furuya, Tanaka & Nakajima, "A Family with Unclassifiable Papillary Patterns," 33 *Proc. Jap. Acad.* 410 (1957).

Furuhata, Furuya, Tanaka, Nakajima, Hasebe, Yokoyama, Nozawa & Fukumoto, "Genetic Investigation of Five Generations of One Family (Second Case) II. Fingerprint Patterns," 33 *Proc. Jap. Acad.* 673 (1957).

Furuhata, Ishii, Hasebe, Yokoyama, Furuya & Tanaka, "Genetical Investigation of a Family for Five Generations. II. Fingerprint Patterns," and "III. Palm Patterns," 32 *Proc. Jap. Acad.* 143 & 147 (1956).

Furuhata & Masahashi, "The Ainos Viewed from the Finger-Prints," 25 *Proc. Jap. Acad.* 219 (1949).

Gibbs, "Finger and Palm Print Alterations Due to Keratosis," *Finger Print Mag.*, Jul. 65, p. 3.

Glanville & Poelking, "Palmar Dermatoglyphics in White, Negro and Mixed Groups," 22 *Am. Jl. Phys. Anthrop.* 407 (1964).

Guirguis, "Determining Paternity Through Finger Prints," *Finger Print Mag.*, Aug. 46, p. 16, and *Finger Print Mag.*, Dec. 1949, p. 3.

Hale, Phillips & Burch, "Features of Palmar Dermatoglyphics in Congenital Heart Disease," *J.A.M.A.* Apr. 8, 1961, p. 125.

Hirsch, "Biological Aspects of Finger Prints, Palms and Soles," *Finger Print Mag.*, Aug. 1964, p. 3.

Hirsch, "Finger, Hand and Foot Prints in Phenylketonuria as Compared with Other Normal and Abnormal Populations," 1 *Humangenetik* 246 (1965).

Holt, "Quantitative Genetics of Finger-Print Patterns," 17 *Brit. Med. Bull.* 247 (1961).

Jelgersma, "Fingerprints and Function of the Fingers in Mongolism," 56 *Folia Psych., Neurol. et Neurochir. Neerl.* 53 (1953).

Kasai, "On the Inheritance of Palmar Patterns," 5 *Jap. Jl. Leg. Med.* 108 (1951).

Mairs, "Finger Prints Indexed Numerically," *Finger Print Mag.*, Oct. 1933, p. 16.

Mairs, "A Study of the Henry Accidentals," *Finger Print Mag.*, Aug. 1943, p. 3.

Nassau & Kallner, "Observations on the Deep Furrows of the Palm of the Hand and the Sole of the Foot in Diseased Children," 191 *Am. Paediat.* 295 (1958).

Ohler & Cummins, "Sexual Differences in Breadths of Epidermal Ridges on Finger Tips and Palms," 29 *Am. Jl. Phys. Anthrop.* 341 (1942).

Okajima, "Studies on the Heredity of the Whorl Finger Patterns," 3 *Jap. Jl. Leg. Med.* 78 (1949).

Penrose, "Finger-Prints, Palms and Chromosomes," *Nature*, Mar. 9, 1963, p. 933.

Pinkus & Plotnick, "Destruction of Fingerprint Patterns by Superficial Late Syphiloderm," 78 *A.M.A. Arch. Derm.* 744 (1958).

Raphael & Raphael, "Fingerprints in Schizophrenia," *J.A.M.A.*, Apr. 21, 1962, p. 109.

Ribeiro, "Dactilo-Diagnose," *Finger Print Mag.*, Jul. 1946, p. 3.

Rubeiro, "Alterations of Papillary Designs by Leprosy," 5 *Arch. Med. Leg. Ident.* 27 (1935).

Sanchez Cascos, "Finger-Print Patterns in Congenital Heart Disease," 26 *Brit. Heart Jl.* 524 (1964).

Shahan, "Heredity in Fingerprints," *Identification News*, Apr. 1970, p. 1.

Takeshina & Yorifugi, "Palmar Dermatoglyphics in Heart Disease," 197 *J.A.M.A.* 97 (1966).

Taylor, "Hand and Foot Prints," *Jl. of Heredity* 511 (1916).

Walker, "A Suggested Association of Mongolism and Schizophrenia," 6 *Acta Genetica* 132 (1956).

Walker, "The Use of Dermal Configurations in the Diagnosis of Mongolism," *Pediat. Clin. N. America*, May 1958, p. 531.

Wolf, Brehme, Baitsch & Reinwein, "Aplasia of the Dermal Ridge Patterns in Mongolism," 2 *The Lancet* 887 [No. 7313] (1963).

Index

About the Author

ANDRE A. MOENSSENS, Associate Professor at the Chicago-Kent College of Law of the Illinois Institute of Technology and founder of the school's Institute for Criminal Justice, is a consulting criminologist whose specialty is fingerprint identification. For six years, he was the head instructor in fingerprinting at the Institute of Applied Science, and in 1967 he was one of the two fingerprint experts to testify at the famous Speck murder trial.

In addition to writing many articles on personal identification and scientific evidence, Professor Moenssens has served as Associate Editor of *Finger Print and Identification Magazine* and as Managing Editor of the *Chicago-Kent Police Law Reporter* and is an editorial consultant for the *Journal of Criminal Law, Criminology and Police Science,* published by the Northwestern University School of Law. He is the author of the book *Fingerprints and the Law*, published in 1969. A member of numerous professional organizations, including the Chicago, Illinois State and American Bar Associations, the American Academy of Forensic Sciences, the Police-Law Society and the International Association for Identification, Andre Moenssens has had over twenty years of experience in fingerprint techniques.